Praise for *Jason Molina: Riding with the Ghost*

"Erin Osmon paints an empathetic and deeply human portrait of Jason Molina, both the artist and the man. A biography that's as beautifully haunting as one of his songs."—**Bob Mehr, author, *Trouble Boys: The True Story of the Replacements***

"*Jason Molina: Riding with the Ghost* acc  examination of Molina's life and work as music he made. Erin Osmon unpacks the that is human, tangible, and deeply mov *The First Collection of Criticism by a Living Female Rock Critic*

"In *Jason Molina: Riding with the Ghost*, Erin Osmon gives us a riveting biography not only of a great musician whose work deserves to be much wider known, but a well-rounded portrait of a fascinating human being, as well as a glimpse into the creative process. It's a ride well worth taking."—**Jim DeRogatis, co-host, "Sound Opinions," and author, *Let It Blurt: The Life and Times of Lester Bangs***

"During his all-too-short lifetime, Jason Molina created some of the most emotionally stirring, soul-enriching, and thought-provoking rock this side of Neil Young, Lou Reed, and Nick Drake. First time author Erin Osmon has crafted a meticulously researched biography infused with both passion and a keen analytic eye. During his lifetime, Molina was criminally under recognized. In a perfect world, Osmon's loving tribute will play its part in rectifying this."—**Rob Bowman, Grammy Award–winning author, *Soulsville U.S.A.: The Story of Stax Records***

"The anecdotal details from *Jason Molina: Riding with the Ghost* are what ring most vividly, exposing a side of Molina that rarely came through in his melancholic music. . . . *Riding with the Ghost* also enriches his songs, illuminating their characters in their own words and supplying context to the places they were set."—**MTV**

"Among *Riding with the Ghost*'s most memorable passages are instances of Molina's fandom, from his unconditional love for Sade and his evangelizing of Kraftwerk to Damien Jurado, to his edict to bandmates to study Neil Young's *After the Gold Rush*. Molina's passion rings through these pages, nowhere more distinctly than in the retelling of the fateful interaction that launched his career while studying at Oberlin College (where he was known as 'Sparky').”—**Pitchfork Media**

“In her new book, *Riding with the Ghost*, writer Erin Osmon accomplishes a tricky feat regarding the late Jason Molina. . . . She presents Molina, whose work can so often seem mythic, as if carved from ancient stone, fully as a person, with faults, desires, humors, and failings. She doesn’t strip his songs of their mystery or allure but rather illustrates the idiosyncratic and personal details that led to his remarkable words and melodies. In doing so, she gives us the gift of more fully knowing Molina, as well as his companions and friends, those who traveled alongside him through life.”—*Aquarium Drunkard*

“Empathetic and informative. . . . Erin Osmon is a great biographer, writer, and critic. She has used new interviews to weave an empathetic and informative story around Molina and his music without turning him into a martyr, without trying to make him even more of a cult figure than he has become. She does not condone or condemn, simply tells it straight. Here is the story of one creative spirit who could not cope. Here is how he lived and made the music he left behind. Read and listen: it is the story of how music is made.”—*International Times*

“Erin Osmon’s new biography of Jason Molina, *Riding with the Ghost*, makes journalism look easy. . . . I’ve found that the more intimate you are with a subject, the more disappointing a book-length examination can be. But through diligent and patient research over the course of nearly three years, Osmon has created the rare essential biography for anyone curious about Molina’s music and legacy.”—*FLOOD Magazine*

“*Jason Molina: Riding with the Ghost* absolutely communicates just what Molina’s life meant to family, friends, collaborators, and fans. . . . Osmon does an excellent job of painting a nuanced portrait of a complex human being. . . . Her interviews with former band members and those involved with the production process yield a lot of wonderful insight into Molina’s singular and demanding creative process and his prolificacy. . . . It was already clear from his immense output that there is endless meaning to be gleaned from Jason Molina’s body of work, but Osmon takes the story of his short, bright time on Earth, warts and all—just like a Songs: Ohia record, ‘no overdubs!’—and puts it in the context of a real human life. And that unveils depths to his music that we're only now able to explore."—**Winnipeg Free Press**

"Osmon's biography is a must-read for anyone who has more than a casual relationship with Molina's work; which, in my guess, would be anyone who has heard Molina's work. . . . Osmon pulls back the curtain and shows us Molina the man."—**37 FLOOD**

"Never short on details, it's a ravenous fan's dream. . . . Osmon provides the deepest of glimpses into Molina's world. All the trinket-filled mysteries left behind by one of the greatest songwriters who ever wrote a note are captured here. . . . Thanks . . . Osmon for a guided tour of Molina's mythological palette, warts and all."—**Popmatters**

"If Jason Molina has ever been important to you, then you need to read the book, because Osmon did a magnificent job detailing Molina's life, struggles, music, and demise. So many lingering questions are answered, and questions you'd never considered are answered as well. Read it. Now."—**Third Coast Review**

"*Riding with the Ghost* . . . captures the heaviness and levity that coexisted in Molina's personality, and it enriches a moving and inexhaustible artistic legacy."—**Decoder Magazine**

JASON MOLINA

JASON MOLINA

Riding with the Ghost

Erin Osmon

Foreword by Will Johnson

ROWMAN & LITTLEFIELD

Lanham • Boulder • New York • London

Published by Rowman & Littlefield
An imprint of The Rowman & Littlefield Publishing Group, Inc.
4501 Forbes Boulevard, Suite 200, Lanham, Maryland 20706
www.rowman.com

Unit A, Whitacre Mews, 26-34 Stannary Street, London SE11 4AB

Distributed by NATIONAL BOOK NETWORK

British Library Cataloguing in Publication Information Available

Library of Congress Cataloging-in-Publication Data

Names: Osmon, Erin.
Title: Jason Molina : riding with the ghost / Erin Osmon.
Description: Lanham : Rowman & Littlefield, [2017] | Includes bibliographical references and index.
Identifiers: LCCN 2016047509 (print) | LCCN 2016048240 (ebook) | ISBN 9781442268678 (cloth : alk. paper) | ISBN 9781538112182 (pbk. : alk. paper) | ISBN 9781442268685 (electronic)
Subjects: LCSH: Molina, Jason. | Singers—United States—Biography. | LCGFT: Biographies.
Classification: LCC ML420.M5558 O86 2017 (print) | LCC ML420.M5558 (ebook) | DDC 782.42164092 [B]—dc23 LC record available at https://lccn.loc.gov/2016047509

∞™ The paper used in this publication meets the minimum requirements of American National Standard for Information Sciences—Permanence of Paper for Printed Library Materials, ANSI/NISO Z39.48-1992.

Printed in the United States of America

CONTENTS

FOREWORD

My eyes are desert
Benny Lava take me now
To my Friday end—WJ

Will lives in Texas
Once in a while he gets out
It is not all talk—JM

These acrylic fumes
Cannot stop me from watching
The View, yet again—WJ

Hey, it still sucks here
A grand old day it isn't
And it's a shit pile—JM

Will Johnson and Jason Molina Haiku exchanges, mid-May 2008

Late one night in March of 2004 I was introduced to Jason Molina at the Northwest corner of 6th and Red River in Austin, Texas. He was wearing a green military-style jacket with a black t-shirt underneath that had some sparkly script on it. I think it had something to do with country music. When we shook hands he said, "Songwriter, right?" I answered, "Yes." We talked for a few minutes, realized a mutual admiration and connected some dots through various folks that had previously linked us from afar. I'd been a fan of his work for five or six years by that point.

I never got around to telling him, but I remember the first time I heard his voice. I was heading out to run evening errands in Denton, Texas, on a late fall night in 1998. It was already long dark, and the first few songs of the Songs: Ohia album *Impala* unraveled on the system in my truck. I kept turning it up in hopes of better understanding it; to get a better definition of this music. There was a lyrical and technical aesthetic that I connected with, but there was also a newness within. I hadn't heard a voice like that before. There was a wideness to it that rattled me on that drive, and it was one of those listening experiences I knew I'd remember for all time.

Before we parted ways in Austin that night, I made sure to convey to Jason that on a recent long tour around Europe, the Songs: Ohia LP *The Magnolia Electric Co.* had become a place of musical sanctuary for me. His expansive, remarkable voice, and those songs, became a crucial source of counsel over those miles and nights. A needed and regular companion just before sleep.

We didn't keep in touch but we'd see each other around here and there, usually in some South by Southwest stew of haste; in a club or makeshift venue we'd never been to before, and probably wouldn't return to again. During those years I was dedicated to seeing Magnolia Electric Co. play any time I could. They'd fast become one of my favorite bands, and their recordings were usually in regular rotation in my truck solo tours. I went to see them at Emo's on September 13, 2007, and they were in astonishingly good, mid-tour form. Afterward Jason and I wound up talking at the merch booth for a while. We discussed the types of hats we were comfortable enough wearing onstage, and found we both had long-running affection for pumpkin orange. He had strong opinions on both topics. He seemed to have strong opinions on everything. When the 2 a.m. house lights went on and we started into our farewells, he flatly said that we should make a record together. I agreed. He suggested that we start the session during the first full moon of 2008. We swapped email addresses on scraps of paper and said goodbye. I drove home inspired.

Jason emailed to follow up on it within 48 hours. I didn't know him well, but I liked him a lot. He was willing to hold to his word, and kept communication strong from the start. He'd meant what he said. There were regular, rapid-fire bursts in his early emails, and his energy was not lacking within them:

I'll start working on a new tune tonight.
I'm inspired.

Energized is more like it.

Am happy to say the tix are bought.

I'm approaching this as seriously as any of my other projects.

We really should not count on cutting corners.

When it gets to money for the studio I'll be quick on the draw.

Once the dates are set in stone, invite anyone you possibly could want to come
    to the studio, no holds barred.

Let's make a legend.

I have no problem writing with you or anyone in the room who's invited.

I'm not talking hippie freak out here.

I am talking precision and with the element of fly by the seat of the pants.

Just get me out of indie rock jail.

We missed the first full moon of the new year, but secured his plane ticket and reserved our dates for February 2008 at the Echo Lab in Argyle, Texas. The idea we talked about was each bringing five songs in, then seeing where it went from there.

When I arrived to the studio he was on the back porch with a cigarette in hand, at the ready. He'd come all the way from London, and I was the one that was late. I gave Jason a copy of *The Stories of Breece D'J Pancake*. He gave me a blue and white Native American bead necklace. He had one, too. We wore them through most of our session together, and I still carry mine in my guitar case for good luck, and for good memory. He told me early on that he took a little something from just about everywhere he went, but he left something, too. He said it in an almost dismissive way, but it held weight—we paid in our ways, but we also got paid. A trade at every turn.

He wanted to get a thesaurus, so I drove us into Denton. We found one that was suitable, along with guitar strings and groceries for the next few days. After that we drove south to the Swisher Road Wal-Mart, where we filled a shopping cart with various types of notepads, packages of colored construction paper, Post-It notes, a box of Sharpies, a box of Mirado Black Warrior pencils, a case of Lone Star beer, a Daisy BB gun, and plenty of BBs for the week. He was very specific about the Black Warrior pencils. He was a natural at throwing forth vapor trails of traveler's wisdom, and could regularly feather lines into conversation or emails that deserved to live in song. I almost started to take it for granted, on drives to the store or while shooting the BB gun from the back porch of the studio. It was a small but crucial part of his energy, and I think it's part of what kept many of us listening closely for so long.

I'd rented a cabin in Mississippi a few weeks earlier to write toward our record, and came back to Texas with a handful of songs I wanted to try.

On that first night Jason recorded a version of "Wooden Heart," and I re-corded a song called "Such Expensive Times" that I later wrote off as a bad fit. I don't recall a formal conversation about it, but over those first hours together I think we realized we wanted to write the bulk of the record on the premises. Clean slate. We both liked the idea of living in the moment anyway—sink or swim—and the setting and energy of the Echo Lab lends itself to that. It's rustic, fairly isolated, with a band apartment across the sidewalk, woods to the west and north, and a hill about twenty yards off the back porch that drops through a line of trees to active train tracks. It's in decent enough proximity to Denton, where if errands need to be run, it's not much of a fuss. It's also comfortable enough to fit plenty of supplies and not feel the need to leave the premises for days.

There was a feeling of great happiness between us at the end of that first night. The next day he set up a writing station in the band apartment, and I set one up in the iso-booth. For the next nine days we workshopped everything. We backed each other readily and worked diligently together. At other times we worked alone. We tried to be the best singers, multi-instrumentalists, and side-people we could be for one another. We were industrious, prolific, and inspired. We barked at each other when a line wasn't right, and left our politeness at the door when it came to the writ-ing. His humor was great, and there was a good balance and rhythm to our days. It felt like camp. Any time there was a needed moment of therapy we stepped out back and shot the BB gun into the woods, or at various targets we'd set up.

Jason was usually the last to go to bed every night, and the first one up. I'd wake up on the lounge futon and often the first thing I would see through the window was his silhouette or shadow on the porch, pacing, with cigarette in hand. Sometimes with a beer. Loyal and ready. He worked on his songwriting with the care and attention of a gifted and obsessed tech-nician. It was an incredible dedication to look upon, this relationship that pulsated between Jason and the song. I learned a lot from him in those days. I watched the way he worked lines and verses over and over, sitting at that little desk, and on occasion found myself in awe of his tirelessness.

Our surroundings were littered with paper. Drafts, chord sheets, frag-ments on pages, notebooks, and final lyric sheets. My longtime friend and bandmate Matt Pence was engineering the project, and was a source of great direction and guidance for us. Mikey Kapinus, Howard Draper, Sarah Jaffe, Bryan Vandivier, and Scott Danbom all dropped by or stayed with us at various points to help see it through. They were all integral to the session's morale and spirit, and they each performed beautifully. We were lucky to have them involved. We recorded and mixed twenty-two songs in nine days.

The last night Jason and I sat down outside, and worked out the sequence of the record. This has often been a lengthy headache of a puzzle in my personal experience, but with Jason we agreed on the order in about thirty minutes. We then took various notes, lyric scraps, and artifacts from the session, put them all in a Ball jar, and buried it out back behind the studio. Our own time capsule. We stacked all of our notes and lyric sheets up on the table and looked through them. He requested that I keep them all together and safe, and we immediately jumped on the idea of making another record together. We stayed up late and said our goodbyes the next morning. I didn't know that I'd only get to see him one more time after that—at a show we played together on October 30, 2008, at the Mohawk in Austin.

Secretly Canadian kindly released our record in November 2009. We briefly discussed giving it a proper title, but instead just went with our names—with the obvious Loggins and Messina jokes. I insisted that his name come first, alphabetical listing be damned. We later agreed that the insert should include images of paintings we'd made.

I won't write much about our cancelled tours. Much of that story is told within these pages. I can only say that I don't think Jason was in any condition to tour then. It wasn't an easy time for a lot of us simply given the fact that we loved him and cared for him. We didn't want to see him struggle.

For the next couple of years I communicated with him through phone calls and emails. My guess is that that's the way it went with most of his friends during that time. We didn't talk often, but when we did it was usually at great length and not without difficult moments. We still discussed the idea of re-circling the wagons and recording again. In 2011, because of his living quarters' regulations, his communication was reduced to letter-writing. We exchanged a few, and it was a practice I liked. His last letter made me grateful for our friendship, the time we had together, his generosity, and the faith he had in his friends and strangers alike. He included two small pieces of art in it, and there was a noticeable tone of peace to it. I hung hope on that for most of the next year. That's what made getting the phone call about his passing even tougher.

These are the last words he wrote to me:

Grandmother's House
17 March 2012
Beckley, W. Va.

Dear Will.

Hello, friend. Thank you so much for the kind words. For reaching out. I've been further down than I thought but man am I inspired to be good. I hope music is again in our future together. No plans yet. I admire your art, what little I've seen, and the songs, the many I've heard over the years.

A horse's mouth account: My father used to deliver newspapers to an old time player here. Name was Homerun Baker. Baker lived here and used to pay for everything with Indian head pennies. There's something to that I guess. They were out of style at the time. I've not heard any music really for a year. I know you are a family man, and I hope it brings you so much joy. Thinking fondly of you.

Here I am camped out for about a month while I figure out my life. Guess I'm moving back to the United States of America. Any good towns left? Don't plan on going to: Chicago, Indiana, but there's lots of other places. Oh, West Coast is not for me. Here comes art first. Songs when I can.

Love, JMo.

Say howdy to Texas for me.

I eventually made a Homerun Baker painting with Jason in mind, but never told him I'd made it. I meant to. Every time I looked at it over in the corner I thought of him, reminded that I needed to write again soon. I don't think reaching out would have changed history. I don't think the story would have changed. It's a matter of being left with the feeling of wishing I'd done something I just didn't do.

There was a regular mystery to Jason. I think most of us who knew him feel that way. I can't say I ever unlocked it, but I'm thankful to have been alongside it in the interest of making something together. He could be difficult, strident, and contrary at moments. He could just as quickly circle back to the camp in the interest of making the best work possible, with a good joke or funny drawing to boot. If we found ourselves in the weeds, he had the ability to lighten the room back up quickly. There could be a duality to him, and I think a lot of us experienced that over the years. I know I will always love his voice, and I will always love his writing. I feel confident that I'll listen to his songs for all my life.

I don't think a better job could have been done with the telling of Jason's story than in these pages. There is a respectful and undeniable grace with which Erin Osmon has conveyed this crucial piece of American music history. I think it's as proper a document of his path as many of us could hope to read, and I am thankful it is in the world.

Connect when the feeling strikes. Work on loving. Work to avoid regret. Because a lot of the time it's hard to tell what the last time looks like.

Will Johnson

ACKNOWLEDGMENTS

This book would not be possible without Darcie Molina. You didn't have to tell your story, but you did. Thank you for trusting me with it. I hope I have done it justice. To the Molina family: Thank you for allowing me into your homes and your memories. I am grateful for the support and participation of the many members of the Spineriders, Songs: Ohia and Magnolia Electric Co. I couldn't have done this without your sharp minds and big hearts. Jason Molina had a unique savvy for surrounding himself with talented and unselfish people. Your friendship is essential to his story. Thanks in particular to Jason Groth and Jeff Panall for championing this project from the start, and for helping me piece together the many scattered pieces. To William Schaff: The world is a better place because of your phenomenal talent and good nature. Thank you Anne Grady for your openness and honesty. A very big thanks to Chris and Ben Swanson from Secretly Canadian for opening the archives and your memories. To my mom, Ann Moore, and my dad, Randy Moore, thank you for instilling a love of music and writing in me, and for not freaking out when I became a weird punk rock kid in high school. I found my people and Molina's music because of your support. Thank you Ken Shipley for your fierce and undying support. Thank you to my agent, Alice Spielburg, for fighting the good fight. Finally, thank you Jason Molina for your talent and hard work. You created an extraordinary catalog of music in a very short amount of time and changed many lives in the process.

INTRODUCTION

The outsider pride beaming from the Midwest's underground music culture of the 1990s is *sui generis*—singular in its aesthetic—the product of tiny and truly independent scenes that sprang up in small towns stretching from Ohio to Oklahoma, detached from the cultural cache and financial privilege commensurate with big cities dotting America's coasts. With factory assembly lines and an evangelical hive mind as the driving force of mainstream culture, the Midwest was often devoid of welcoming spaces for teenage punk bands, artists, and anything outsider. As such, upstart acts from the Midwest convened after hours in church basements, park shelters, and VFW banquet halls, blazing musical trails based solely on reimagined sonic cues from cassette dubs and radio-rock record collections inherited from parents. In the pre-Internet era of do-it-yourself music making, many Midwestern kids had limited-to-no access to record store bins and touring bands, which bred creativity through a lens of isolation and fostered a unique community not found outside the confines of the Midwest's pastoral plains and industrial emptiness.

Jason Molina's story is a paragon of this Midwest isolation and pride. A musician reared in the heart of the Ohio Rust Belt with a big, singular voice, he both shunned his humble roots and wore them like a badge of honor. Hailing from a tiny town and holding a torch for great country and roots-rock artists, much like Townes Van Zandt and Gram Parsons before him, Molina was a songwriter's songwriter, acutely attuned to the beautiful and the absurd in the everyday, penning volumes of profoundly simple lyrics in his abbreviated 39-year life. His self-taught style was charmingly unpolished and noncommercial and his record sales were commensurate with that ethos. Still, the artists, musicians, and appreciators of Molina took to him with fervor, recognizing the prodigious and prolific talent torpedoing from the young man with the old soul. Like Van Zandt and Parsons, Molina left earth largely unheralded in the mainstream, save for his rabid fan base and scant higher profile musician-peers who covered his material after his death. He was neither fashionable nor amenable to the terms of his era, rejecting trends and corporate cash ins, favoring instead a very singular vision centered on his unique and unwavering tenor voice, which shot out of his diminutive 5'6" frame like a rocket. As the '90s gave way to the '00s, Molina looked increasingly to the past for inspiration. As skinny ties returned to vogue, Molina sported bolos. He flew fast from his hometown of Lorain, Ohio, but never really left; its Great Lakes shorelines and oxidized industrial landscape lived forever in his spirit and in his songs.

After worshipping heavy metal and alternative rock acts in the '80s, Molina reached college and focused on becoming a singer-songwriter. He'd find a trusted coterie of brother-bandmates who'd remain loyal throughout the innumerable pranks, pitfalls, and paradoxes that were inevitable when working with Molina.

He found his footing in the progressive campus of Oberlin College, a liberal arts school a stone's throw from his hometown, where influential '90s underground bands were incubated. Unlike Molina, these acts tended to favor a louder or faster approach to music making. His stripped down and plaintive performances at house parties often captivated or sank the collective heart of the room, his sets brimming with equal amounts of hope and sadness.

Jason Molina's story cannot be told without that of his label Secretly Canadian, which found its first successes by issuing Molina's records and considered him their flagship. Though the label and Molina parted ways ideologically—the label climbing and expanding into the global indie realm as Molina increasingly crawled inside of himself—the partnership lasted into Molina's final days. While Molina continued to churn out low-fidelity music cloaked by depression and uncertainty, the label and its siblings Jagjaguwar and Dead Oceans turned their sights to bigger names like Bon Iver and Antony & The Johnsons, expanding their humble Midwest offices to New York, Los Angeles, and the UK in the process. Still, Secretly Canadian's partnership with Molina spanned about thirty records, split among LP, EP, and seven-inch single formats. As Molina traveled from Ohio to Chicago and London, the label's humble home base in Bloomington, Indiana, served as a de facto musical community and incubator for Molina, its tight-knit web of DIY musicians and recording engineers aiding the singer-songwriter into his last days. It's where Molina found his bandmates, his wife, and himself.

Molina's biggest success was his 2003 album *The Magnolia Electric Co.*, which has been canonized in the contemporary roots-rock songbook. Its songs have been covered by both Grammy nominees and nobodies. Its lyrics and cover art have lasting permanence in CD and vinyl pressings, but also in tattoos on the limbs of Molina's fans.

The album's second song, "I've Been Riding with the Ghost," contains one of Molina's most pointed observations on the human condition. In it he explains the turns and trials along life's journey to acceptance with oneself, with lovers, and with spectral forces unseen—the many ghosts that ride with us along the way. Molina himself was highly superstitious and convened with both literal and metaphorical ghosts his entire life. These came in late night bed rattlings and homemade altars he fashioned from found objects as well as the ghosts from his troubled childhood and from friends who died in tragic accidents. Molina's own ghost, the alcoholism that pulsed through his family's bloodlines, begat his end. Though his swan sang of tragedy, today he lives on through the songs, his continual ability to write at a hummingbird's clip his only personal measure for success during his short life.

Molina often relied on a preferred collector's set of metaphors, which mirrored the very real events of his life. He sang of moons, trains, ghosts, flowers, wolves, and bells, providing a sort of tactile connection to his studies and surroundings and to the celebration and suffering he felt inside of himself. He was heralded as a balladeer of heartbreak, but in reality found tremendous hope in the sad songs he wrote and recorded. Molina often spoke in parable, encouraging his fans to keep the lamps trimmed and burning, and today the multitude of songs he left behind continues to burn. He was a man of supreme solitude and of supreme silliness and every contradictory, hilarious, and devastating thing in between. Today, his name is praised by contemporary roots, Americana, and folk musicians who grew up with his records or discovered them after it was too late. Molina never sold out big theaters like his fans in the Avett Brothers, Band of Horses, and the Frames, but his spirit remains a gigantic presence in the tiny clubs and DIY spaces he inhabited in his many years of road dog touring. His is a story of misfortune but also of achievement, from the heavy metal kid winning battle of bands competitions in Lorain, Ohio, to a man whose extensive oeuvre continues to woo and deeply affect fans old and new.

①

LORAIN

Lorain, Ohio, is a town to move away from. A prototypical notch in the Rust Belt, it's a place where the city and its school system became the largest employers in the aftershocks of a shuttered Ford plant, a closed shipyard, and layoffs at the local U.S. Steel plant. Growing up in this blue-collar enclave of northern Ohio, Jason Molina felt little hope for a future as an artist. Little did he know, however, that the town's working-class motifs and lakeside setting would leave a lasting imprint on his musical oeuvre. His future wife Darcie explained, "Jason hated Lorain, but he loved Ohio."

Nestled on the banks of Lake Erie, the village christened the "Mouth of the Black River" was settled in 1820 by pioneer John S. Reid before it crawled east toward Cleveland and was renamed Lorain. Its current population hovers around sixty thousand. The town's most famous former resident is novelist Toni Morrison, who described her childhood in the Ohio town as segregated not by law but by de facto attitudes toward people of color in her debut novel, *The Bluest Eye*, which takes place in Lorain. Today, a local elementary school bears her name.

Molina spent his childhood in Lorain but was born at a hospital in neighboring Oberlin, Ohio, on December 30, 1973. For thirty-five years his father, William "Bill" Molina, taught science in the Lorain public school system. It's what brought him to the Ohio town after graduating from West Virginia University in his home state in 1967. In college he played baseball and had a keen interest in science and history. His first wife's uncle was a teacher in the Lorain area and recruited the couple westward with promises of jobs in science and coaching. In 1971, Bill Molina split from her and met Karen Foster, another West Virginia native, whom he married that same year. Jason came as a surprise to the couple. Karen didn't realize she was pregnant until she was five months along.

The Molina patriarch was a music enthusiast and maintained an extensive collection of country, classic rock, new wave, hard rock, and metal LPs. He spun his favorites for his oldest son when he was in utero, placing his over-sized headphones on Karen's belly so that the firstborn Molina could enjoy his dad's favorite tracks such as "Stairway to Heaven" and cuts by Black Sabbath. Due to these blastosphere listening parties, Jason Molina often told his friends that his first-ever concert was Ozzy Osbourne's heavy metal mouthpiece. "Jason would kick and kick, and I would say to Karen that I think we have a boy who loves music," Bill said.

Molina's younger brother Aaron was born three years later, and the two shared a bedroom into high school. The boys were inseparable, their close age gap and mutual interests in the outdoors, history, music, and art keep-ing them close, intellectually engaged, and generally noncombative well into adulthood. The two also eventually shared the same affliction with alcoholism, a problem that ran deep in their bloodlines. A doctor once told Aaron that if he ever took to drinking, he'd be a goner. Though he was eventually able to manage the disease, in his brother's case, the doctor was right. "Jason had the kind of alcoholism that kills you," Aaron explained.

Their sister Ashley arrived six years after her oldest brother and claims she remained twelve years old in Jason's mind. She didn't share her broth-ers' mutual interests and was instead regarded as a bratty little sister for most of their upbringing. Less introverted than her brothers, the outgo-ing and gregarious youngest Molina took to cheerleading and '90s rap and R&B, while her brothers slid full tilt into art and rock 'n' roll.

When the kids were young, their mother stayed home while dad taught school. By the time Ashley could walk, Karen had taken a part-time job as a bookkeeper at a local heating and cooling company, where she worked out of the owner's house. "She could take us to work, so I basically grew up there," Ashley remembered fondly. Molina had less favorable memories of his childhood under Karen's watch, like the times she picked the kids up from school under the influence and young Jason sat in the backseat won-dering if he'd make it home alive.

Jason didn't speak until he was three years old, when suddenly his squeaks and coos turned into full sentences. His first was an astute pontifi-cation from his car seat as he looked out the window. "Don't you think the trees get tired of standing all the time?" he said. Soon after, he explained to a family friend, "The rainbow is so beautiful, I can see it in my heart."[1] Around the time Molina began speaking, his father gifted him a bugle he said was a relic of the Civil War, which Jason "tooted and tooted." Young Molina's full head of long blond hair was cut into a ubiquitous late-'70s "bowl" style and was often tucked under a pint-sized Confederate soldier hat given by his father. He became enamored with the horn, and the budding musician often concentrated intently on his practice, lifting the horn skyward as he blew into it. His dark brown, almond-shaped eyes conveyed the old soul living inside him.

Though Molina lost interest in the bugle in elementary school, the historic war between the North and the South served as a lifelong fascination for both father and son. The Molina family's West Virginia heritage, and the Civil War's battles, battalions, and jargon comprised many of the lyrical motifs of Molina's first full-length, self-titled album, anecdotally known as the *Black Album*. The song "White Sulfur" was a reference to the Battle of White Sulphur Springs, while "Dogwood Gap" and "Big Sewell Mt." reference historic West Virginia sites the Molina family visited. Local legend maintains that Confederate soldiers hid a cannon in a ridge in Fayetteville, West Virginia's Cotton Hill, which they used during a withdrawal from a post overlooking the New George River in Gauley Bridge. By virtue of that lore, Molina's songs "Cotton Hill" and "Gauley Bridge" come as no surprise.

Molina was especially captivated by history and antiquities and read everything he could get his hands on as soon as he was able. When he became interested in a subject, there was no stopping his appetite for information, a pattern identified as obsessive by his dad and siblings. His scholarly interests extended beyond history and the Civil War, though. He consumed massive volumes of poetry, classic literature, and art books. A devout visual artist, as committed to drawing as he was to music, Molina counted Cy Twombly, Sol Lewitt, and Joseph Cornell among his favorite artists. Molina's penchant for fashioning collages and collections of vintage trinkets in old cigar boxes was reminiscent of Cornell's assemblage technique. Molina also devoured tomes on magic and the occult and often fashioned little shrines or totems out of tarot cards, chicken bones, crystals, or any other small, and often found, object to which he assigned meaning. And he assigned meaning to nearly every object he found, gave, or was given.

Trailer parks often evoke visions of despair and decay—dilapidated rectangles scattered among rusty detritus and garbage, just waiting to be scooped up by a tornado's fury. But where the Molina's lived, lot 19 at 3708 W. Erie Avenue in Lorain, was well kept and a stone's throw from the picturesque banks of Lake Erie. It's a breathtaking shoreline wealthier residents of the Lorain area paid healthy sums to live upon, and perhaps why to this day Bill Molina refers to the grounds as a "trailer court" and not a "trailer park." Aaron and Ashley explained that although their home was unusual in the landscape of their peers, to this day they feel fortunate to have had the run of the Great Lake's shoreline and neighboring grounds as they came of age. Jason later memorialized his fondness of the trailer park's scenery in his song "Blue Factory Flame":

When I die put my bones in an empty street to remind me of how it used to be
Don't write my name on a stone bring a Coleman lantern and a radio
Cleveland game and two fishing poles and watch with me from the shore
Ghostly steel and iron ore ships coming home

Where I am paralyzed by the emptiness
Clearly iron age beasts you can tell by the rust and by the chains
And by the oil that they bleed the crew and crows fly the skulls and bones
They fly the colors of their homes I fly the cross of the blue factory flame
Stitched with heavy sulphur thread
They ain't proud colors but they're true colors of my home

Bill and Karen Molina moved into the wooded lot before Jason was born. At the time, a sign that specifically stated "no children" hung from a tree, but when Jason came along, they didn't want to move because they'd made friends and weren't mentally or emotionally prepared for a tethering to Lorain vis-à-vis a home mortgage. So they negotiated a deal with their landlords. "The trailer court was filled with older people, retired professionals," Bill explained. "They became Jason's grandparents in a way." Ashley remembered spending a lot of time with the older residents. "They were probably looking out for us," she added. "Not knowing what kind of condition our mom was in."

Despite the idyllic scenery and responsible retirees, the lot came equipped with its fair share of trailer park stereotypes, too, though Aaron and Ashley remembered feeling pretty sheltered or oblivious to seedy elements that might have surrounded them. This was primarily because they weren't allowed to play with most of the other kids who moved in. What they weren't sheltered from was their mother's addiction to alcohol and the ensuing chaos it caused in the Molina household.

For much of their childhood, Bill and Karen's marriage seemed touch-and-go to the children. The trio of young Molinas were never quite sure if and when it might implode. "I think my mom felt very homesick," Ashley added. "Before she got pregnant with Jason, she would go back to West Virginia almost every weekend, and when he was born she realized she was stuck in Lorain." This homesickness deeply affected her relationship with Jason and created a chasm between mother and son. Molina grew up convinced that his mother resented him. The palpable divide between mother and oldest son caused Bill Molina to overcompensate. "He just doted over Jason," Ashley said. "The running joke was that Jason was always the golden child to our dad."

The Molinas' trailer was uncluttered and sparsely decorated in used furniture and rust-colored carpet, which complemented the paisley in the curtains. "It was reasonably clean—as clean as three kids, two smokers and a pet can be in a trailer," Aaron added. A peculiar feature was that none of the bedrooms had doors on them, until one day Bill fashioned a makeshift set for Ashley's room. But what they lacked in privacy they made up for in music pumped through a mid-end hi-fi stereo system, Bill's prized possession.

The Molina boys took turns spinning platters ranging from Neil Young to heavier acts like Metallica, along with classic country, which served as an early source of inspiration for Jason. He idolized Hank Williams and was enamored with the Carter Family's mixing of religious and secular music. Despite their lower middle-class standing, Jason's seemingly insatiable appetite never suffered. "My brother ate like a hobbit," Aaron explained. Pumpkin pie ranked among his favorites, and he often requested it instead of cake for birthdays.

A small house stood at the end of the trailer park near the lake, shrouded in a few large trees. Here a man the kids called "Mean Joe" saw his last days. "I don't know if he was actually mean, because I never talked to him," Ashley explained. "But that's what everyone called him." Mean Joe had a great effect on Jason, as he recounted in a 1995 interview:

I can remember walking down the street in the wintertime and he'd be outside. And we were the only two people outside. I'm this little boy that's like five, and he's, you know, in his nineties maybe. He seemed really nice to me, because I always wanted to stop. I knew that he used to be a fireman. And he used to tell me about how he used to be a fireman when they had horses to pull the things to the fires. And one day, cold-ish autumn, rain—not deep winter, but cold and like freezing rain sort of time of the year—I was out by myself, you know, walking around, and he hands me a handful of black Crayolas. Black crayons. And they were all used. And I never thought anything strange about them—I was little—and I took them home and drew with them. And that day he killed himself. I was little, and no one told me. I found out through someone else in the neighborhood or something. And so that always sticks with me. Surely that man wasn't trying to do anything evil. But if you think about it, if he's a man who lives so close to me, and no one knew him, and everyone in the neighborhood calls this man "Mean Joe," and this little boy may have been the only person that this man ever had any contact with. And I hadn't judged him as anything. Old Men were cool as hell to me.[2]

The tale of Mean Joe underscored Jason's attraction to both the supernatural and the outsider and serves as a very early example of his convening with both. Jason never feared the spirits and ghosts he claimed to see around him, both in the living like Mean Joe, and from the other side, such as when he woke up his brother with screams that a ghost was shaking his bed. The trailer court's confines informed Jason's lifelong struggle with feeling like the odd one out on an emotional and spiritual level. Throughout his life he both clung to the status and actively eschewed it, mostly through the formation of bands and the unspoken brotherhood that is cultivated within those creative bounds. That's not to say Jason would have turned out differently had he grown up in a standard subdivision with block parties and backyard barbecues, free of trailer spirits and haunted old men. Still, the isolation of his childhood had a lasting effect on both his need for privacy and his need for attention, and on his lifelong rapport with apparitions.

A path in the northwest corner of their family's lot led down the small bluff to a beach, where Jason learned to swim by fire after Bill tossed the kids into Lake Erie's shallow shoreline. On the beach, brothers Aaron and Jason built lean-to shelters and sometimes slept under them at night in the summer. This setting birthed Jason's very early infatuation with washed up relics and detritus, including old cans, stones, and fossils the boys plucked from the lake's banks. Jason often arranged his findings atop the boys' shared dresser. "He always had flags and bandanas, and he'd wrap what he found in them, until our mom would throw them away," Aaron said. Karen's disposal of Jason's collections only fueled his fire for finding replacements. He toted and arranged his found wares with a near-religious precision.

Bill recalled one instance where Molina found a couple of rusty wrenches near the shoreline and became obsessed with tracing their origin. After conducting research in the local library, Jason discovered that they were likely from a seafaring tug that sank in Lake Erie in 1913 during a massive storm known as the Big Blow. Jason and Bill later donated the World War I–era tools to the Inland Seas Maritime Museum in Vermilion, Ohio. The feeling that he had contributed to the preservation of a historical relic was one of boy Jason's proudest achievements.

Throughout his life Jason amassed piles of historical trinkets, war-related ephemera, and outdoor gear. He carried collections of compasses, tiny brass cannons, animal bones, whistles, Boy Scout badges, original G.I. Joe dolls, pendants, bandanas, flags, football cards, pewter figurines of presidents, antique coins, Roosevelt dimes, Confederate dollars, and cigar boxes from city to city. At one point he lugged around old manhole covers. His collection of antique books weighed hundreds of pounds.

On Erie's banks, Jason's interest in the outdoors took form as he watched raccoons scour the grounds and kingfishers and golden eagles take flight overhead. He and Aaron walked the nearby railroad tracks and fished until nightfall. Jason became a Boy Scout under the tutelage of his father. When they weren't roaming free outdoors, Aaron and Jason convened under the spell of their VHS collection, which included a copy of Led Zeppelin's *The Song Remains the Same*. Jason spent many hours, over many repeat screenings, perfecting his impression of Robert Plant, the band's curly-topped, astral sexual frontman. Aaron believes this is where his brother's singing voice began to evolve, though Jason wouldn't use it in any serious way until much later when he entered college. The family's isolated confines pushed Jason's imagination into overdrive, and though he spent many hours lost in the company of books and records, he also became extremely performative and increasingly eager to sing or play guitar for anyone who would listen.

By age five he entertained for the neighbors with classic songs Bill taught him, such as the 1905 traditional "Low Bridge, Everybody Down." "I've got an old mule and her name is Sal / Fifteen miles on the Erie Canal," he sang with a small guitar. Jason developed a lifelong love of the Great American Songbook that blossomed into the influences for some of Jason's greatest works. He once explained, "I'm always attracted to older music. And not just a little older. It's not the '80s that I'm going back to. If I could get recordings from the 1880s, I'd be just happy as hell. I like that huge break off when popular music in the classical violin-bass-drum arrangement, like the huge classical arrangements of musicians, sort of broke down."[3]

The same year, Molina was crowned the Woolybear King of nearby Birmingham, Ohio, after winning the fifth annual kid competition championed by local weatherman deity Dick Goddard. The Molinas stumbled upon the festivities after going out for an evening drive, and the officiants plucked Jason from the crowd. "They put him up on the stage and the applause-o-meter shot up," Bill remembered. Young Jason, wearing Cleveland Browns–inspired orange-and-brown pajamas his mom had designed and hand-sewn, made the front page of the local paper, rendering him famous for a day. He carried the official "Woolybear Watcher" certificate bestowed upon him that day for the rest of his life. It was addressed to "King Jason Molina."

Bill's first twenty years teaching were spent with gifted students at Hawthorne Boone Elementary School on W. 20th Street in Lorain, where he utilized music and storytelling in his classrooms as teaching devices. Jason and Aaron had him for seventh-grade science. Bill also coached baseball, wrestling, and track and led outdoor expeditions for his students. Young Jason often tagged along. "He was my shadow until he was about twelve," Bill explained. "He never left my side."

Though Jason clung to his father, the kids were also accustomed to making themselves scarce in the midst of their mother Karen's binges, which happened fairly consistently—about four or five days a week, often Monday and Tuesday, and then again Friday through Sunday. In a fit of rage or sadness, she'd send the kids out of the trailer until evening. Ashley often headed across the path to her best friend's trailer, who she later realized lived with two drug-addicted parents, while Aaron and Jason headed to the beach to fish or explore. "I've always been like, 'Okay, see you later. I'll go out and do my own thing,'" Jason explained of his childhood. "I rarely got into trouble, though. I was always in my own little world."[4] This physical and emotional separation from their mother is something Jason clung to for the rest of his life. "I don't think she ever bonded with him," Ashley explained. Being the oldest, Jason was also the most defiant, which led to sparring between him and Karen as Jason grew older.

The Molinas took sabbaticals in West Virginia when Bill was on break from school. They often traveled to Bill's hometown of Beckley to visit Jason's grandmother, Mary Molina. Jason never knew his grandfather, Andrew Molina, who died before he was born, but was enamored with his grandpa's Spanish heritage. Jason often recounted tales of Bill's Spain-born kin, calling them gypsies, a poetic embellishment to explain his propensity for incessant touring and moving from city to city. He explained,

> I never met my grandparents. But I'd heard stories about how they were magicians and charmers, and did things that the more orthodox, more religious Christians in my family hated. They wanted to keep it a secret that they had all these traditions and these "things" that they did from Spain. As far as I know they weren't musicians. I heard they were good singers, they had a vocal oral music tradition.[5]

During some of the family visits to West Virginia, Karen took the kids while Bill stayed behind, even though he was from the Mountain State, too. Despite her struggles, she also made many attempts at fostering and participating in her children's day-to-day lives—cooking, sewing, and running errands. Karen quit drinking by the time Ashley was in middle school and became active in their school district's Parent Teacher Organization. Whereas Ashley found a best friend in her mother, Jason only remembered the instability, which he'd remain mum about throughout most of his life.

Regardless of their individual relationships with Karen, summers away were a great reprieve for the Molina children, who were free to roam the vast expanse of the countryside and get away from their mother's unpredictable emotional and physical states. Bill recalled that when Jason was three he hiked eleven miles wearing a kid-sized backpack and never complained.

On one of the trips Jason's maternal grandmother, Daisy Foster, shared with him family lore that his great-great-great-grandfather fired the last cannon shot on behalf of the Confederacy in the Civil War, before they surrendered to Robert. E. Lee in 1865. This of course impressed the budding Civil War buff. Bill remembered that Jason's constant inquiry about the legitimacy of the claim sparked a decades-long search for this truth that led Bill and Jason to courthouses all over West Virginia and Virginia. Bill eventually learned that Jason had two great-great-great-uncles, brothers Isaac Edward French and Rufus French, who were with a Virginia artillery company that surrendered at Appomattox. Like many of the stories Jason dropped like bread crumbs throughout his life, this particular family mythology had just enough truth to be believable.

Jason's fascination with history and the Civil War grew so strong that at age eight he voluntarily participated in several reenactments at the Battle of Carnifax Ferry, wearing a light blue Confederate uniform, often donning a kepi outside the replicated battlefield. Around the same time, Jason realized he had been born above the Mason-Dixon Line and wasn't a Southerner, despite the large chunks of time spent in the Mountain State. This distressed him deeply, to the point that he pleaded incessantly with Bill about becoming a citizen of the bucolic West Virginia grounds he'd come to adore.

After some lobbying on behalf of his father, on November 4, 1983, Jason received a letter from the Office of the Secretary of State, from A. James Manchin himself, commissioning Jason a "Captain on the Ship of the State," a rather studious reference to book 6 of Plato's *Republic*, likening nine-year-old Jason to a philosopher king. "We need young people like you who are intelligent, enthusiastic and concerned for a better Nation," the letter explained. "Always remember, Jason, honor and obey your parents who love you very much, study hard in school, respect your neighbors, and success will be yours."

Figure 1.1. Molina and his brother Aaron playing the part at Pioneer Days in Vermilion, OH. *Photo courtesy of Ashley Lawson*

Jason and Bill often attended antiques shows and scoured for Civil War relics and gold using metal detectors. "He was a sponge," Bill explained. "It was amazing how much he knew about battle flags and calibers of canons. When we'd pull an old bullet out of the ground, he would say, 'Oh, Dad, that's a three-ring .58 caliber.' Or 'That's a Pritchett, that's very rare.' Or 'That's a Tower; that's the biggest shell they fired in the Civil War.'" One time Bill and Jason dug up a class ring from 1914. After diving headfirst into research, Jason returned the ring to its deceased owner's son.

An expedition on a family friend's land had a particularly profound effect on the young explorer. Upon entering the grounds, Jason almost immediately located an old coin. When Bill asked him how he found it, as such a score was rare, Jason explained, "The old man with the gray hair told me where to find it." Bill hadn't seen any man. When the two Molinas told the property owner the story in more detail, his face turned ghost white. "He was describing the original owner of the house, who died a long time ago," Bill explained. The story still gives Aaron goose bumps: "Jason was so incredibly freaked out about that," he said. "He and my dad are both kind of tall-tale tellers, so it's easy to dismiss the story. But seeing Jason so freaked out sold me on it."

Jason also claimed to feel spirits or to have encounters with supernatural beings in the family's trailer. "He would wake up sweating and screaming and claim that someone was shaking his bed, and he wasn't faking it," Aaron said. "Whether or not it was true, he really believed it was true." This relationship with ghosts and the supernatural became a through line in Jason's writing, and in his storytelling, for the rest of his life. In a 2000 interview, he explained that he truly believed in ghosts, and that many people are ghosts. "Nothing to me seems to be on a straight narrative path, i.e., birth to death, especially in art and music. There are immediate directions that are strongly pulling, so something says we owe it to ourselves to give each other space, especially ghosts."[6]

It also illustrated a very early propensity to not allow facts to get in the way of a good story. Jason's strong belief and charismatic delivery often outweighed any skepticism the story's recipient might have about its truthfulness, and he would often talk himself into believing a story, even if deep down he knew it was untrue.

Though he never stood taller than 5'6", Jason was a dedicated athlete who excelled on his middle and high school teams. Though Bill would have loved for him to follow in his baseball-cleated footsteps, Jason's athletic interests were more cardiovascular. "He was a good soccer player and an even better football player," Aaron said. By the time he had risen to the ranks of upperclassman at Admiral King High School, Jason had given up both. "Back then you kind of had to choose between being a jock or being in a band," Aaron added.

Keeping company with each other in their early years, Jason and Aaron thought they might meet other kids at the church that had been evangelizing on the grounds of the trailer park. On Sundays while Bill was fishing and Karen was drinking, the boys boarded a bus to a nearby Baptist church where they attended services and Sunday school. They participated in church plays and were both baptized without their parents being present. "There's something really good and passionate about religion and devotion and stuff," Jason later remarked. "All the honesty, and a lot of times the simplicity, and the passion of devotion to something is what I like in music. I go and play music even before I seek the company of other people. But that gets to be such a downward spiral. You have to be careful not to be such a loner that you can't live. Because living as such a lonely person, you're not getting to experience life!"[7]

This very early isolation contributed to a dichotomy that became a through line in Jason's life, sowing the seeds for both his desire for privacy and his desire for attention—call it the lonesome performer effect. Aaron speculated that genetics played a role, too, and explained that both Jason and Bill always desired to be the center of attention, until they actually were, at which point they would become extremely uncomfortable and squirrely. These feelings of awkwardness often led to the half-truths and over-the-top storytelling commensurate with Jason being the focal point of conversation. "Jason would turn into a character outside of his personality that I knew, and my dad is the same way," Aaron explained. "If you asked me if my dad or my brother are dishonest, I'd say no. But do they tell bullshit stories incessantly? Absolutely."

Outside of his wild but harmless storytelling, Aaron described the Molina patriarch as the "hillbilly version of a Tiger Mom," hyperfocused on the development and success of his three children, injecting his own interests in fishing, the outdoors, and Southern culture and history in the process. Because Bill was a teacher, he knew all the kids' teachers and regularly checked in on his boys' progress. Much like the phenomenon of the preacher's son, the Molina boys felt both compelled to perform but also to rebel, particularly Jason, who took to a heavy metal look and persona in his tween years and by high school had distanced himself from the shared activities he had once engaged in with his dad. Given Jason and Aaron's studious natures, grades weren't a problem. Jason was accepted into gifted programs and maintained high grade point averages through high school, even when he was forced to take his dad's science class in the seventh grade.

Bill's hands-on nature was no doubt a broader attempt to counteract the negative effects of Karen Molina's alcoholism, as the Molina children grew up with a mother in varying states of sobriety until Jason graduated from high school, when she cut back on drinking considerably and then eventually quit. "And she was never a fun drunk," Aaron explained. "She was a mean drunk or a sad drunk, but never a fun one." Though it wouldn't take her own life, the tragedy associated with her alcohol abuse would extend to her two boys. Aaron was eventually able to manage the disease, but Jason could not. And like his mother, he was never a fun drunk.

Ashley, who rarely touches alcohol given her family's history with it, fondly recalled that she had a wonderful mother for about ten years before Karen died suddenly of complications from a brain aneurysm at age fifty-five. For three months Karen lived in the care of the assisted-living wing at Anchor Lodge Retirement Village, which stands on the lakefront grounds of the former trailer park where the Molina kids grew up. After Karen passed, Ashley had no idea that her oldest brother would exhibit a near-reversal of their mother's experience with alcohol. Instead of quitting the bottle, by the age of thirty-five, Jason was crippled by it, and he would end up in the care of his baby sister during the last years of his life. Today, her two young daughters have only memories of the pair of relatives they barely knew, now known among them as "Ghost Jason" and "Angel Karen."

2

METAL

By the time Molina reached middle school, his love of heavy metal transcended high volumes and heavy distortion. He listened to his dad's Black Sabbath and Metallica records incessantly as a child, usurping command of the hi-fi in his tween years. By the time he was thirteen he'd perfected the hairstyle, with feathered bangs and tendrils in the back that passed his shoulders. He repped business up front and a party in the back through his sophomore year in high school.

This impressed his friends Todd Jacops and Carl Raponi. The Admiral King High School freshmen took guitar and drum lessons at Ron Zehel's Guitar Center in nearby Amherst, Ohio, where musically inclined kids from Lorain purchased gear and refined their chops during in-store lessons. Like many kids who were post–middle school but pre–driver's ed, the pair often rode bicycles long distances after school. One day they dropped by Ron Zehel's to browse. There they happened upon a short kid wearing a Black Sabbath T-shirt who was trying out bass guitars. "He kind of looked like [heavy metal guitarist] Randy Rhoads," Raponi remembered. "He was full on metal." The young guitarist and drummer didn't know any kids who played bass, so Jason stood out right away.

The pair immediately connected with Molina's weirdo factor, as they were both a part of the "alternative" crowd at their high school. "He turned me on to a lot of music," Jacops remembered. "We really relied on each other in that way." This was in 1987 when U2's *Joshua Tree* and INXS's

Figure 2.1. Jason Molina at an early Spineriders band practice. *Photo courtesy of Todd Jacops*

Kick dominated the airwaves. The Smiths had just dropped their fourth and final album, *Strangeways Here We Come*.

It was a year before Everett True's 1988 coverage of the Seattle music scene for British rag *Melody Maker* led to the explosion and exploitation of the term *grunge*. "It was before the labels grunge or alternative or indie existed to us," Jacops explained. Though Molina was younger and finishing the eighth grade, the older pair of friends knew they had found a peer. They called him "Jay."

Soon after the encounter at Zehel's, the three got together along with Jacops and Raponi's friend Dave Williams, a singer, to form their very first band. They called themselves Chronic Insanity. Because Molina was still in primary school, the band often met after school at Hawthorne Boone

Elementary, where Molina studied and his dad worked. They even played an overnight "lock-in" that Bill Molina chaperoned, as well as a talent show at Admiral King High School. But they didn't have a lot of ambition beyond practicing and refining their sound. "We were more about learning what we wanted to be musically at that point," Raponi explained.

By the time Molina upgraded to Admiral King, the four boys were actively dipping into sounds outside the metal genre. Molina and Jacops were into Soundgarden, and singer Williams introduced the rest of the band to Jane's Addiction. But that didn't stop Molina from sending Ozzy Osbourne a fan letter in 1988. He had hopes of being accepted into Osbourne's fan club, which unbeknownst to Molina didn't exist at the time. He was instead given a typed response on Ozzy letterhead, along with an autographed publicity photo. "If you have waited a long time for a reply to your letter, we apologise, but as you know, 1987 was very busy for all of us," the letter said. "Ozzy is currently recording his new album which at the present time is due for release later this year," it added. The album was *No Rest for the Wicked*. Molina loved it.

Molina also grabbed a copy of metal rag *Hit Parader* and headed to a local hair salon, where he requested a style similar to Ozzy's *Bark at the Moon*–era locks, pointing to photos in the magazine. It required a perm. "Unfortunately the hair stylist did a really good job," Aaron Molina said. "He caught so much hell for that . . . so many people made fun of him," Jacops added. "It was awful." Molina's wavy mullet met its fate during a show he played in Cleveland, when it caught on fire after a concertgoer attempted to set the stage ablaze. As a result, he cut his long locks into a shorter, swooped-over skater style, which eventually grew into the ubiquitous, Kurt Cobainesque '90s "butt cut," parted down the middle. It worked well with the two jean jackets he often wore—one with the Misfits skull logo hand drawn on the back in black Bic ink. The other with a hand-drawn, life-sized human spine.

There were a few other bands at Molina's high school, but the most popular was the Sneezing Weasels, fronted by senior Mike McCartney. Molina's band Chronic Insanity marveled at the upper-class brothers-in-arms, who were full of attitude as they towed the line between punk and hardcore. Molina, Jacops, and Raponi wanted to sound more like the Sneezing Weasels . . . less hair metal and more punk rock.

"The singer of Chronic Insanity sort of sounded like he belonged in a bar band," Molina's childhood friend Reilly Lambert recalled. Given that their singer's style didn't match the rest of the band's increasing interest in punk and hardcore, the trio let him go and began pursuing the Sneezing Weasels' frontman.

Chronic Insanity opened up for Sneezing Weasels a few times, becoming friends in the process. After the members of Sneezing Weasels matriculated from Admiral King and the band fell apart in the tire tracks of college-town commutes, Chronic Insanity recruited McCartney as their new frontman. They called themselves the Spineriders, a nod to that prickly feeling when a chill catches a ride down one's spine.

Though outwardly he projected a tough image, and socially he was goofy and in general a bit weird, Molina kept diverse company. His sister Ashley explained that even though he was quite noticeably "cut from a different cloth," one of Molina's very best friends in high school was prom queen. "Whether it was the jocks or the preppy people, everyone liked Jason," she added. Outside of music and school, Molina also held a part-time job at a local pizza parlor, which kick-started and nurtured his love of the marinara-and-cheese-covered pie. Later on in life while on tour overseas, Molina would often eschew trying new dishes in favor of vending-machine pizza or a corner slice. A friendly weirdo who told good stories, Molina was a magnet for anyone who'd have him. Once he got through an obsessive stint with metal, his musical and artistic interests became quite varied. His culinary preferences, however—pizza, fried chicken, barbecue, and pumpkin pie—remained the same.

By the time they could drive, Molina and his brother Aaron were aligned on their interests, as Aaron wasn't on board the metal train either. Both had become obsessed with visual art and anything esoteric. It started with the Bauhaus school of art and developed into a love of large-scale works such as Sol LeWitt's wall drawings and Cy Twombly's automatic writing. Oftentimes instead of reading fiction or nonfiction they tore through technical manuals for electric typewriters and typesetting machines, as well as complete encyclopedia sets.

Molina was infatuated with German experimentalists Kraftwerk and covered a number of the group's songs with his self-taught guitar playing. His favorite was a version of "Das Model," the group's best-known single. The brothers were also enamored with the occult, aliens, and the supernatural and often stayed up late for crackly radio broadcasts of *Coast to Coast AM*, listening intently as electronic music pioneer Giorgio Moroder's hi-NRG classic "Chase" introduced the host's tales of aliens, conspiracy theories, and ghosts.

When Molina was a senior in high school, he made his brother a mix tape that was one-third Merle Haggard, one-third Elvis Costello, and one-third Soho, the British pop band behind the song "Hippy Chick." "Any mix tape snob would go nuts," Aaron laughed. "But for us it made perfect sense." Molina also played in a school-sponsored swing-jazz act dubbed the Rhythm Section, which made regular rounds at area nursing homes and even played at Disney's Epcot Center. "We had eight mostly female vocalists, and we got to dress up in tuxedos," Molina explained.[1]

Spineriders singer Mike McCartney brought a love of thrash and hardcore to the band and introduced its younger members to the likes of Corrosion of Conformity and D.R.I. The songwriting was a group effort, though sometimes the lines were blurred between what McCartney wrote for the Spineriders and for his college band Gordo. That was a point of contention, but in the early days it was a fairly typical suburban teenage affair. Molina, Raponi, and Jacops spent hours in their parents' garages working out three-minute fire drills centered on anticonformity, angst, alienation, and the general malcontent they felt toward Lorain. McCartney joined in on weekends and on breaks from college and served as the resident antagonist, chiding Raponi to drum faster or razzing Molina and Jacops to get in sync.

One fight broke out after Raponi snapped at Molina after a harsh critique of his drumming. "That was a bad one," Raponi said. "I really tried to mend the fence on that before Jason left and got into his parents' minivan." But for the most part the four friends were chummy, though it often seemed that Molina was at odds with his bandmates' recreational activities. "Jason was not a partier at all," Raponi explained. "I cannot recall him drinking at all."

They all agreed that Lorain was a dead end and sang about it in songs such as the Black Flagesque "I Wanna Be," in which McCartney insists, "I don't wanna be like you!" The equally West Coast hardcore–influenced "Adult" maligns the trappings of grown up life, while "Six Coffins High" goes off template with wild guitar and keyboard solos. Bass-forward "Closer" represents the start of many rhythmic instrumental tracks the group later dove into. This was no straightforward metal band. These guys were wild.

When Molina was in school, the regional decline in manufacturing increasingly threatened the identity worn proudly upon Lorain's blue collars. The anxiety and animosity among Lorain's citizens was palpable. Classmates' parents' lost their jobs, and the full factory parking lots and postwork neighborhood bar spillover went from swollen to downright anemic. "There was a real factory mentality," Molina's friend Reilly Lambert recalled. "In the eighties and early nineties those factories were clearing out, and that caused a lot of anger."

In 1982, U.S. Steel Corp.'s Lorain energy pipe plant laid off half of its 8,600 employees. The next year New York Yankees owner George Steinbrenner shut down his American Ship Building Company in Lorain when overburdened employees rallied to unionize. In the early '80s, recession manufacturing jobs across all of the Great Lake states slid from 5.2 million to 3.8 million, the lowest level since World War II.

Though Molina dreamed of leaving the depressed confines of Lorain, once he did, he wore them proudly, metaphorically, as a sort of outsider's badge of honor. Later while attending Oberlin College he wore a cowboy hat, which he viewed as a symbol of simple men. He worshipped at the thrones of classic country singers, music of the everyman, like George Jones, Willie Nelson, and Hank Williams. He hated the small-mindedness of Lorain's factory mentality, as it wasn't particularly kind to artists or anyone who dared to look beyond the template, but he also didn't deny where he came from. It would most obviously manifest itself in his musical identity through his first chosen name as a recording artist: Songs: Ohia, the descriptor being the way in which his family pronounced the name of his home state.

Molina found some reprieve from Lorain's small-town treatment of artists in Cleveland, just a forty-five-minute drive east on Interstate 90. His friends and bandmates often traveled to see touring acts they loved in the neighboring big city, which encouraged them to set their sights on the horizon beyond the boundaries of the dead-end factory town where they lived. They saw nearly anything they could, shows ranging from Dinosaur Jr. to Jesus Jones. In high school, Jason also took a field trip to Oberlin, Ohio, to visit the Allen Memorial Art Museum. The undercurrent of creativity and artistic expression was a revelation, and he left longing for its spirit, which was a far cry from the stifling oppression he felt in Lorain.

The handful of punk and alternative bands in Lorain and neighboring towns Avon Lake and Westlake, on top of a few metal acts from nearby Amherst, traded members and supported one another on shared bills. Because there were only about fifteen or twenty kids to choose from, this caused somewhat unusual age disparities among band members, like college students playing with high school freshman. But the spirit of musical solidarity was what got many of them through the taunting and feelings of extreme outsiderness that go with choosing a punk lifestyle in Lorain. Raponi's younger brother had a band, Neo Nothing, that was respected. The UnKnown from neighboring Westlake, Ohio, remain a perennial favorite and still perform today. Reilly Lambert explained,

I can go on for hours about how Lorain, Ohio, is a shit town, but I won't. Jason and I would talk about how much we hated it, about how we never wanted to go back. When I listen to the Spineriders now, I remember that period as such a creative time for the band and for everyone involved in the scene. Going to their shows and listening to their music gave me my best memories of Lorain.[2]

Once the Spineriders had a few songs in its back pocket, the four boys brought their racket to their high school's talent shows. One was a Gong Show–style affair where Jason and comrades were met by immediate boos, the stage's curtain closing over their screeching din mid-song. "We weren't offended," Todd explained. "It was actually sort of invigorating, because we didn't like many people at our school anyway."

The response emboldened the group to take their antics to a higher level at an upcoming battle of the bands in neighboring Avon Lake, Ohio, sponsored by the Avon Lake High School PTA. It was the second incarnation of the annual competition and widely considered the pinnacle of musical talent in the region. The band entered in earnest, but with a knowing wink—armed with the knowledge that their music could bring onlookers to close curtains. They auditioned February 3, 1990, in the high school's main cafeteria and were judged on musicianship, sound quality, sound dynamics, stage presence, and originality/creativity. Points were added if the band played original songs.

The Spineriders passed the screening and on March 3 took to the Avon Lake Community Center for the real-deal skirmish. Five hundred kids and parents watched as they performed with hopes of nabbing the top prize: five hours of studio time at Cleveland's Magnetic North recording studio. "They were really advanced technically and stylistically," Magnetic North engineer Chris Keffer said of the Spineriders. "They were kind of like the punk attitude of Jane's Addiction crossed with the weirdness of Frank Zappa."

The Spineriders swept up that evening. The quartet went from being booed offstage to being boosted up in the *Lorain Journal*. With their five-hour prize, the boys recorded five tracks and self-released *Like Eye Care*, its cassette debut, later that year. A hand-drawn eyeball with a safety pin through it graced the cover.

Following their win, the Spineriders organized their first DIY show, outside the confines of the school districts. The boys rented the local El Rey Grotto Park community center, charged a few bucks at the door, and sold refreshments. The place was packed with kids and parents. "We ended up breaking even on that one, which felt great," Raponi remembered.

The group reentered the Avon Lake Battle of the Bands the following year and came in second to their friends in the UnKnown. Having become friends with recording engineer and judge Chris Keffer, Molina received some extra feedback on their scorecard. "The bass player is a babe," Keffer wrote in his best girly script.

Along with third-place finishers the Others, the Spineriders and the UnKnown booked their first gig at Peabody's DownUnder in Cleveland, formerly the Pirate's Cove, where Devo, Dead Boys, and Pere Ubu cut their teeth in the late '70s. On April 28, 1991, it cost just five dollars to take in the all-ages triple billing from Lorain County. It was a big deal for the teen band to play on Cleveland's storied punk stage. And it opened up a lot of doors for other shows in the region. The Spineriders began to play regularly at Pat's in the Flats, a sullied dive bar in Tremont beloved for its unpretentious atmosphere, which hosts punk bands to this day.

Despite the Spineriders momentum, Molina grew anxious about this role as bass player and backup vocalist. He had been gravitating toward lo-fi indie and folk music and wanted to pursue the material he wrote at home outside of Spineriders practice. Adding to his discontent was the fact that he didn't drink, and quite often his bandmates were far deeper than half in the bag. "He wasn't cool with us partying," Jacops said. Molina was also very serious with his girlfriend Shannon Dickson, a sophomore at neighboring Avon Lake High School, who had musical aspirations of her own. During his senior year, Molina made an unremarkable exit from the Spineriders, and Jacops shifted over to the bass duties in his stead. He also joined up with Molina in two new musical pursuits.

Molina chose the name Bleem for his first solo project. The aim was to make music that was homespun and DIY like punk, but sonically more aligned with folk music or Lou Barlow's lo-fi emotionally driven band, Sebadoh. Jacops had graduated from Admiral King but stayed in Lorain to complete a year of community college. In the process he became enamored with Molina's stripped-down compositions and happily joined him on guitar, drums, or whatever Molina needed at the time. "The songs were already there, whether he had a band or not," Jacops said. "They were so good that I never felt the need to fix them or overpower them at all."

Bleem set the template for Molina's preference to play with a rotating cast of characters instead of choosing a steady band, though his rotating cast at this time largely consisted of Spineriders personnel. In a 1997 interview, Molina explained, "If you have rotating people . . . see I'll probably never get any better," he said. "But this way I get better by the company that I keep."[3]

Perhaps the most interesting element of Bleem? Whirly Tubes. Molina and company swung the thin corrugated tubes over their heads at different speeds to vary the pitch, for a unique accent to Molina's increasingly sparse compositions. Mike McCartney from the Spineriders remembered being home in Lorain over a Christmas break and swinging the things in Todd Jacops's parents' basement, which resulted in the Bleem song "Tess." The song trades in teenage angst lyrically, with Molina singing about murdering the world in a softhearted near whisper filtered heavily through vocal effects. The innovation lies in the pairing of Molina's ukulele strumming with Todd Jacops's fiercely distorted electric guitar lines. And of course, the whirly tubes. It's as if Molina took cues from Lou Barlow's style but stripped out the rudimentary drums and added electric guitar. Though Bleem hinted at the cryptic, extremely lo-fi acoustic banner displayed by the early work of his band Songs: Ohia, Molina mostly played bass in the band, his ukulele notwithstanding.

Molina also formed Green, his band with girlfriend Shannon Dickson. He played bass, and Todd Jacops joined in on guitar, though it often felt like the roles were reversed. "Jason always kind of played his bass like a guitar, even in the Spineriders," Jacops explained. "He was always kind of soloing on the bass, which was really impressive." Dickson's style of singing was heavily influenced by the late '80s and early '90s sounds of Throwing Muses and Cocteau Twins. The sound was much softer than the Spineriders, though rhythmically the music was complex. Although Green never played a show, the quartet linked up with Chris Keffer at Magnetic North in Cleveland to record three songs for a cassette they distributed to friends, one written by Jacops and two cowritten by Molina and Dickson.

Molina was resolutely dedicated to Dickson for the two years they were together. A photo of the pair from Molina's junior year at Admiral King shows Dickson, in a black spider web–like sweater, planting a smooch on Jason's cheek ahead of the Spineriders' second go at the Avon Lake battle of the bands. "Jason Molina, 17, of the Spineriders of Admiral King High School, gets a kiss from his girlfriend, Shannon Dickson, 15, of Avon Lake High School," was the caption. What's odd is that Dickson was clutching a bouquet of flowers, despite it being Molina's big send-off. Molina's siblings explained that this perfectly illustrated their relationship. "He once walked ten miles in the snow just to take her to lunch," his sister Ashley Molina recalled. Molina's endless dedication and giving of himself to Dickson seemed at once respectful and romantic but also worrisome, particularly to his family. This was especially true when Molina considered forgoing college so he could stay in Lorain, work, and save money for Dickson's tuition.

Even as a teenager Molina kept his worries close to his chest, so when he and Dickson split he didn't discuss it with his friends or family. Molina instead focused on the future, aided by a generous scholarship he was awarded near the end of his senior year to study art at Oberlin College. Though the school was just a twenty-minute drive, it felt like a faraway land and a creative sojourn along the path to a permanent out from the trappings of Lorain. As his high school peers deliberated over potential next steps at regional colleges or factories, many remembered Molina being unflappable about his plans for the future. Jason Molina was going to be a rock star.

3

OBERLIN

Oberlin College is a recognized left-leaning private school tucked in the midst of blue-collar Lorain County, known for its student activism and progressive policies. Its trailblazing dates to its founding in 1835 under president Asa Mahan, an educator known for his pro-abolitionist stances. By 1844, Oberlin had become the first college in America to admit and graduate both black students and female students, in addition to white male students. By the 1970s it had become the first American college to hire black coaches and have co-ed dorms, banning fraternities and sororities in the process. Today, the school mandates gender-neutral bathrooms on campus.

In the fall of 1992, Jason Molina began his four years at Oberlin College as most students do, in the campus dorms. He had been awarded a scholarship to study visual art and art history. His passion for art was the only rival to his passion for music making. A part of his scholarship afforded him the opportunity to be a resident advisor, which provided a private dorm room. His tiny quarters were meticulously organized with the trinkets, relics, and ephemera he collected and situated like altarpieces to the past. In the dorms he continued to write songs under the Bleem name and recorded them with his high school friend Todd Jacops, who'd left Lorain to study at Kent State. It also provided a home base away from Lorain. His sister Ashley recalled that after Molina left for college she never saw him, unless she traveled with their brother Aaron to visit him on campus or attended one of his shows. "Oftentimes over holidays when all the other kids went home, Jason stayed on campus," Jacops explained. "So we would have the run of the dorm." Molina also began tinkering with the ukulele after realizing its four strings were an easier way to achieve the sounds he wanted than his thuds of the electric bass.

Molina entered Oberlin near the end of the college's post-rock musical renaissance. Beginning in the mid-'80s, groups comprised of highly trained students from the conservatory melded with highly conceptual visual artists to create sounds that eschewed rock's traditions and trappings, sort of like an undergraduate version of Patti Smith's Chelsea Hotel, but with meal plans and cheap beer instead of scurvy and hard drugs.

Punishing post-underground hardcore act Bitch Magnet formed in 1986 at Oberlin, paving the way for other loud-soft, slowcore, and conceptual melting pot bands such as Codeine, Trans Am, Bastro, Oneida, and Golden, whose members met or were educated in Oberlin's halls. Oberlin grad Liz Phair's bedroom cultivations met the world in 1991, with encouragement from fellow Oberlin grad and Codeine drummer Chris Brokaw. A few years after Molina's time, Oberlin students Karen Lee Orzolek and Brian Chase continued the college's rock 'n' roll tradition by forming the Yeah Yeah Yeahs in Brooklyn after they graduated.

The synthesis of the Oberlin music scene occurred in two places. On campus, live sets by emerging acts were broadcast from student-run radio station WOBC, its studio B serving as a hub for recording student and touring bands. Off campus, ubiquitous student house parties hosted bands that set up in kitchens and living rooms to play for, quite literally, a packed house. Molina quickly made friends in the scene, his unrelenting energy and earnest enthusiasm for song craft a standout trait among the throngs of jaded art kids who traded in sarcasm and irony.

Upperclass students Dan MacAdam, Rob Sullivan, Jeff Panall, Carl Kumpke, and Eben Burr played in a metal band called Thighmaster, re-named Thigh Mastersssen on their only release, a split single with robotic post-rock trio Trans Am, who gained greater visibility after graduating. Molina *loved* Thighmaster and was an enthusiastic audience member at all of their shows. In turn, the band members grew to know Molina as "a weird metalhead kid from Lorain." Dan MacAdam and Rob Sullivan, Molina's two redheaded friends known for their acerbic wit, also played in a bluegrass act called Rufus Crisp, named for the storied banjo player and raconteur, with their friends Jennie Benford, a vocalist and mandolin player, and Phil Manley, who went on to play in Trans Am. Molina attended their gigs, too, and was particularly enamored with Benford's singing.

During Molina's tenure in progressive Oberlin, the underground music circuit on campus was vibrant and thriving. The centrality of social life for upperclassmen was the off-campus shared houses, where many of the conservatory-trained and scrappy independent musicians crossed over. "He [Molina] was this little weird guy with a teenage mustache," MacAdam explained. "He'd set up in the corner at parties with his ukulele, totally uninvited." Some chalk this up to renegade-style performance art on Molina's part. Others say that Molina didn't have the sharpest awareness of social cues. Either way, Jason Molina, poet troubadour, became a known presence on campus—the long-haired kid with a ukulele, belting out cryptic poetry laced with inside baseball insights about the Civil War and the Ohio and West Virginia landscapes of his childhood. His oddities and high energy were adored more often than not, and a budding talent was recognized among his peers.

Molina was literally swinging from a lamppost on the sidewalk when friend Max Winter met him in the spring of 1993. His frenetic energy was like some sort of prewar cartoon. "His voice just sort of shot out of him, like a dog's bark or a loud bird," Winter remembered. "He was energetic, goofy, and very joyful." Molina had seen Winter's fledgling rockabilly band play on campus, and the two hit it off immediately, bonding over a shared love of country musician Johnny Cash, swamp-rock pioneers Creedence Clearwater Revival, and bluesman John Lee Hooker. Molina's unsparing energy earned him the nickname 9 Volt.

He was not only enlivened by the college's musical breeding grounds but also by its art scene and museum, and he immediately took advantage of the Allen Memorial Art Museum's unique rental program. For five dollars a semester, Oberlin students could check out works of art by masters such as Renoir, Picasso, and Dalí and hang them on their dorm room walls to study. The first time Bill Molina visited his son on campus, he noticed a black-and-white drawing on the wall of Jason's room. "He said, 'Dad, that's a Picasso,'" Bill recalled. "He had special white gloves to wear to handle it. I couldn't believe it." Molina was so proud of the program that he couldn't help but brag to his friends from Lorain. His friend Carl Raponi from the Spineriders was so impressed that he included the program in a paper and presentation he gave during his own college art studies.

Outside of his RA duties, Molina worked at the beloved local coffee shop the Feve, which was a stone's throw from the heart of campus life at Main and College Streets. A hole in the wall that hosted open mic nights, the Feve was where Molina gave his first solo performances under various monikers. "Bleem was him singing and recording on his own," Bleem contributor Todd Jacops explained. "But what ultimately lead to [Molina's first band] Songs: Ohia was him getting out and performing." It would be a few years before Molina would adopt the moniker Songs: Ohia, though. Instead he performed under his own name, or an endearing nickname he would soon earn that followed him for the rest of his life.

Molina's job at the Feve afforded him the opportunity to perform, and it was also where he earned his infamous nickname. "He ran around like crazy when he worked at the coffee shop," owner Jason Adelman explained. This sprightly behavior lead Adelman and crew to christen Molina "Sparky." At first he hated the name, but soon embraced it and used it as his stage name before landing on Songs: Ohia. He often signed letters and e-mails to his Oberlin friends "Sparks," "Sparx," "Sparkletone," "Sparxiphone," or plain "Sparky."

At the Feve, Molina also befriended brothers Geof and Bruce Comings, two musically inclined townies who became lifelong friends and collabora-tors. Bruce Comings got a job at the coffee shop when he was a senior in high school. On his first day, he was scheduled to work with Molina. "He [owner Jason Adelman] called him Sparky, and so forever more he was Sparky," Bruce Comings explained. "He had a really jumpy energy, so it made sense." When his brother was working, Geof Comings often came in to hang out and chatted with Molina during his breaks, when he'd often sketch and write lyrics in notebooks. Molina and Geof Comings soon real-ized that they went further back. Geof had broken Molina's foot during a collision in a high school soccer match.

The two friends connected over a shared love of heavy metal, but also alternative acts like Dinosaur Jr. "He took it a step further by saying he only liked the Lou Barlow songs," Comings laughed. He also remembered hearing slowcore acts Red House Painters and Codeine for the first time in Molina's dorm room.

After one of their listening parties, Molina ran into a neighbor and stayed back to talk to him while Comings walked on. "Suddenly the kid ran up, shook my hand, and thanked me for being there," he explained. "Sparky told him I was Lou Barlow." To this day Comings has no idea why Molina told his neighbor a blatant lie other than for the pleasure of both his amuse-ment and the kid's amazement. These sorts of displays became a mark of both Molina's humor and his penchant for mythmaking, as he never al-lowed the truth to get in the way of a good story. Though his siblings knew him as a storyteller, Molina was known for stretching the truth among his high school crew, which regarded him as hilarious and enigmatic, a heavy metal bass player, and an undying romantic, but never a liar.

In the dorm, Molina met Anne Grady, a raven-haired anthropology major who was one year his junior. "One day he came by my dorm room to look at my tapes," she explained. "I asked him his name, and he said 'Sparky.'" Refusing to accept that answer, she pressed him further, but Molina wouldn't budge. "Not just in that conversation, but for days," she added. "When I saw him in the hall, I just called him 'you.'"

While those around him tended to look to the future of rock music, Molina stood firmly in the past, inspired by Hank Williams, the Carter Family, Tammy Wynette, and others. As many of his friends took to over-the-top antics circa death metal, punk, and heavy rock 'n' roll bands—an arena where more is widely celebrated—Molina exercised restraint and became increasingly committed to sparsity and simplicity. As his friends wailed on solos, Molina hushed into meditation.

Perhaps the most extreme example of his friends' antics was Chicken Hatchet, the tongue-in-cheek death metal band his friend Jeff Panall formed after Thighmaster, with friends Eoin Russell, George Patterson, Eben Burr, Eric Eidsvik, and David LaCrone. Molina participated in a stunt where the group nailed a haul of chicken carcasses to a large crucifix during a show at the 'Sco, the Oberlin student union. Though it elicited loads of attention and laughs, the group got in even more trouble—near expulsion-level trouble. Molina immediately regretted his onstage role slapping around a blindfolded guy, his friend Christian Oates, who was tied to a chair and was palpably embarrassed by any mentioning of the event.

In contrast to the boldness of the Chicken Hatchet stunt, Molina's first solo gig at an Oberlin house party was markedly apologetic. During the performance he played an electric guitar borrowed from Chicken Hatchet friend Dave LaCrone and wore a masquerade-style mask to shield his face. His demeanor was shy and reluctant, opposite the exceedingly mature songs he belted out. "His stage banter left a lot to be desired, but his work was incredible," friend Max Winter explained. "He was the first person I met who had kind of arrived as a fully formed musician and songwriter." The autodidactic quality of Molina's work was unique in the sea of Oberlin's conservatory elite, and his oblique poet-songs were pearls in the barnacled sea of aggressive metal- and prog-steeped bands blasting from basements of college kid houses. He didn't write in standard verse-chorus-verse format and instead sang snippets of scenes he'd penned in a notebook, or a tribute to the Civil War or another historical battle. An oblique customer rooted in musical tradition, Molina belted out folk songs for anyone who'd have him, his long, straight hair accented by a mustache—a truly unique aesthetic at the time, established far prior to the bevy of irony-laced T-shirts and tote bags that would start to pop up in urban coffee shops and cutesy indie-folk bands in the late '90s. He'd ditched metal and punk almost entirely in his performances, confining them to the turntable and cassette decks in his bedroom, though Black Sabbath remained a favorite. Throughout his life he'd often refer to himself as a heavy metal bass player.

Oberlin's leftist confines and palpable nonconformity allowed Molina to ditch any hang-ups he had about the trappings of his hometown, but he clung to his blue-collar roots in what he saw as a sea of privilege on Oberlin's campus. He captured his angst about Oberlin students in the song "Rich Kids":

> Laboring, I first chose you for my all-star team
> and you have been advised
> where power and rich kids find ways to unite
> it is virtue who's sitting the bench
> by not talking, I shouldn't have to say it
> I said get out, I mean get out this minute
> I don't trust you more than
> the weight of your shadow
> rich kid I'm talking to you

Molina worked various jobs on top of his studies while attending the school on a scholarship, as there's no way his family could have afforded the tuition otherwise. He insisted to friends that his background was so blue collar and so insular that he hadn't even heard of the town of Oberlin, which was about a twenty-minute drive from Lorain, until his high school guidance counselor encouraged him to apply to the college. A few facts got in the way of that story, primarily that Molina was born in an Oberlin hospital, and his high school soccer team played in Oberlin when Geof Comings broke Molina's foot. But like most things with Molina, his friends almost appreciated the mythologizing, preferring his story craft and cultivated persona to the banality of the truth.

Though he had found many musically inclined peers and supporters, Molina had an outsider persona . . . never really fitting in . . . never really revealing too much . . . towing the line between fantasy and reality. He began his personal mythologizing in earnest through stories, but also drawings he'd leave in the backs of library books and cryptic hand-dubbed cassettes. He began drawing the frequently used Songs: Ohia crossbow insignia in 1993, inspired by a 15th-century watermark used by Italian papermakers. He also compulsively drew the fleur-de-lis, a symbol of French heraldry that spans religious, political, artistic, and dynastic connotations. Nearly every notebook, paper, and book Molina got his hands on became ingrained with one of the two images, which he never explained but spoke of in oblique historical terms, which perfectly suited his persona.

In his sophomore year he befriended Tom Colley, who had a show on Oberlin student radio station WOBC. On October 18, 1994, the gentle, ponytailed art student, who became a lifelong friend of Molina's, recorded the singer-songwriter's first session in the station's Studio B. In a brief interview before his set, Molina explained that his two biggest influences were Ozzy Osbourne and Hank Williams. "That doesn't mean I'm going to be covering any Sabbath here tonight," he added.[1] That didn't stop a joker from crank calling the show to request Black Sabbath, which Molina eventually appeased with the opening riff from "Paranoid."

After an "okeydokey," Molina launched into what he described as a chronological set, starting with his oldest songs, including "Tess," "Nosebleed," and "1943," which he had written under the Bleem name with Todd Jacops. Instead of his distorted bass, Molina strummed a ukulele and sang without any affectation. His twenty-year-old voice was cherubic and choirboy like, a clean canvas awaiting an onslaught of paint. He played eight songs that never made it to a proper recording, including one titled simply "Ohio." He dedicated the song to his best friend and his home state, which he pronounced *Ohia*. He also played songs "45 Degrees" and "Bath," which eventually made their way to his 1998 LP *Impala*, both examples of Molina's poetic worldview. In the latter song, he sings,

> So here's your bath tub, Christmas lights
> Add the water, seven pints
> Face down in silver, white Christmas light
> Wednesday found you,
> Your hair was white as a kite string
> So here's your story, as you would have said it
> Leave out the sad parts
> As bright eyes fill with Novocaine
> And chandeliers with fire flies
> You won't know
> You won't know
> I'm not sure

Before Molina's last song in the set, another prankster called in to request the Troggs' "Wild Thing," to which he replied, "I think whoever called knows that I'm not such a wild thing, and I don't know if I know any songs called 'Wild Thing.'"[2] He ended with a song he described as being from the eighteenth century and written by the poet Isaac Watts. Lyrically it more closely aligned with the traditional "Wayfaring Stranger," though not exactly. Regardless, it was a cogent statement of his outlook and his influences, a sort of precursor to the materials he'd record leading up to his first two singles and LP. He explained, "This is a song sung by soldiers in America, kind of after they get a little bit toast and then they're real sad to see each other go, because they reckon they might not see each other again."[3]

Molina and Todd Jacops released a six-song cassette under the Bleem name in 1994 titled *The Halfdoll EP*. The songs inside are a direct reflection of Molina's adoration of Sebadoh frontman Lou Barlow, its pairing of homespun discord and melancholy lyrics perhaps the most obvious reference point. The seven-song cassette opened with "Halfdoll," a sped-up and warbled psychotropic nugget clocking in under two minutes, Molina's voice resembling that of Alvin the chipmunk. The plaintive second track, "1943," eases the listener into the heavy distortion of "Where All the Pain Goes" and "Tess." Jacops helms vocals and acoustic guitar for "Fistfull of Wishfull," a more subdued song than its predecessors. Its style mirrored the next song, "Nosebleed," sung by Molina. The last track, "Sleeping Wartime," truly opens the door for Molina's future musical endeavors, as a reimagined version of the song would appear on his second LP under the Songs: Ohia banner. Strictly looking at the parts, the songs were incongruent. But the lo-fi recording quality and bathtub vocal vacuum created a uniformity easily adored in the early '90s.

In the contemporary landscape of GarageBand home recordings, the fuzzy, tape-recorder quality of the EP is utterly enigmatic. But for anyone of the pre-Internet era, it's a fitting capsule of the time, when lo-fi was king and indie rock got weird. The idea that punk's spirit could be embodied by two guys pairing folk whispers with shredding electric guitar and ukulele plunking seems utterly preposterous. But in 1994, among certain circles of basement show–throwing, mix tape–trading, indie chosen family, the sound was cozy and familiar, like a favorite thrift-store cardigan or bedraggled Chuck Taylors.

A handwritten track listing appeared on the tape's inside, which was signed "Jacops/Molina 1994." The hand-dubbed TDK D60 cassettes were stocked in the Oberlin Co-Op Bookstore, an important hub for discovering new music, which had just opened in a newly constructed three-floor building in the summer of 1993. The owners of the Feve ran a coffee shop in the space called Irene's, where Tom Colley from WOBC worked. The space also sold textbooks and art supplies. Molina and friends often shopped for

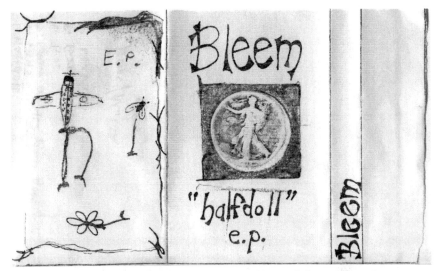

Figure 3.1. The hand-drawn and Xeroxed j-card from Bleem's cassette tape, *Halfdoll* EP. *Photo courtesy of Tom Colley*

records at the co-op, scooping up favorites like the first 7" by heralded recording engineer Steve Albini's band Shellac, titled *The Rude Gesture: A Pictorial History*, as well as Oberlin-related slowcore band Codeine's second album, *The White Birch*, which endured as one of Molina's favorite records.

Another band that had made its way into the collective consciousness of Molina and his friends was the mysterious folk act the Palace Brothers, Louisville-born singer-songwriter Will Oldham's pre–Bonnie Prince Billy outfit. Oldham's 1993 debut LP for Chicago-based indie label Drag City, *There Is No One What Will Take Care of You*, reverberated throughout Oberlin's dorm rooms, shared houses, and student radio airwaves. The same year Molina tipped into the realm of Visible Musician on Oberlin's campus, the Palace Brothers' sophomore 1994 LP, *Days in the Wake*, was a unanimous favorite, it's ghostly Americana a contemporary amalgamation of new and traditional sounds.

In the 1994–95 school year, Molina moved from the dorms into a shared dive at 181 West College Avenue—dubbed "House of Boys" due to its lack of women roommates and the maturity level of its inhabitants. Here, Molina wrote the song "Boys" as a jab at his older roommates who treated him like a little brother. Tom Colley from WOBC lived there, along with Jeff Panall and Dave LaCrone from Chicken Hatchet and a few other roommates. The house was an incubator of creativity and hijinks, where local bands often played in the kitchen or living room. "That house was ground zero for a certain gang," explained roommate Eoin Russell, who became infamous for wearing his Harley Davidson black leather pants 666 days in a row. "We just started hanging out and overlapping, and here was an extended crew of about 50 people." Russell and Molina especially bonded over their deep affection for heavy metal and classic rock, acts like Metallica and Motorhead, but also Deep Purple and Boston, "which were not the coolest things in the mid-'90s," Russell added. Russell and Molina looked the part, too, with their long hair.

The friends bonded over music and art, but also teenage-boy mischief. This often involved drinking, and to excessive amounts. But no one witnessed Molina partaking beyond one or two beers. "I knew him as sort of a teetotaler or a total lightweight," friend Max Winter said. "In the fall of '94 some buddies and I went to Cleveland to go to the Great Lakes Brewery, and he wanted us to bring him back a growler of Elliot Ness Amber Lager," he added. "He drank like a quarter of it and passed out. He seemed really unfamiliar with the process of drinking."

Though he was surrounded by creative peers, many felt that in general Molina was a loner. Laser focused on music, he rarely spoke of his life outside the artist and musician persona he was cultivating. In college Molina became obsessed with the notion of authenticity, the product of feeling stifled by the conformity that he felt in Lorain, where many of his peers didn't appreciate the making of art and music. In contrast, at Oberlin Molina was allowed to be anything he wanted. And the blue-collar artist image he became was, to him, his true self, even if others felt it was performative or meticulously crafted. Friends often razzed him for the cowboy hat he wore, as there was nary a ranch to be found in northern Ohio. But Molina developed a lifelong love and fascination with headwear and often asked for recommendations for the best hats to wear onstage and the best haberdasheries in the cities where he toured. He especially admired Hank Williams's short-brimmed Stetson.

Molina made friends through playing music, but he held most everyone at an emotional arm's distance. Conversations never ran much deeper than records and the stories that helped shape his personal mythology. "I think Jason befriended me because of my gear," friend Eoin Russell said. The only person who knew much about Molina's personal life was Anne Grady. Even then, she never saw where he grew up or met his parents, even though they were a short drive away. Instead they meshed largely under the banner of art and art making. Grady, and her academic cum no bullshit outlook, was at once a very romantic and very grounding presence for Molina. She could accompany him to museums, but also help him with life logistics like financial aid. And oftentimes she did, as Molina was horrible at managing money and often spent his paychecks as soon as they arrived.

Molina's penchant for storytelling cranked up to ten in the company of his housemates and their extended friend group. One of the most beloved Molina tall tales involved his high school prom photo with then girlfriend Shannon Dickson. His roommates Jeff Panall and Tom Colley found it in a box in their living room shortly after Molina moved in. "He was in a tux and his hair was all done up," Panall recalled. "So of course we put it up on the wall." When Molina returned home and received the de facto razzing about the pubescent relic, he responded soberly that it was difficult for him to look at the photograph because his date had died in a terrible car wreck soon after that night. Guilt-ridden, Panall and Colley left the photo on the wall but eased up on the teasing. That is, until Shannon Dickson showed up on their front porch. "Our housemate was home one day, and someone knocked on the door," Colley explained. "It was the woman from the picture." Dickson was very much alive and living just twenty minutes away in Lorain.

"There's a guy named Molina in the band Crazy Horse [drummer Ralph Molina] that Sparky would say is his uncle or some sort of relative," Colley said. "I don't know if that's true or not. I never figured it out." Molina told some friends that Cincinnati Reds outfielder Bernie Carbo was his cousin and that his dad was a professional baseball player. He also insisted that he overheard a member of the Oberlin city council saying that their friend Rob Sullivan was going to be evicted from his house, which never happened. "He was this insane instigator and clown who was very attuned to the absurd in everyday life," friend and future bandmate Dan MacAdam added.

There were also stories that didn't serve Molina at all. "He claimed that a friend of ours whose last name was Porter, that her family ran an inn called the Porterhouse Inn, and that's where we got the name of the steak," Max Winter recalled. "That wasn't true, but I believed it. It took a while for me to realize that he was constantly making things up." Molina's story weaving rubbed some people the wrong way, but most simply accepted it as an extension of his eccentricities—with affection, even. "People love to hear stories, and Jason loved to tell stories," his friend Geof Comings said. The best raconteurs never allow facts to get in the way of their craft.

Shortly after Molina took up quarters at House of Boys, another roommate, Todd Renschler, moved in. "I was practicing drums in the living room, and Jason came downstairs from his room and plugged in," he said.

"We didn't say anything to each other, just began playing." Though the two never spoke much of their process or goals, Molina, most often on ukulele or a four-string Stella tenor guitar he'd grown fond of, and Renschler on drums, traversed campus in search of shows, playing anywhere they could, like dormitory commons areas, the radio station, house parties, and the Feve. They became an inseparable duo.

Molina was relentless in his pursuit of music. "I never knew him to be studying," Renschler added. "I never knew him to be anything but walking around playing his guitar or ukulele." He often joined Molina in one of his preferred recording locales—the bathroom in the dorm across the street from House of Boys. Molina grabbed a tape recorder and his ukulele, and Renschler a hand drum or a metal pot, and the two worked out Molina's sparse songs among the sinks and toilets, recording the results on cassette. "He'd song write in any bathroom," friend Eoin Russell added. "He must have tried 100 bathrooms on campus."

Before he landed on the name Songs: Ohia, Molina performed publicly under Bleem, his own name, or his nickname Sparky, often recording to cassette tapes adorned with his sketches of crossbows, fleurs-de-lis, or whatever insignia intrigued him at the moment. He often labeled the tapes with the antecedent *Songs:* and then a successive descriptor of the mood or inspiration of the songs, such as *Songs: Goth* or *Songs: George Jones*. At Oberlin he began in earnest his pattern of waking up early to write, sing, and strum, like 5 a.m. or 6 a.m. In a 2010 interview he explained, "Sometimes I really do wake up with a song in my head and I have to race to an instrument or write down a few lines."[4] He certainly didn't operate on a College Dude Standard Time, which didn't always bode well with his friends and roommates like Tom Colley, whose bedroom window faced the front porch of House of Boys, where Jason got ready for his morning ritual. "He slept as little as any person I've known," friend Max Winter noted.

In love with Will Oldham's newest LP at the time, Tom Colley, Jeff Panall, and a few of Molina's friends bought tickets for a Palace Brothers show November 13, 1994, at the Euclid Tavern in Cleveland. Molina couldn't attend because he was about a month shy from twenty-one. The friends had decided that the Palace Brothers and their friend Sparky were kindred spirits, and so Molina placed a demo in Colley's trust with instructions to hand it to Will Oldham. "I can't remember if it was his idea or if someone else told him to do it," Colley added. "But I remember I was somewhat embarrassed and shy at the end of the show when I was like, 'Here's my friend's cassette, you should listen to it.'"

Figure 3.2. Molina on the porch at the Big 5 house, near the campus of Oberlin College. *Photo courtesy of Darcie Molina*

Inside was a note from Molina, which he signed Sparky. He invited Oldham to send him letters. Intrigued by Molina's demo, Oldham penned a response postcard requesting more songs. Molina sent another tape and labeled it "Songs: Ohia." Among the two tapes were songs "East Hearts Divided," "Soul," "Freedom Pt. 2," and "September Is 17." Oldham chose "Soul" and "Freedom Pt. 2" for Molina's debut single on his Palace Records imprint of Chicago-based indie label Drag City, which also doled out sublabels for its artists Jim O'Rourke (Dexter's Cigar) and David Grubbs (Blue Chopsticks).

The two songs embody the spirit of Molina and roommate Todd Renschler's bathroom jam sessions. "Freedom Pt. 2" opened with a heaving

scream from Molina's gut, which introduced stripped-down, ghostly ukulele repetitions and Renschler's hand drumming. "And I must walk these
roads to freedom / Cause I can hear them call my name," Molina sang
straight, like a battle cry from a previous era. "Soul" is confessional, Molina
explaining much of himself through the lyrical repetition:

> I love what I know about passion
> I love what I know about mercy
> I love what I know about patience
> I love what I know about soul
> And I know you

Molina's voice was pure and unafraid, particularly for an artist who'd
never been pressed to record. It was as if that voice had been waiting for the
moment since Molina summoned it from within himself when he sat in his
car seat as a three year old. The opportunity to be on Will Oldham's record
label was the stuff of dreams to Molina and his friends, though Jason, notoriously private, kept the news close to his chest, boasting of it to practically
no one. News made the rounds, though. A flier for a 1996 Oberlin house
show would even tout Jason as a "Palace Records recording artist."

Molina spent the summer of 1995 in Providence, Rhode Island, where
his friends Bruce and Geof Comings had relocated to play music with
some locals in a rock band called Pranger. Their Oberlin friend Max Winter had also moved there after graduating but didn't live in the Pranger
house. Molina showed up with only a knapsack and the clothes on his back
and spent the summer sleeping on the kitchen's linoleum floor without a
pillow or blanket, which suited him fine as it was a devastatingly hot summer for New England. Molina had received a fellowship from Oberlin
to study in the summer term at the Rhode Island School of Design. "He
basically got someone to give him money to spend time in the library and
look up stuff that was interesting to him, which is pretty much what he
did all the time anyway," Geof Comings said. Molina brought so few possessions and had so little money that he wore his one pair of dress shoes
to the beach.

When he wasn't in the library, Molina sought out as many open mic
nights as possible in pubs or coffee shops. He'd even perform on street
corners. He played under the name Sparky, Jason, or sometimes the Guard-
ian. "He'd carry his tenor guitar and I'd carry his chair," Bruce Comings explained. This was in an era when Molina sat in a chair he had adorned with
a crossbow insignia and an American flag-inspired design done in pastel col-

ors. Much like at Oberlin house parties, Molina tended to show up near the end of the evening, after a line of high-energy strummers, and completely sink the mood of the room with his downtrodden solo sets. "We just knew him as Sparky, but in Providence he really played up the enigmatic side of himself, this guy from the 1800s sort of thing," Geof Comings explained. "He kind of looked like a pirate," Bruce Comings added.

Molina continued in his pattern of waking up extremely early, writing songs, and then singing at the top of his lungs on the front porch or in the backyard. When he wasn't wailing solo, Molina practiced in the basement with Bruce and Geof or Max Winter. "One time Jason and I played for hours a song I'd written that was pretty terrible," Winter remembered. "Jason was playing lead guitar, and it was incredible. He said something like, 'I can play those Neil Young guitar solos all day, it's the most fun I have playing music.'"

A writer for the local zine *Wingnut* took notice of the short guy with long hair stomping around Providence's campuses and coffee shops in old corduroys and a cowboy hat and interviewed Molina for a Q&A that ran in the zine's third issue. It was Molina's first published interview and quite possibly his most honest and least guarded. The writer asked if Molina was lonely:

> Sure, still am. Always. And it's not by choice, it's just de facto. It just happens, I think. Like the nature of always needing to go out and write more songs. And always needing to go out and read. I read like a maniac. When I think about what I do for fun, it tends to be go buy a book of poetry and read it in a day. Or two days. And I've gone from buying a single book to buying these huge anthologies, because I need something that challenges me. Like I really need 10,000 pages to work through and read and read. And I've always had more company with musicians and artists and writers, and people who are out creating and stuff. I like to be around those people and not really talk about what we do. It just, sometimes I like to be around a lot of musicians but not really talk about music. I like to acknowledge that I'm bordering on some sort of an average normal person, but there's a certain safety in knowing that I can go home and just write more songs, you know?[5]

The scene at the time was building what became recognized as the Providence Sound, in the form of disruptive, arty noise bands such as Six Finger Satellite, Lightning Bolt, and Arab on Radar. But it also reveled in its poppier side. The alternative rock band Scarce was huge on the scene, and Molina found a friend in its drummer, Joe Propatier, who sometimes accompanied Molina at the open mic nights. By chance, Will Oldham was also in Providence that summer, where his girlfriend was studying at Brown University.

Oldham attended Molina's performance in a parking lot behind the coffee shop Ocean City Roasters, where Molina shared a bill with Bruce and Geof Comings's rock band Pranger. Oldham also showed up to see Molina at the venue Millhaus on July 24, where he played a slew of new songs and a particularly alluring cover of country siren Tammy Wynette's "Still Around." In Providence, Molina became enamored with Oldham's art-centered lifestyle and DIY ethos and often romanticized it to Anne Grady when he returned to Oberlin. To his friends, though, Molina never discussed Oldham or the Palace Records deal. "I don't know if he was nervous about comparisons, or if it was just another example of him being weird," Geof Comings explained. "For the most part he denied any awareness of current music once he started touring and recording. The only band I can remember him seeming interested in that summer was Dirty Three."

In the beginning Molina had a deference for Oldham, but eventually the two butted heads, dating back to their shared time in Providence. "Jason liked Will, but he never thought he was an easy person to get along with," Anne Grady explained. Friends also remember Molina vehemently denying that he had even heard the Palace Brothers or Will Oldham. Whether it was a part of Molina's mythmaking or a dogged attempt to skirt comparisons, the likening would haunt him for much of his early music career. During most of his run as Songs: Ohia, Molina was often tagged as some permutation of the "singer-songwriter who sounds like Will Oldham" in the press.

Despite their differences, Oldham invited Molina to open for him in Manhattan, at the newly formed Macintosh New York Music Festival, which came to life in the murky wake of the defunct New Music Seminar, NYC's longest-running showcase of independent music. Molina performed under the name Sparky with his temp drummer Joe Propatier from Providence, and he sang out from under a cowboy hat and on top of a chair, as was his style that summer.

On July 20, 1995, Molina opened for Oldham again, at NYC venue Tramp's. There he made a new friend in Edith Frost, a country-leaning folksinger from San Antonio who'd fronted a rockabilly band and who'd recently moved to Manhattan in the wake of that band's falling apart. The two became e-mail pen pals, as she, too, was about to release her debut 7"—on Drag City, Palace Records' parent label. For Frost, it was her first time playing her original material onstage. "We were both completely green, out of our elements and very excited to be there, so we had that in common," she said. "I thought Jason was a great singer, but I wasn't wild about that name Sparky."

Figure 3.3. Molina performed under the name Sparky at this show opening for Will Oldham's Palace Music. *Poster courtesy of Max Winter*

Will Oldham wasn't wild about it, either. By the time Molina's first single, *Nor Cease Thou Never Now*, reached the pages of the Palace Records mail-order catalog, its cover was graced with a new sobriquet. In a postcard to Molina, Oldham suggested he use the name scrawled on one of the first cassettes he'd sent. "It is a good idea not to use 'Sparky,' but may I suggest replacing it with 'Songs: Ohia' at least for this first record?" Oldham said. "It is a gem to nibble on for the listener and would make a compelling pairing with the record's title."[6]

Speculation attributes the name *Ohia* to the Hawaiian plant *Ōhi'a lehua*. Jason's ukulele performances and penchant for drawing palm trees in the late '90s fuels the speculation, and it's entirely possible that he adapted it as part of the name's origin narrative over time. In a 1997 interview, Molina even quickly said, "The name is a reference to some flowers in Hawaii called *Ohia*."[7] It's a nice line for a newspaper article and a way for Molina to quickly skirt having to fully explain himself, something he grew to loathe in interviews and in life.

People who actually knew Molina attribute the name to his tendency to label his home-recorded tapes and notebooks with "Songs," a colon, and an adjective. Jason tagged a 1996 photo of friends assembling his first LP "Songs: Working." Before a show in Spain, he sent Geof Comings a cassette of songs they were to play and labeled it "Songs: Spain." And of course there was that tape he'd sent to Will Oldham in the spring of '95 from Oberlin, Ohio, labeled "Songs: Ohia."

Molina's simultaneous embracing and dismissal of his humble origin story during his tenure at Oberlin, and his commitment to crafting an image of a working-class balladeer, furthers the idea that the name *Ohia* is a nod to his roots. Quite simply, it's the way in which Molina, his dad Bill, and his West Virginia kinfolk pronounced the state. Molina loved *Ohia*.

Before Molina left for Providence, he had been accepted into a study-abroad program in London. His friend Anne Grady was accepted, too. The focus on the program was on architecture and math, subjects not nearly as enticing to the anthropology and art majors as the prospect of going to London on Oberlin's dime to tour art museums and the city's ancient streets and royal parks. Before Molina departed for the Big Smoke, he recorded two sides for his Palace Records debut, "Freedom Pt. 2" and "Soul," both songs recounting the logistical and emotional conflict of the Civil War.

"How does it feel to be signed?" he asked Todd Jacops over the phone before Jacops and Mike McCartney from Molina's high school band the Spineriders convened in Oberlin, along with Molina and drummer-roommate Todd Renschler, to record the *Nor Cease Thou Never Now* single, his only record for the Drag City imprint. The 7" was released in January 1996 and pressed in an edition of one thousand copies. Two more newcomers to Will Oldham's label, Scottish singer-songwriter Alasdair Roberts's project Appendix Out, and Louisville post-rock alumnus David Pajo, founding member of Slint, released singles at the same time. Molina was particularly impressed with his new label mate Alasdair Roberts.

That fall of 1995, during their study abroad in London, Anne Grady and Jason Molina fell in love. The morning of her birthday, September 1, Molina woke up Grady early, explaining that he had a present for her. The two had been out the night before in a pre-birthday drinking reverie—though Molina did not imbibe—and Anne, commensurately inebriated, had crashed in his flat. Ever the romantic, Molina slept on the floor so Grady could feel comfortable in the bed. The next day, her birthday, in the wee morning hours, they walked London's wet, foggy fall streets to Regent's Park. He led her through the rose garden and to the duck pond. "We'd been walking for hours," she explained. "He took out his guitar and said something like, 'I don't have any money for a present, but I can give you this song." He played his song "The Eagle," which he had recently written:

> Deny the eagle the right to be weary
> Though she bears your nation a breast
> Thrush cries, thrush here
> The cardinal mistrusts me
> Divides the gray sky with fire roads to ride
> Hey, with fire roads to ride
> Hey, with fire roads to ride

Molina had been writing heaps of songs and recording them in his flat in London. His preferred recording method was to stick his small tape recorder in the oven, leave the door open and then sing toward it. It was the first time Grady had ever heard Molina's singing voice. "I was totally entranced. I'd never heard anything like his voice . . . beauty, stubbornness," she recalled. "He really should have kissed me then, or I him." But the kiss didn't happen for weeks. After the private concert in the park, the two simply went out to breakfast, silently knowing that from that point on they were for each other. By the time they got back to the States, they were inseparable.

Molina had many nicknames for Anne: Grady, My Anne Grady, My Lady Grady, Jones, Jonesy (a reference to the Cary Grant film *His Girl Friday*), and Grady Bones Jones. Grady, however, never ever called him Sparky. She refused to. The pair often joked about a fake television show they'd dreamed up that chronicled their adventures: *Grady Bones Jones & Mud-*

flap Molina: Harebrained Adventures, Hotwire Love. Molina's seriousness about living an authentic artist's life greatly impacted Grady, who was enamored with touring art museums and discussing what she saw with Molina. He changed the way she looked at herself, giving her the confidence to not only study but also make visual art.

Grady never met Molina's family, other than the times his brother Aaron would visit campus. They didn't visit Lorain, and Molina rarely spoke about his childhood, except for scant instances when he'd recount the peril associated with his mother's drinking. "I don't think he was completely comfortable sharing the hardships of his childhood," she said.

In London, Molina and Grady met up with Alasdair Roberts, of Appendix Out, also signed to Palace Records, who lived a five-hour train ride away in Glasgow, Scotland. "One day out of the blue I got this beautiful letter asking if there are owls in Scotland, because there was one sitting outside his window as he was writing," Roberts said. "We exchanged a few letters and then I went to visit him in London." The two new friends, along with Grady and some of the other exchange students, toured London's streets, discussing art, music, and literature. On the last day of his visit, Molina gave Roberts a collection of poems by Edna St. Vincent Millay and a cassette of his home recordings.

When they left London, Molina accompanied Anne home to her parents' place in Waltham, Massachusetts, for a visit. It didn't go well, but the drama between Molina and her parents seemed wildly romantic to Grady, who defended her new love vehemently.

When the couple returned for the spring 1996 semester at Oberlin, Jason's older comrades like Jeff Panall, Tom Colley, Rob Sullivan, and Dan MacAdam had graduated. After feeling liberated by the palpable opportunity and freedom in London, Molina felt stuck in Oberlin. He retained his spot in the shared house dubbed House of Boys, though it had been renamed Big 5 by his friend Eoin Russell—a tongue-in-cheek tribute to an overtly sexual song by Jamaican singer-songwriter Prince Buster. Molina slept in the attic. "That house was really memorable because it was always a huge mess," friend Jennie Benford said. It was so messy that trash bags often piled up throughout the house and even fell from the drop ceiling panels. There was crap everywhere. Molina, however, kept his quarters clean and tidy and put a padlock on his bedroom door to keep out the trash bag riffraff. Benford also recalled Molina captivating audiences at parties with his ukulele. "I was always impressed that he could just play solo like that," she said. The place was unbearably hot but free of rent, and Molina spent most nights at his girlfriend's place anyway.

Despite Molina's musical momentum and art school community, his mood took a dive. He became increasingly depressed and dependent on Anne. His emotional state turned on a dime, and he even sometimes threatened to kill himself if she ever left him. "I didn't take it as a serious threat, just more as a sign he wasn't happy," Grady explained. She added that his downtrodden mood never came out when other people were around. "I remember how crazy it drove me, how controlled over his emotions he could be in public," she recalled.

When Molina was in England, he began working on his senior thesis, which he finished by spring's end. A collection of 150 small drawings in waxed crayon and a companion series in mixed media synthesized his takeaways from Oberlin's art program and presented the origin of an iconography he'd use for the rest of this life. The vessel for the drawings was traced from a credit card and cut out, resulting in small, inch-wide canvases. The aesthetic themes of the drawings were twofold. Half of the series features a white Nordic-style cross with a red border, and the other yellow-and-white drawn abstractions.

The mixed-media component of his thesis was another series of small works featuring crosses that were fashioned from newsprint, with a button sewn in the middle of each one. The crosses were framed by a circle Molina cut from a square of white cardboard, which he sometimes spray-painted black. When Molina was living in Providence, he spoke of finding buttons everywhere on the street, and it is very likely that those buttons made their way into these pieces. He had a great eye for scavenging—finding a metaphorical jewel in a pile of rubble—and he attached great sentiment to every trinket, antiquity, or bits and bobs he scooped from the street or flea market. He could easily spot a four-leaf clover in a field of thousands.

When he was in England he also began affixing a white cross symbol to the cases of his four-string tenor guitar and ukulele, something he would do for the rest of his life. Most often they were formed in white medical tape. Grady remembered it being the symbol for a Nordic snow rescue squad, but it also resembles the cross featured on the flags of many Nordic countries. Later, Molina became fascinated with hobo symbols—the chalk or coal markings of impoverished, traveling migrant workers. He specifically drew close to the equilateral cross that symbolized a safe area, which he sometimes called a "protection spell." Other times he referred to it as the Southern Cross, in reference to the constellation Crux, a cross-shaped grouping of stars featured in a bright part of the Milky Way.

Molina wrapped up his studies at Oberlin in the spring of 1996, with two credits to spare. Instead of leaving, he opted to take a pass/fail course in the fall at Oberlin in order to stay close to Grady. He also took a job at the Oberlin library working in the conservation lab. Molina loved the job almost as much as he loved his girlfriend, and he constructed piles of hand-stitched diaries and little blank books for her to sketch in. Like their time spent discussing art in London, Molina's work in the conservation lab greatly influenced Grady. "The woman who ran the lab had gone through a program in Boston, and I decided to go there too after I graduated," she explained. "I became book conservator, eventually I got a graduate degree, and now I'm a sculpture conservator. I credit it all to Jason."

In the fall of '96, Molina began playing in earnest as a trio under the Songs: Ohia name with his friends Eoin Russell and Todd Renschler, working out new arrangements and sonic stylings of his material that ranged from Crazy Horse–inspired '70s-era roots rock to jazz-combo dinner music. Molina gave Grady a copy of Bruce Springsteen's *Nebraska*, which they listened to incessantly, along with such favorites as X, the Clash, and George Jones. In October Molina sent an e-mail to his new musician friend Edith Frost that inquired, "What or who is catpower [*sic*], it arrives here in my town next week."[8]

One weekend Molina enlisted his new bandmate Eoin Russell for a trip to Cleveland to peruse a used record store where every LP cost twenty-five cents, and then a used music equipment store, where Jason bought a tiny Fender Champ amplifier. "It was like four watts or something," Russell explained. "I remember teasing him, like 'What are you going to do with this toy?'" When they returned to Oberlin, Molina plugged his four-string tenor guitar into the Champ, and it emitted a lush, spectral tone, which came as a shock to everyone who heard it. His friends couldn't believe that Molina had conceived of the combination, let alone pulled it off with such a degree of beauty. And of course Molina never explained himself.

The act is a poignant representation of Molina's philosophy on music making and a forecasting of his process in the studio. He was an unabashed fan of the *aleatoric* process in song craft and performance, leaving elements in the recording to chance or to the individual tastes and intuitions of his band members. But he was meticulous in songwriting and highly selective in the people he chose to flesh out the sound in the studio and onstage, though he'd never admit to the latter. "He projected this image of it being coincidental. That was very characteristic of Jason," Russell added. "But he was a showman. He was not accidentally doing this stuff."

Molina loved to be the conductor of his friends and always encouraged those in his life to make and explore their craft. He reveled in bringing people together under the auspices of creating, and to this day his friends cite this tendency as one of the greatest acts of Jason's generosity. Molina's brother, Aaron, remembered him being supremely disappointed when he gave up photography. "In his mind I was always a photographer and visual artist, even though I wasn't very good," Aaron said. He went on to join the military and then the corporate world, two fields very far removed from his early interest in art.

Molina wrote volumes of songs in the summer of 1996, when Anne Grady was away exploring Portland, Oregon, leaving her musician boyfriend in Oberlin rather heartsick. In the fall, Molina took those compositions to Eoin Russell's house, where they recorded on an early Macintosh computer. Todd Renschler played drums, and Russell played bass and auxiliary instruments. By this time Molina had a single under his belt and was increasingly prolific. Still, he felt stifled by the confines of Oberlin's undergraduate trappings.

He began ruminating on his next projects and especially desired to collaborate with his new Scottish friend Alasdair Roberts on a project he tentatively titled "Songs: A Out." Molina also reached out to Cleveland independent label Happy Go Lucky about putting out one of his records. "When Rick from Happy Go Lucky gets back in touch with me we'll be working out the next record by us," he explained to Anne Grady. "Perhaps a 4-song 12"? What do you think, wouldn't it be better not to jump into doing a full length right now?"[9] The Happy Go Lucky album wouldn't come to life for a few more years, but little did Molina know, his life as an independent musician was about to change dramatically.

❹

SECRETLY CANADIAN

Five-and-a-half hours away from Oberlin, in an Indiana college town, two brothers and two friends were starting a record label. Indiana University juniors Chris Swanson and Eric Weddle met through the local basement punk scene and bonded over mix tapes, CD-R rips, and 7" records they traded in the hallways of the Collins student dormitory where they lived on campus. They both worked at the campus radio station, WIUX, and sometimes helped book punk shows at area clubs and houses. Swanson's younger brother Ben had been recently admitted to Indiana University, and the three, along with their friend Jonathan Cargill, whom Chris Swanson met at his job in the Collins cafeteria, were focused on starting an indie record label akin to their underground favorites like Kill Rock Stars, Drag City, and Dischord. It helped that they were all students of the Simple Machines' DIY record-making tutorial *Mechanic's Guide*.

Underground music was thriving in 1996. Indie rock was still considered a sonically nebulous movement rooted in an independent, do-it-yourself ethos, not the tag often synonymous with "bearded" and "hipster" that it would morph into by the mid-2000s. The nearby Chicago scene was at its peak with independent labels like Drag City, Thrill Jockey, Touch & Go, Bloodshot Records, Skin Graft, and Southern Records cranking out LPs that would leave a lasting footprint on their legacy by revered and varied artists across the folk, punk, post-punk, post-rock, indie rock, alt-country, and other assorted micro-genres.

The Pacific Northwest was booming in the post-grunge explosion of Seattle's Sub Pop records, with labels such as K Records, Kill Rock Stars, and C/Z working independently of the increasingly rabid majors looking to cash out as many alternative-leaning acts as possible. On the East Coast, the rosters of New York's Matador and North Carolina–based Merge continuously swelled, while in Washington, D.C., Dischord continued in its ethical sales spree with figureheads Fugazi and friends occupying shared houses and throwing five-dollar shows in and around the nation's capital. Down south in Athens, Georgia, the scene was an increasing presence with its coterie of psychedelic and freak-folk acts birthed from the ever-evolving Elephant 6 collective. On the West Coast, the Bay Area teamed with punk acts signed to Lookout! Records, Fat Wreck Chords, and Alternative Tentacles, while Sympathy for the Record Industry, Revelation, and Epitaph attracted punks in SoCal. That's not to mention the heaps of heartland and coastal indie labels born of their respective hardcore and emocore music scenes. The CMJ Music Marathon in New York remained a hub for discovering bands springing from these independent nooks and crannies, as did Austin's South by Southwest music festival.

In the mainstream, the concept of the traveling music festival was picking up steam in the wake of the success of Lollapalooza, which made its debut in 1991. By 1996, the punk-focused Warped Tour, sponsored by classic skate shoe cobbler Vans, made the sold-out rounds. Crunchier music fans headed to Willie Nelson's Farm Aid or the Tibetan Freedom Concerts staged by the Beastie Boys. In 1997, Sarah McLachlan's female-centric Lilith Fair would form.

"The Midwest Has a New Music Haven," *Billboard*[1] proclaimed of Bloomington, Indiana, in a May 1996 article that likened the swelling underground music scene to that of an early Seattle or Athens, Georgia, in no small part due to the number of working musicians who moved there after graduating from college or after being priced out of more metropolitan locales, not to mention scene spillover from the music school and recording programs at Indiana University. The article narrowed in on the recent contract inked between the major label RCA and the Mysteries of Life, the indie-pop act formed by singer-guitarist Jacob Smith and drummer Freda Love (who also played in Boston's Blake Babies with grunge goddess Juliana Hatfield), after their band Antenna disbanded. They were the first act from Bloomington to sign to a major since "Jack & Diane" heartland megabrand John Mellencamp. The article covered less-visible bands and up-and-coming DIY acts, too, and observed, "There is an intimacy to Bloomington's rock scene, with many of the local musicians playing in several bands simultaneously and regularly guesting on each other's albums."[2]

Bloomington became a regular stop on the indie-rock touring circuit, its bands and booking agents keenly aware of the number of licensed and unlicensed DIY venues from which to choose, including the all-ages club Rhino's and more traditional clubs like the Bluebird and Second Story. The John Waldron Arts Center hosted both traditional performing arts and bands.

In 1996, MTV2 launched as a source for continuous music video play as its patriarch channel dove headfirst into reality television. Its sister station was inaugurated with Beck's pastiche of vintage clichés, the music video for the *Odelay* single "Where It's At." As the sonic aftermath of grunge grew more commercial, the underground became an accessible and unbiased platform for youth dissatisfied with the prepackaged angst aesthetic pumped through conventional channels. For every alternative rock, nu metal, or rap-rock whiner championed by Universal, Warner, or Sony, there were dozens of punk or indie-rock start-ups forming in revolt. And then there were the singular, acoustic protestations of Jason Molina, helping to carve a folk-centric superniche in the greater alcove of independent music. Like Will Oldham of Palace Music, Bill Callahan of Smog, and Jeff Mangum of Neutral Milk Hotel, Molina turned from traditional rock 'n' roll and looked to folk, blues, and gospel musical traditions for inspiration.

Unlike the monikers of some overtly aesthetically driven labels, the Bloomington-based foursome of Chris and Ben Swanson, Jonathan Cargill, and Eric Weddle didn't want their label name to nod to any specific musical genre. Because they found the breadth of "hidden Canadians" in the landscape of American popular culture amusing, they landed on the name Secretly Canadian for their new record label. Its first release was a CD reissue of the album *Glory Hole* by North Dakota outre singer-songwriter June Panic. Growing up in Fargo, the Swanson brothers followed Panic's live performances and cassette-tape output on the local scene and felt his work could be an impactful and easily attainable debut for Secretly Canadian. Ben remembered feeling incredibly awkward at seventeen years old, sitting at his parent's kitchen table attempting to hold a "business meeting" with June Panic before packing up his hoodies and notebooks to begin college in Indiana. When it came to their second release, the quartet of label heads were set on an artist they'd never met, but whom they collectively adored.

Chris Swanson was an obsessive fan of the Chicago-based record label Drag City and bought anything they released. After scooping Molina's Palace Records 7" debut, he became captivated by Molina's cryptic verses and vulnerable trill and likened him to a mysterious poet. "He seemed so mythological at the time," Ben Swanson explained. "We thought his music was perfect." He also seemed far out of the infant label's reach. "I was eighteen and my brother Chris was twenty-one, and we had no idea what we were doing," Swanson added. "We thought because Jason had a 7" out that he had this massive hookup." An indie poet-mystic working under the tutelage of heralded loner-rock icon Will Oldham? It seemed like a stretch.

Undeterred, Chris Swanson—the label's resident extrovert who hovers around 5'8" but has the moxie of an NBA point guard—thumbed the rolodex of his mind for a possible in with Molina. How could they pull this off? Enter Edith Frost, from Molina's New York City show with Will Oldham. Chris Swanson knew her through mutual friends, and she provided Molina's e-mail address. The brothers huddled over their old Macintosh computer, nervously crafting an e-mail introducing themselves, their upstart label, and their adoration of Molina's work. He responded more quickly than they would have expected via a series of short, cryptic electronic asides. Molina was intrigued.

A lasting relationship didn't seem in the cards with Palace Records. Dan Koretzsky, cofounder of the Drag City label, explained in a handwritten note to Molina that the label had no future plans for Songs: Ohia, perhaps because of the many comparisons to their label's sonic figurehead, Will Oldham. So Molina took Secretly Canadian up on their offer to do a 7". But not without a challenge. Molina required that Chris and Ben Swanson drive to his upcoming show in Manhattan to pick up a two-song DAT (digital audiotape), even though he lived basically next door in Ohio. "It was the first in a long line of Molina tests," Chris Swanson said.

Todd Jacops and Mike McCartney from Molina's high school band the Spineriders, as well as Molina's classically trained, leather pants–wearing friend from Oberlin, Eoin Russell, packed up and hit I-90 West for a show at the Empty Bottle in Chicago with Molina before the quartet headed east to Manhattan. They were totally unaware of Molina's plans to meet the Swansons and only knew that Molina had recently booked the NYC gig with the help of his new friend Edith Frost. "Jason let me know that his friend Ali Roberts was going to be coming to America, and we should try to set up a show together while he was here," Frost said. "The best I could do was scrounge an unpaid gig at a record store called Adult Crash, a cool indie record store long gone now."

The four-member Songs: Ohia just barely beat the two geeked-out Swanson brothers, who drove nearly eight hundred miles straight to get there. The two Secretly Canadian reps and Molina had a series of awkward and hilarious exchanges before and after the set, and in them Molina revealed his storytelling prowess. "He kept telling us about Eoin his pirate bass player who had pledged to wear leather pants 666 days in a row," Ben Swanson explained. "He kept calling him a pirate and kept talking about the leather pants." The tale presented a theme to the Swansons that they'd eventually come to expect in Molina: oftentimes the wildest, most outlandish, and most unbelievable stories Molina told were actually true, while the more tepid, pedestrian tellings were lies. What could have easily been a mythologizing of his band, or at the very least a grab for attention, turned out to be completely true—Eoin had committed to wearing the same leather pants for 666 days, an extension of his own larger-than-life persona. At one point after an injury he even walked with a cane, adding to the pirate effect. Chris

Figure 4.1. Alasdair Roberts, Eoin Russell, Mike McCartney, Todd Jacops, Jason Molina, Edith Frost, and friends after performing at WFMU. *Photo courtesy of Todd Jacops*

Swanson explained that he believed everything Molina told him for at least the first three years of their relationship, before realizing his inclination toward the telling of tall tales. "The fans from Indiana were perfectly nice people, not freaks as I had feared," Molina wrote in a letter to Anne Grady. "They will take smiles back with them, I hope."[3]

The show afforded another opportunity to Molina, outside of the start of a partnership with Secretly Canadian. "A WFMU deejay named Robin Edgerton came to that show and invited us to play on the air a few days later," Edith Frost explained. "Tonight we play at what people say is the coolest radio station in the country," Jason said to Anne Grady.[4] He played the radio show solo, to the slight chagrin of his band.

In New York, Molina handed over DATs for two songs for his Secretly Canadian debut, *One Pronunciation of Glory*, which became the label's second release, SC2. "Waltham: Simply Unite the Name" and "Napoleon: How We Have Ranged" were gifts for Anne Grady, Waltham being the name of her hometown in Massachusetts. On the cover again appeared Molina's favored insignia: the hand-drawn crossbow that had also graced the cover of the Palace Records single. The songs were a natural extension of his Palace Records debut, as they'd been written around the same time, but through the lens of his intense and flailing romance with Grady. In "Waltham" he sings of her no-nonsense personality over hushed drums and Todd Jacops's wobbly slide guitar work: "And the most honest one / With the razor wit tongues."

Molina's first 7" record on Secretly Canadian took off like a pack of rockets. It sold out quickly and allowed the label to pay Molina and fund their next record, a 7" single by Bloomington-based math rock outfit Ativin. Based on the success of the single, Molina agreed to let his new label release his first full-length record. His only stipulation was that Secretly Canadian allow his Chicago-based friends from Oberlin, who ran a DIY art and music space called Crosshair, to design and print the cover, as they had done for *One Pronunciation of Glory*. The label eagerly agreed to Molina's terms on a handshake deal. A new partnership was formed.

Molina's college friends Tom Colley, Dan MacAdam, Rob Sullivan, and Jeff Panall had all moved to the Second City after graduating from Oberlin and posted up in a warehouse loft on the city's west side soon to be known as the Butchershop. There, they ran a screen-printing shop called Crosshair and hosted rock shows and art openings, mostly centered around their friends' music and art. "It was very much the DIY dream-slash-nightmare where none of us were technical or businessmen and we were trying to do something technical as a business," MacAdam said. Molina often visited his friends while on tour with early Songs: Ohia, where he would play an informal show at the Crosshair space and then crash on the floor overnight.

Molina had written a lengthy catalog of songs in 1996, many centered on his relationship with Anne Grady. Though his first two singles sold out and were generally well received, they also came with unwelcome comparisons to the Palace Brothers, something Molina had stridently tried to avoid. It came as a point of anger for his friends, when their peers tried to write Molina off as an imitator. "First of all, Jason's songs were fantastic," Eoin Russell explained. "And second of all, having some lo-fi recording of you strumming on an instrument and wailing away with your voice isn't the sole domain of the Palace Brothers. It's not like they invented that."

That fall of 1996, Molina and Grady both lived in the catastrophically messy shared house Big 5, which had gone from untidy to utterly bedraggled, with trash bags thrown everywhere and food smeared on the walls and stored in the panels of the drop ceiling. Upstairs, Molina kept a padlock on his tiny, closet-sized room, which was organized and immaculately kept, decorated by a small turntable, a cot, and a writing desk.

Due to its post–natural disaster state, the house became memorialized in the video archives of daytime talk show *Jenny Jones* after being nominated by neighbors Joseph Friedman and Micah Hughes for the show's annual "Messiest Houses in America" episode. Among hundreds of submissions, Big 5 was chosen along with five other flophouses across the country. For the episode's debut, Grady and roommate Jackie Linge were flown to Chicago to explain themselves. The "award" also included a makeover for the heinous crash pad, which didn't go over well with the eccentricities of its inhabitants. "It looks like the lobby of a Ramada Inn," Linge told the *Oberlin Review*.[5]

By Christmas 1996, perhaps the only thing messier than Big 5 was Anne Grady and Molina's relationship. Molina's emotional states became increasingly erratic. He engaged in stalking-like behavior, often following Grady around campus or staring at her as she slept. Whereas his undying devotion and attention once felt romantic, at this point it was overwhelming. As she pulled away, Molina reeled out of control, though Grady admits her behavior was nothing to be proud of.

The only time anyone ever saw Molina drunk was during a house party in the fall semester of 1996. In a fit of frustration, Molina hurled a jar of mustard across the kitchen in Grady's direction. It sailed past her nose and then smashed on the front of the house microwave, shattering its door. He immediately regretted it. "I never saw him drink again after that," Grady said. During winter break of '96, Grady and Molina called it quits.

In the wake of the split, Molina scrapped much of the batch of songs he had planned to use for his Secretly Canadian full-length debut and penned almost an entirely new bunch. The fourteen songs that made the cut comprised his self-titled debut, which became known as the *Black Album* by fans. Much like his previous two singles, many of its tracks were bathed in Molina's encyclopedic knowledge of historic American wars, particularly the Civil War. "U.M.W. Pension" is a textbook example of this: many recruits of the Civil War were uneducated farmers. They didn't know left from right, but they did know hay from straw. So they affixed a swatch of hay to one leg and a patch of straw to another so they'd know left from right during marching orders. "It goes hay-foot with strawfoot ya thrown down (throw down)," Molina sang. The record also traversed a new battle, fought much more recently. "A lot of it is about our personal Civil War," Grady explained.

The *Black Album* was recorded to eight-track tape in one afternoon at Eoin Russell's new house, a little college dive at 231 W. Lorain Street, though Molina later mythologized that it was recorded in a historic mansion. Unsurprisingly, many of the songs were captured in the bathroom, Molina strumming and singing on the toilet. Others were played live in the living room, with Molina on his magic tenor guitar–Fender Champ combo and Todd Jacops on drums. Mike McCartney from the Spineriders added banjo flourishes on opener "Cabwaylingo." Russell overdubbed the bass and out-of-tune organ a few days later and brought friend Peter Hess in to play woodwinds on "Blue Jay," "Our Republic," "Cotton Hill," and "U.M.W. Pension." Molina wasn't present for the overdubs or the mixing. His only request? No edits. He insisted the tracks represent the spirit of the live playing.

A number of the *Black Album*'s songs reference Molina's homeland in West Virginia. Some were about Anne. In "Gauley Bridge," he used her nickname Jonesy. "Blue Jay" references a phone call the pair had while Grady was in Portland, where she explained that she couldn't get a job "into sin and death," meaning she was struggling to find work. Molina told her she was the captain's bride in "Dogwood Gap." "Our Republic" stems from a motif throughout many of the couple's conversations: the source of life's passions. That song fell apart at the end when one of Russell's housemates walked into the room and disrupted the session. At the end Molina is heard greeting him with a "hey," which he didn't want to erase. "He liked the warts on everything," Russell said. In "Our Republic," Molina sings,

> You should know,
> Trouble comes from a passionate word and
> You should know,
> Passion comes from a passing word
> Dark blue they, our banners flayed
> And burning to the base

Submit to draw closer
The glance you'd once given me
An attempt of the old position
They impose their pushing in steep heroics
These fine others
I owe my lifted, though wounded head
And every side of you to a man
There have been signals
these are now joined by a future
And only say which decayed
Not live opposite the failed republic
Time will meet and pass you by
You should know
Trouble comes from a passionate word
You should know
Passion comes from a troublesome word
You should know
Trouble sounds like a comforting word
You should know
Passion comes from a passing word

In line with the long-standing tradition of oblique musical poets, Molina's lyrics were delivered in a way as to mystify their origins. Like Bob Dylan, poet-jester, he often blurred the lines between fantasy and reality, between earnestness and farce. But in the real reality, most of Molina's words were drawn directly from his interest in history and his daily interactions, most often his interactions in love. "He told me for a long time he was going to send the [test] pressing of his first record to George Jones," Grady said. "But he gave it to me even though we were so rocky, or maybe because of it."

For the *Black Album*, Molina ditched completely the distorted electric guitar of his Bleem material and created a sort of mystical aura around his tenor voice and his tenor guitar. The fidelity of the recording, while better than his previous efforts, still reeked of DIY—the vocals were hot and the drums were hollow. At the same time, it was spectral and timeless, as if it could have been recorded in 1920 or 1990. He sang poems. Verse-chorus structure was nowhere to be found, let alone a bridge or a hook. And it worked beautifully, the quality of the record, with its limited run and limited distribution adding to the mystification of its origins.

In Chicago, Dan MacAdam and Tom Colley designed and screen printed the outer sleeve for the LP, which featured another of Jason's favorite images printed on black card stock—an owl perched on a limb as if staring into the eyes of its listener, a rabbit jumping through a wooden hoop below it.

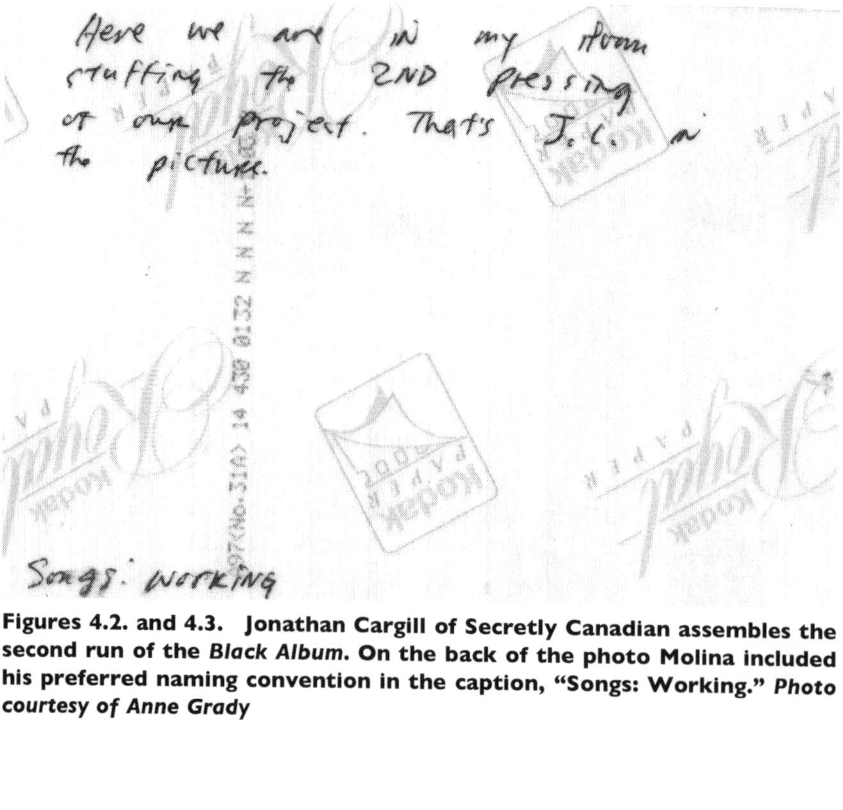

Here we are in my room stuffing the 2ND pressing of our project. That's J.C. in the picture.

Songs: WORKING

Figures 4.2. and 4.3. **Jonathan Cargill of Secretly Canadian assembles the second run of the** *Black Album.* **On the back of the photo Molina included his preferred naming convention in the caption, "Songs: Working."** *Photo courtesy of Anne Grady*

A black-and-white painting by Colley was printed with a red border and included in an LP version of the album that was hand numbered and limited to five hundred copies. Each LP and CD was hand assembled by Ben and Chris Swanson, Jonathan Cargill, and Eric Weddle at Secretly Canadian. The initial CD and LP runs of SC4 were released in April 1997 and sold well enough for the label to repress five hundred copies of the LP version again in 1998. Secretly Canadian the label was officially a thing, and Jason Molina's Songs: Ohia was their flagship.

5

DARCIE

Jason Molina and Anne Grady resumed their romance for a few months after splitting over Christmas break of '96. By the end of the spring semester, though, they were done for good. Grady graduated from Oberlin and headed back to Waltham, Massachusetts, to crash with her parents until she figured out her next move. Molina had become close enough with the Swanson brothers from Secretly Canadian to move in with them in Bloomington, Indiana, though he viewed it as a last resort. Grady and Molina, former lovers, vowed to remain friends.

Molina left Oberlin with his foldout cot and few possessions and decamped to the swampy, unfinished basement of the Swanson's house on North Maple Street in Bloomington, which doubled as Secretly Canadian's offices. They charged him $150 a month in rent. "It was a cinderblock basement, but he liked it," Ben Swanson remembered. "In a way it was his aesthetic."

Molina made many acquaintances in Bloomington, both through the swelling musical community and at his jobs at CD Exchange and Roscoe's Cafe, a coffee shop that also sold records, where Ben and Chris Swanson worked. He played many local shows in support of the *Black Album* and began working on new material, writing at a hummingbird's pace.

Though he enjoyed the musical camaraderie the town offered, he often thought of his Oberlin peers working in New York, Boston, and Chicago with envy. No sooner had Grady returned to her parents' house than she moved into a hip, illegal artist loft in Boston, and a number of Molina's friends were working in warehouse spaces in Brooklyn and Manhattan. The Crosshair space in Chicago, run by Molina's friends from Oberlin, Dan MacAdam, Tom Colley, and Jeff Panall, was thriving as an important underground hub for local and touring fringe art and music. Many of Molina's friends from Oberlin crashed there while on tour with their bands, and he'd anecdotally hear stories from the impromptu jam sessions, shows, and gallery openings that he was missing out on. He was envious. A theme in Molina's letters to Anne Grady during this time was how impressed he was that she was pursuing her love and interest in art unabashedly. He constantly encouraged her to keep working and pushing herself, even though he felt he was falling behind her in Bloomington. In a July 1997 letter, he explained,

> This town reveals its fucked up ness [sic] more and more, this weekend they are closing down the square and having a go kart grand prix right in the street. I will leave here when I have $3,000 saved up. It's an arbitrary number, it could change, but with that I'd feel good moving. If I can stay in the $150.00 a month basement and eat very little, it should take less than a year. We have a big order for 300 more records and I should get $500.00 at least from that + the $300.00 they already owe me. Perhaps the new one will do really well + I could get $ from some rock shows as well. I hope when I get out of here I still can catch up to you.[1]

That summer Molina mobbed Grady with letters—about three or four a week—and the two visited each other a couple of times when Molina played shows on the East Coast. Remaining in the friend zone proved difficult for the pair, as they couldn't seem to keep sex out of the equation. Physical attraction was never part of their problem.

To circumvent his uncertainty about his new living situation and flip-flopping relationship with Grady, Molina took off on tour for six weeks, with just his friend Geof Comings from Oberlin on drums for most of the dates, after Todd Jacops and Mike McCartney from high school band the Spine-riders bowed out of the Songs: Ohia touring equation. Molina was generous with sharing funds and split everything down the middle with Comings after paying for gas. "In the beginning he was mindful that it was his friends who were helping him get where he wanted to go," Comings explained. "But it was our dream, too, to play full time in a rock band." In his touring infancy, Molina was also generous to fans and often stuck around for hours after shows to shake hands, swap stories, and answer questions. Comings recalled that one of the most hilarious and absurd questions that constantly arose was about groupies. "I'd explain that our groupies were young men in glasses who asked if Faulkner was our major influence," he laughed.

Molina and Comings meshed well, though Comings admits there wasn't a lot of depth to their many, many hours spent on the road and in the air on tour. Molina never shared too much of himself or delved into anything that was difficult. No one in his band was aware of the ups and downs with Anne Grady. "He was constantly performing," Comings explained. Most of the time, the goal was to make people laugh. In Molina's comedic repertoire was a goofy interpretive dance he called "jazz dance," which consisted of him making up a ridiculous, improvised song in a high-pitched voice, reminiscent of Meatwad from *Aqua Teen Hunger Force*, and combining it with spontaneous choreography. "He had probably half a dozen moves he'd string together in hilarious combinations," Ben Swanson remembered. He often referred to the act as "Songs: Jazz Dance." He also developed a character, Mr. Squirty, who appeared when Molina wiggled his finger and spoke in the same high-pitched voice. His friend Max Winter remembered Molina saying, "I think I have Tourette's," after one particularly wild outburst. "Mild Tourette's," he revised. Among his many quirks, all of his bandmates recall that he never carried gear. Not ever. Not with Songs: Ohia, and not with his next band Magnolia Electric Co.

As much as he wanted to entertain, Molina also required considerable time alone. He made sure to give himself the space he needed in order to be a tolerable presence for others and often stayed up late at night writing alone, or taking long walks early in the morning. In line with his behavior at Oberlin, Molina was always the first person to rise in the morning and often took off without warning, often to sit in a diner, drink coffee, draw, and scrawl lyrics in notebooks.

On the tour, Molina and Comings fell in love with a venue in Louisville where they played one of their best shows. And of course Molina, with his Hobbit-like appetite, especially loved the meal that came with it. He wrote in a postcard to Anne Grady, "We played at this entirely female run and owned place called the Sugar Doe and it was the best food. Here they say 'do you want it stepped on or do you like lumpy oatmeal?'"[2]

When Molina returned from the tour, he had a long period of time off in Bloomington and flew Anne to his new home for a friendly visit. He was chomping at the bit for her arrival, not knowing she accepted the trip for closure, even though she sensed his motives might have been a bit different. "His letters always ran the gamut from ecstatic to very sad, but some of the letters he sent me then had been disturbing," she explained. "I was overwhelmed by the volume, so while I was there I asked him to stop sending them, a pretty horribly selfish thing to do." His letters tapered off after that, and they kept in touch occasionally over the phone. "I was really trying to push him away," she added. "I regret that now."

After Grady's visit, Molina recorded and released his first CD EP on Secretly Canadian, *Hecla & Griper*. It featured contributions from his high school friend Todd Jacops, as well as drummer Geof Comings. Secretly Canadian's Jonathan Cargill, who worked closely with Molina on all aspects of his new recording career with the label, also stepped in on whatever additional instrumentation was needed. The album chronicled Molina's foray into louder rock band territory, the product of learning to play over bar noise on tour. The informal session was held in a massive recording studio on the campus of Indiana University and engineered by Molina's SC label mate Dan Burton of the bands Ativin and Early Day Miners, who was studying recording engineering at the school. The studio was a step up from the home-recorded quality of the *Black Album*, Burton's amateurish recording technique grabbed Molina's raw compositions with a homespun quality, though they were captured in a high-end studio. Because the room was so big, the drums boomed and bounced, adding a sort of unusual cheeriness to the album. Molina's tenor trill lived front and center, hot in the mix, an apropos representation of the heat in his belly in the aftermath of his parting with Grady. Though the tenor guitar–centric songs are cloaked in lyrical obliqueness, it's safe to assume they center on the long, drawn-out dissolution of his relationship with Anne.

This is particularly evident in "Defenders," where he muses, "I'm still no one's darling / at least they're saying / got nobody waiting / though I'm pale and I'm young." The song references a baseball-style T-shirt Molina borrowed from Grady, which had the word *Defenders* written across it in iron-on letters. His completing the eight-song EP with a cover of Conway Twitty's "Hello Darlin'," one of the most iconic breakup songs in the country music canon, is perhaps the most powerful evidence in this hypothesis. The bouncy quality of many of the songs, openers "Pass" and "All Pass" and "Declarer," act in contrast to the heartworn quality of the lyrics. Unlike the *Black Album*, *Hecla & Griper* sounded more 1990s than 1890s, returning Molina to the modern era.

Grady was supposed to be part of the production, too. "The animal drawing on the back is something I did in Kentucky," Jason explained in a letter to her. "It will be on the backside of the art you send, please try to send the hat girl from your print as well as the other things you've worked on."[3] She never sent Molina artwork for the cover of *Hecla & Griper*, so the rabbit Molina scrawled was promoted. In an early handwritten sketch of the credits for the album, he included the following credits: "Artwork by Anne R. Grady" and "with due credit to C. Twitty."

Figure 5.1. A version of the animal that appears on the cover of Hecla & Griper is included in this letter Molina wrote to Anne Grady. *Letter courtesy of Anne Grady*

By the end of the summer, Molina had under his belt his first big tour, a new EP, cheap rent, and a promotion at his coffee shop job. Still, he was restless and dissatisfied. In one of his last letters to Grady, he explained, "I feel so strange here in this town, maybe I would anywhere, but even with all the people it's lonesome."[4]

In November 1997, Indiana University student Darcie Schoenman stopped by Roscoe's at the behest of her friend, who had a crush on one of its employees. "She was like, 'Let's see if Ben is working,'" she explained. The Swanson brother wasn't on duty, but the mysterious songwriter who lived in his basement was. The two friends chatted with Jason Molina, and he invited them to his show at local all-ages club Rhino's, which was happening a week or so later. The night of the show, on a white fast-food napkin, Molina penned the guest list: "Laura Flannegan +1." On the next line was a note with an arrow pointing upward that said "Darcy, her room-mate." He didn't yet know how to spell Schoenman's name, but that would change soon enough.

After the show, Molina and Schoenman succumbed to a magnetic pull between them. They talked for hours. Soon after the show she called the Swanson brother's house to see if he would answer. After chatting for an hour, Darcie explained that she needed to pop to the grocery store, and the basement-dwelling singer-songwriter offered to keep her company. She agreed to pick him up.

The trip to the Marsh supermarket that day in November would become memorialized as Molina and Schoenman's first date, and it's the meet cute of an indie rom-com. "He kept putting a turkey in the cart," she said with a laugh. No matter how many times Darcie returned the bird to its freezer home, it reappeared. Molina also deliberated endlessly about what to buy, as he was trying to eat as little as possible on top of his $150-a-month rent. His final choice was as silly and nonsensical as almost any Jason Molina thing Darcie would ever experience. "He ended up with a wedge of brie cheese and a six pack of cream soda," she explained. "Not exactly staples." After the trip, Molina wrote "Darcie November 24, 1997" on a dollar bill and kept it for the rest of his life. Today, Darcie doesn't remember whether their date was actually on Thanksgiving but entertains that it might have been in reference to the turkey. "He assigned meaning to everything," she added. He also kept the label from the brie and the bottle caps from the soda.

Darcie was immediately taken with the sweet, hardworking, and oddball musician who treated his song craft like a job, but who also wasn't above punching a clock to get by. She admired his tenacity and was amused by his quirks. She felt for his troubled past. They fell for each other fast and furious. "We didn't have that thing where we were friends first," she said. Molina echoed this sentiment in his song "Captain Badass," which he wrote shortly after meeting his future wife. "Resistance failed / And friendship failed / And friendship failed / As lovers we did not fail," he explained of their early courtship. Captain Badass was a nickname given to Darcie by a friend from her math program, which Molina latched on to. He thought it was a perfect moniker for the crimson-topped pragmatist with a sharp wit and romantic outlook, who generally excelled at everything she pursued, including her relationship with Molina.

The two didn't immediately connect on a musical level, though. Darcie was the rare combination of theater nerd and math geek and joined the two fields in perhaps the unlikeliest of double majors. When she met Molina she listened almost exclusively to Broadway musicals. However, she enjoyed hitting up local shows at the campus radio station and at house parties, though oftentimes she wasn't familiar with the music. Molina was impressed with her creative drive as an actress. They both had performative aspects of their personalities that meshed well, which is why Molina pushed to introduce her to the musical world that was so important to him.

Molina wrote a passage for Darcie to recite over the opening track for his 1998 EP, *Our Golden Ratio*, which he titled "There Will Be Distance." "I didn't want to let him down, but I didn't feel entirely confident," she said. "I have listened to it only a handful of times since we recorded it, and I cringe every time. But I guess in a way I'm glad it exists." The pair recorded on a cheap cassette recorder in Molina's bedroom at the Swanson's house, where he had recently graduated from the basement to the first floor after one of them moved out to shack up with a girlfriend.

The title of the EP is a mathematical principle and a nod to Darcie and her studies. On the cover, Molina placed two silver hearts among a sea of stars, imagery he often scrawled during this period, along with moons. It's a personification he used for Darcie and himself throughout his song craft. In "Love & Work," he sings, "We are constellations in our own way," capturing this new love as luminous spheres. Molina released the EP on Madrid-based label Acuarela Discos, which had also issued music by American indie acts ranging from Will Oldham to Molina's Secretly Canadian label mates June Panic and Early Day Miners. The label gained a shady reputation, however, after not properly compensating its artists, which is why this project became a one-off deal.

In 1998 Molina also released a split 7" with his Scottish friend Alasdair Roberts, whose band Appendix Out contributed four songs to Molina's one. The slow-burning meditation "Nay Tis Not Death" questions mortality and the afterlife in a call-and-response: "Is it death? / Nay, tis not death." Its sound is a return to the spirit of Oberlin, when Molina strummed a ukulele in bathrooms around campus.

The Songs: Ohia lineup of Molina and drummer Geof Comings also recorded and released the band's sophomore long player in 1998. *Impala* was not an album that Comings was entirely sure Molina wanted to make, but he pressed for it as a means for Molina to capture the near entirety of his back catalog of songs—all of the stuff he'd written during his time at Oberlin that hadn't been pressed on CD or vinyl yet. Molina forgot to mention to Comings that many of the songs had indeed been recorded by his friend Eoin Russell during the "Nor Cease Thou Never Now" and *Black Album* sessions. This wasn't out of character as Molina often forgot songs he'd just written or recorded, and when reminded of them would swear that they were written by someone else or by the bandmate who brought it up. Regardless of his faulty memory, Comings convinced Molina to capture the Oberlin-era songs. For *Impala*, Jason went electric, with a twist: he played the guitar with just four strings, a nod to his tenor guitar and his days as a metal bass player.

Molina and Comings decamped to the north side of Louisville, Kentucky, to work at the home studio of Eric Stoess, who played in the band Hula-Hoop with Louisville-based indie-classical darling Rachel Grimes, most famously of the Rachels. Stoess was very familiar with the waters in which Molina tread, as he'd recorded Will Oldham's Palace Brothers in 1994. In turn, Molina had played with Hula-Hoop in the past and was familiar with Stoess. Happy Go Lucky, the Ohio-based label Molina tapped for the CD version of *Impala*, arranged for the session. "Jason mentioned to me that he liked the open and slightly dark and raw sound of Palace's 'Stable Will,'" Stoess explained. Stoess had recorded that Palace Songs single on the third floor of a vacant warehouse in downtown Louisville and conjured its spirit with a similar setup: open windows, wood floors, and no close mic'ing.

The trio set up in Stoess's shotgun-style single-family home, using the living room and dining room as the "studio" areas and recording to a Tascam Portastudio 488 cassette recorder. As was typical of Molina, the vocals and some guitar parts were captured in the bathroom. Molina had an Ampeg bass amp that he ran an old Harmony guitar through, his new electric, in addition to the four-string tenor guitar setup he maintained and had affection for. "It was bizarre because it was just a tiny little bass amp and a cheap electric guitar with no effects at all," Comings remembered. The instrumental personnel produced the bleak midrange tone that became Molina's signature in this period, which was unique in the landscape of acoustic strummers, acrobatic indie rock, and hardcore punk's chugging. "I love the sound," Stoess said. "It was and is really odd to my ear, but it establishes a great platform for his voice and the whole vibe of that album."

Molina used the quick session, which spanned just the course of two afternoons, to begin in earnest to examine his preferred ways of working in the studio. Stoess remembered Molina saying that he was drawn particularly to the ambient sounds creeping in through the open windows. Because there wasn't a full band, Molina used overdubs to capture the bass. In retrospect it was a strange thing to do because the record is extremely stripped down and simple. Still, it was a major step in the evolution of his recording preferences—most notably, that he really didn't like overdubs.

The pump organ on the record, featured on track 8, "The Rules of Absence," looked and ran like it was from the 1800s, which Molina, antiquity fetishist, loved. "It had a mind of its own," Stoess remembered. "I got it from my mom's antique shop. It was in the front room of the house next to the porch and had a nice airy quality to it whenever I recorded in there with the door windows open." Geof Comings sweated bullets jumping up and down on the organ's pedals at twice the speed of what appears on the track, the only way to achieve the tempo he wanted. Comings didn't hear the mix of the record until it was released, as Molina had no patience during that phase of album craft, and he's not entirely confident that Molina was present for it himself. Stoess recalled the session fondly, saying Molina was serious, but with an overall positive, creative vibe.

Forever keeping Secretly Canadian on its toes, Molina shopped *Impala* around to other labels and found an offer from Ohio-based Happy Go Lucky, who also released electronically driven post-rock cum performance art outfit Trans Am from Oberlin and Stoess's Hula-Hoop. Molina liked the idea of being on an Ohio-based label with his Oberlin peers and took the deal, which was CD only. Secretly Canadian sweated collective bullets thinking they were about to lose their anchor. "Molina very casually mentioned that he wanted to release his next record on another label, and we totally panicked," Chris Swanson said. Thinking on their feet, the label negotiated the rights to release the LP version of the record, which was issued the same year.

CMJ reviewed Molina's sophomore platter in its July 1998 issue and observed, "The songs on *Impala* drizzle out like cold maple syrup," and concluded, "Chances are you've heard indie-folk bands like this before, but Molina's pining falsetto makes Songs: Ohia a little better than the rest."[5] While it's humorous that the review described Molina's increasingly deeper tenor vocal tone on *Impala* as a falsetto, which is something he definitely didn't use on this record or probably ever, the writer was right about one thing: Molina's vocals made the music distinctive in the en vogue indie landscape of nasaly emo, guttural punk and hardcore, and wispy twee. He was none of those things and yet embodied the spirit of all of them, from the perspective that he unabashedly carried the torch of independence, carried by so many minor music makers in the era. But instead of aligning with a sound, he increasingly crept away from any one genre, adding electric guitars and a midrange tonality that was difficult to pin down.

The opening track, "An Ace Unable to Change," set the template for the record, its seven-plus-minute time span and glacial pace a pivot from the alternating bounce and blues of *Hecla & Griper*. The home studio setting flattened Comings's drums a bit, as Molina's voice again took center stage. The organ accents and ambient murmurs from open windows added a depth of composition missing from the previous EP. The record plays out in four parts, an opening full-band sound that drips into solo Molina, his guitar and vocals recalling the bathroom-recorded qualities of his college days. Act 3 brings Comings back into the mix for a series of slow-burning minimalist tomes before Molina again emerges solo, wailing over his electric guitar setup, which echoes throughout the end of the record's grooves. It was as if the two musical sides of himself were engaged in a faceoff: solo Molina holding a torch for his roots, and bandleader Molina becoming increasingly confident with collaborative experimentation and auxiliary instruments. The two teams took turns throughout *Impala*, the record's unhurriedness uniting each side to cohesive effect.

Press coverage picked up after the release of Impala, and Molina read all of it, though he often claimed that he didn't. The Will Oldham comparisons increasingly infuriated him. In a letter to Anne Grady from on tour he wrote,

> I've been wondering what kind of shit you would talk to me if you could see the press I'm getting. The *Village Voice* says I'm like Cormac McCarthey without the violence. In Virginia the caption reads "Down on the farm, Jason Molina takes a break from the cornfields to play here tonight," and there are other fucked up things. *A.P.*, *Option*, *Magnet* and other are reviewing for sure and No Depression has a big article I'll try to send you. Gladly the Palace references are dwindeling [*sic*]. His Disco tour really helped me out in that way.[6]

Molina was likely referencing the Mayatone drum machine credited as "Maya Tone" on Palace Music's 1996 album *Arise Therefore*, which accompanied Oldham on the commensurate tour. Though it might have provided momentary reprieve, the Oldham comparison mudded Molina for much of his career, most steadily through his sixth long-playing album as Songs: Ohia, *Didn't It Rain*. Even though Molina had been siphoned into the same indie-folk silo as Will Oldham, *Impala* caught the attention of an impressive set of ears.

Ivo Watts-Russell, tastemaking founder of British independent label 4AD, added a song from *Impala* to his fabled "list of songs to cover." These lists most famously manifested themselves as the project This Mortal Coil, in which acts from 4AD covered songs handpicked by the label head. The project produced three studio albums. The debut, *It'll End in Tears*, being the strongest. Its cover of Tim Buckley's "Song to the Siren" by dream-pop pioneers the Cocteau Twins became a smash hit in the alternative rock arena.

"I fell in love with 'An Ace Unable to Change,'" Watts-Russell explained. "The song reminded me, still does, of some of the more melancholy, possibly ponderous, songs from the first three Richard and Linda Thompson records." He liked it so much that he sent it to Mark Kozelek of 4AD-signed band Red House Painters, which Molina had played for Geof Comings all those years ago in his Oberlin dorm room. Kozelek never covered the song but would soon cross paths with Molina who, like Kozelek, hailed from Ohio and held the state close to his ticker.

Molina had been working on a series of love songs for his new, red-headed sweetheart in late 1997, despite the fact that their future seemed uncertain. Molina was focused on ditching Bloomington for Chicago, where he'd be closer to his friends from Oberlin. Molina and Schoenman even broke up for about thirty-six hours at one point, because Darcie still had a year of school to finish and Molina was aching to leave. He soon realized that he was more miserable without her, though, and vowed to stick it out until she graduated.

To capture Molina's new batch of songs in February 1998, Molina and labelmate Rory Leitch from the band Ativin headed north to Chicago to Michael Krassner's Truckstop Studios in the industrial South Loop neighborhood. Krassner, who formed the musical collective the Boxhead Ensemble, worked with notable names from the flourishing post-rock, free jazz, and folk music scenes within Chicago's city limits. His collaborative spirit and artist-centric principles were a good fit for Molina, who signed his first legitimate contract with Secretly Canadian for the forthcoming album. The details were short—only two paragraphs long—and to the point: Molina would get 50 percent of royalties after the record recouped. Secretly Canadian always covered up front the costs of Molina's recording sessions, a 2009 collaborative project with singer-songwriter Will Johnson being the only exception.

Like *Impala*, this session was quick and spanned no more than two days. Molina borrowed one of Krassner's guitars for the session, a rare 1970s Gibson, and liked it so much that he took it home to Bloomington on Secretly Canadian's dime. The label paid $300 for it, the same amount they budgeted for the entire session. "He took off the low E and the high E strings to create these really cool chord voicings that were kind of different," Krassner remembered. "I don't know how he discovered that, but he definitely played with just those four middle strings." The technique harkened back to Molina's tenure with the tenor guitar and his work with the electric on *Impala*, its midrange tonality a sound he continued to favor.

After Molina returned home to Bloomington and reviewed the tapes, he became dissatisfied with the sound of Leitch's drumming. Consequently, he compiled a short list of additional personnel he'd like to have on the album. He tapped his friend Edith Frost for vocals. He also desired violin parts by Julie Liu, who played with slowcore act Rex, with whom Molina would release a split 7" in January 1999. After gathering his thoughts, Molina called Krassner, explaining that Secretly Canadian had no problem covering the cost of an additional weekend session.

A few days later Chris Swanson from the label dialed Krassner to suss out the recording details. "Chris says, 'I'm so sorry to hear about the flood you guys had, and that all your tapes got ruined,'" Krassner explained, laughing. "Once I realized what was going on, I just went along with it. I thought Jason was such a funny guy, and I always side with the artist anyway." In the landscape of Molina's stories, this might have been one of the most self-serving. "I was like, 'Oh yeah, the flood, it was awful,'" Krassner added. Though the flood story doesn't sound uncharacteristic of Molina, Chris and Ben Swanson say that they don't remember it.

The second round in the studio was not terribly dissimilar to the first, with Molina and Comings both playing live and largely unrehearsed. Like much of the whole of Molina's existence up until that point, the studio was devoid of alcohol, drugs, partying, or any other such rock 'n' roll clichés, the product of his general disinterest and the band's limited time allotment due to anemic recording budgets. Molina did have one weakness, though. "The thing I remember most is the insane amount of Coca-Cola we consumed during that session," Comings said. "We probably went through four two liters, which doesn't make any sense given how slow that record is."

Overdubs with Edith Frost and Julie Liu were an early example of Molina acting as a conductor of his friends, their parts laid down under his direction. "He'd play part of the track and I would sing or hum along with some harmony I thought might work," Frost remembered. "And he'd go yeah, yeah, do that, and I'd bang it out and move on to the next one. I don't think I must've been in the studio more than an hour or two." After they wrapped, Krassner had a few ideas for the album and consulted Molina over the phone. With Molina's blessing, Krassner recorded his friends Dave Pavkovic and Joe Ferguson playing ambient organ parts, which helped to fatten the overall sound of some of the more sparse and plodding songs. Krassner made a quick, rough mix of the album and mailed a cassette to Molina under the auspices that he would return to Chicago for a follow-up, real-deal mixing session.

Molina worked hard on the touring circuit in 1998, his first truly concerted effort to travel extensively behind new material with a full band. In March he rounded up Oberlin friends Max Winter and brothers Bruce and Geof Comings for a short jog around the Midwest. Before the tour, the quartet convened in the Comings brothers' grandmother's house in Oberlin, which lay empty after she moved into a retirement facility. The quartet practiced and slept for a few days in the basement, during which time Molina took to an antique desk in the house, which was purportedly where the Louisiana Purchase was signed. "He'd sit at it and write letters and claim to be inspired by it," Winter said.

Throughout his entire life his friends were always up for the next thing, regardless of pay or circumstances. From his earliest days in high school to his latest and last days, the friends that Molina surrounded himself with were always wildly loyal and wildly living, often eschewing their own musical ambitions in favor of his. "We all recognized that what he was doing was better and more important than our own bands, and we were excited to be a part of it," Geof Comings explained. Knowing that many of his friends were excited about the momentum of his career, Molina made a point to never stick with one group of friends over another, in terms of a band. He wanted to spread the proverbial wealth, in addition to his desire to inject spontaneity into the recording sessions and live performances.

Winter recalled Molina explaining that he wanted to share Songs: Ohia with everyone he loved. Molina even planned a tour, that never happened, during which he intended to stop in every state to record a song with groups of local musician friends in tribute to the coterie of folks who befriended and influenced him along the way. Though this penchant for personnel changing didn't help dispel the constant comparisons to Will Oldham, who employed the same model of bandmate shuffling, it did fulfill Molina's desire to share and create art with his friends and, as a result, capture the free-spiritedness of live performance that he adored. Molina loved the tipping point where a song became a song among a new group of collaborators—the moment when it gelled, that unique and spirited essence of new collaboration that can rarely be re-created after frequent rehearsing.

The tour game plan for the Oberlin-originated four piece was to hit Chicago for their first show at the Empty Bottle. While in town, Molina was to meet up with Michael Krassner to mix his new record. What instead befell the band was a blizzard on I-65 between Indianapolis and Chicago, quite an unexpected phenomenon in March. On the back of a packet of Ernie Ball Custom Gage 26 guitar strings, Molina wrote,

> Currently trapped on 65 in middle of the highway. Totally whited out, semis wrecked, constant 40–50 mph at least NOT IN GUSTS. Master bitch ass weather. Unbelievable. But Winterlong by Neil Young is in and god bless the man. If I die here it's a great soundtrack.[7]

The group spent seven hours traveling just a quarter of a mile down the highway before being directed off the road by state troopers, who encouraged them to seek shelter. "We tried knocking on doors in suburban Indiana to see if anyone would let us sleep on their floor," Winter said. That went about as well as one might think. Power was out for miles, so the foursome pulled into the parking lot of a darkened motel. They huddled together in Geof Comings's beat-up Chrysler minivan, sleeping collectively about one hour, before realizing the southbound side of the highway was considerably clearer than the northbound side.

Figure 5.2. The Songs: Ohia lineup of Molina, Max Winter, Geof Comings, and Bruce Comings. *Photo courtesy of Max Winter*

They turned around and headed back to Bloomington and canceled the Chicago, Madison, Minneapolis, and Ypsilanti dates of the tour. Molina would later recount the story to a fan, who inquired about "crazy" stories from the road in a Q&A session posted to Molina's website. "I spent about 20 hours trapped in a blizzard on the highway," he explained. "It was the first day of the tour and playing bass was my friend who is named appropriately for that kind of adventure—Max Winter."[8]

Molina never made it back up to Chicago for the *Axxess & Ace* mixing session. "The cassette I sent him that took like less than an hour to mix . . . that's the record," engineer Michael Krassner said. In a much later conversation between the two friends, Molina recalled somewhat embarrassingly how much of an amateur he was during that 1998 session, but also how fond of that record he was and how much it felt like a major milestone in his recording career. Its quality isn't unlike the impulsive and spirited live quality that he grew to adore. "We always talked about these Neil Young records or Springsteen records or certain Dylan records where you can hear the mistakes," Ben Swanson said. "And how honest that was or how much energy that gave the recording. He was kind of searching for that spontaneous inspiration all the time."

Molina, Geof and Bruce Comings, and Max Winter hit Detroit on March 14, 1998, and then met up with their friends from Oberlin in Oneida on April 1 for a ten-show run. On tour the band of brothers had as much fun as any guys in their early to mid-twenties could have, cranking Metallica and Iron Maiden cassette dubs in a wood-paneled minivan with a broken speedometer. "We're traveling at the speed of metal," Molina said.[9] On the tour, Molina's rabid appetite and complicated relationship with the truth prompted a regular pattern of forgetting—or claiming he'd forgotten—to eat lunch or dinner. Instead, he'd buy two or three lunches or dinners, shoving a series of sandwiches, fried chicken, or pizza down his gullet. Or he'd push the numerous junk-food meals aside after being confused as to why he wasn't hungry. When the tour concluded, Max Winter and Bruce Comings found about forty Reese's Peanut Butter Cup wrappers and as many empty bottles of Coca-Cola shoved in the well where a spare tire formerly lived, the area christened Molina's nest.

"We're just a bunch of plain ol' guys doing something that a lot of people should be doing," Molina said of the tour, adding, "I think I'm a professional rocker right now. Even though I had a job until a month ago, I kept on playing music straight through. I quit my job to go on tour."[10] He explained that he had just recorded a new record of love songs, which didn't have a title yet:

"We have to know [a title] before we go to Europe though," Molina said.

"Meet Me Where We Survive," Max Winter suggested.

"It's good. It's possible. It's just too long. People will never get it," Molina replied.

"People will just shorten it to Meet Me. That doesn't sound good," Winter added.

"That's catchy!" Molina replied.

"We could just call it Full Metal Jack-Ass!" Winter suggested.

"That's probably the name of it: Full Metal Jack-Ass," Molina concluded.[11]

The album, which he titled *Axxess & Ace*, is a major development in the maturity of Molina's singing and songwriting. It's his first proper long-playing album written completely outside of his undergraduate confines at Oberlin College, its contents an extension of his first real-life experiences as an adult, living independently of meal plans and college houses. Molina was never a self-conscious singer and always positioned his tenor voice front and center, oscillating between hushed incantations and fearless decrees. But on this record, his voice absolutely wails. From the opener, "Hot Black Silk," to the ending track, "Goodnight Lover," his vocals seem to stretch into infinity, the notes pulled like taffy, the volume nothing higher than what might be expected from songs with such romantic titles. In the press release for the LP, Molina explained,

There is no bullshit on this record. It's a love song record, so I wrote as directly to the point as I could. There is nothing snarling or cynical anywhere on the record. It is not invented stuff, either. It's a desperate record. It's a jealous record. It's an imperfect record. It is also as incomplete as a man. This record wasn't made to rid me of any doubts, or to heal me. The end result should show a man, anxious to learn, anxious to share, anxious to curtail all that is selfish.[12]

Two matching silver hearts appeared on the cover of the album, which were nearly identical to the two silver hearts that appeared on the cover of the *Our Golden Ratio* EP. Darcie's certain they represent the two of them, though Molina never verbalized it to her. He rarely entertained lines of questioning about the meaning or symbolism within his music. "He would always say something like, if you'd listen to the music you'd know," she said.

In 1998, a fledgling music zine out of Minneapolis was gaining momentum after launching a website, where its often sarcastic reviews of indie-rock albums stood out among corporate rock rags. Though criticized for favoring the writer's voice over substantive insights or commentary about

Figure 5.3. Darcie and Molina at the Songs: Ohia merch table. *Photo courtesy of Darcie Molina*

an album, *Pitchfork* and its then snark-first approach to music criticism was becoming a player on the overall landscape of independent music. When Molina's *Axxess & Ace* was released in the spring of 1999, the website ran its first review of Songs: Ohia, likening Molina to Will Oldham with a caveat: "Admittedly, Molina is more emotionally explicit and vocally polished than Oldham, but the two both employ the same sparse musical structure and evoke the same mood."[13]

Though the comparison most likely made Molina see red, the review and 8/10 rating wasn't a total wash. The writer seemed uniquely tuned in to Molina's intent, however wrong the article was about the album's logistics in its reporting that everything on the album was played live and totally unrehearsed.

It was an unfortunate fate that Oldham's widely heralded album *I See a Darkness* was released just two months before *Axxess & Ace*. It made the comparisons by writers all too easy to make—not necessarily because the two records sounded alike, but because Oldham and Molina were two visible contemporary figureheads of folk-influenced, sparsely arranged songs. The success of Oldham's album bled into the coverage of Molina's new effort. Whereas Molina earned an 8/10, *Pitchfork* awarded Oldham's LP a rare perfect score. Secretly Canadian's collective heart sank at the news. Though they never thought much of the comparison, they knew the implication of the unfortunate album release timing. Molina was unquestionably a better singer, but Oldham was a bigger and more recognized character. It was becoming a veritable David and Goliath situation.

In April 1998, Molina and Geof Comings headed overseas to the Netherlands for the Rebound Festival, which was in part funded by the Dutch government, notoriously generous to the arts. So generous, in fact, that it paid for the two-piece Songs: Ohia's airfare, which to Molina and Comings felt like a coup and an indicator that momentum was building. "We couldn't go play any other shows, though," Comings explained. "They didn't want us touring on their dime." Molina did manage to sneak in a live session for Dutch National Radio, VPRO Amsterdam, where he played a plodding set comprised of slowed-down ballads such as "East Last Heart" from *Hecla & Griper*, which he introduced as "a song called 'Laboring'"; "Redhead" from *Axxess & Ace*; and even "Gauley Bridge" from the *Black Album*. The thirty-minute set crescendoed with a spirited version of the ballad "Good Night Lover" from his new record before reaching its apropos-to-Molina denoue-ment—a cover of Black Sabbath's "Solitude." Though flecked with older material, the set marked a sonic shift in his songwriting style, something he mentioned lightly in interviews and with friends. The songs were getting slower. The tone of his vocal delivery was dropping. Molina was entering into a new era, trading in complex minor key chords for three-note dirges.

It also marked a willingness to play older material that Molina would soon find incredibly tedious. From the release of *Impala* forward, Molina had an increasingly complicated relationship with his fans who often re-quested their favorite, older songs at shows. The emotional attachment he held to the songs aside, Molina was confounded when audiences yelled out requests or expressed disappointment after the show if he didn't play their favorites. He hated bar noise, which was nearly impossible to escape, and would often yell at the crowd from onstage if they were talking dur-ing his set.

In a 2003 interview, he explained his frustrations with audiences: "I don't play music for other people," he said. "I don't appreciate the pressure from audiences who come expecting something of me, because I don't expect anything of them except the minimum courtesy to listen and watch and not throw shit at me. When I do get up there it's something really special for me, so I try to give it the best I can. But there are a lot of expectations of me, as I'm learning."[14]

Molina also began to develop a paranoid streak. He often insisted that a venue or the label was trying to rip him off. Bandmates remember him scream-singing a "song" with one line: "The people of the world, they'll try to jack you!" "This was a common response to bad drivers, soundmen, promoters and during a brief period when he was questioning Secretly Ca-nadian's treatment of him," bandmate Geof Comings explained. Molina's brother Aaron said that Molina inherited a fatalistic view of the world from their mother.

It was an odd sentiment given that Secretly Canadian offered him a fifty-fifty split on royalties after his records recouped, a generous deal in the late '90s—one that sustained throughout the entirely of his career with the label. It's one reason Molina was hesitant to sign contracts and often wrote a note on a piece of paper instead. One time he signed a tea bag as a sign of good faith to the label.

After extensive touring in the winter and spring, Molina used his savings for a one-bedroom sublet in Bloomington in the summer of 1998. It was the first time he'd had his own space since being a resident advisor at Oberlin College. That summer he and Darcie solidified their bond, spending much of their free time together, creating many positive memories and inside jokes. When he was out of town or even just across town at home, Molina wrote letters to her constantly. The romance and chemistry of that summer, due largely in part to their solitude in that little apartment, yielded one of the best periods in their relationship.

That summer Molina also became a force in the Bloomington basement scene and played as many local shows as possible. He took to wearing a pair of glasses at Darcie's behest, who thought they suited his dark eyes and furrowed brow. He wore them at least the rest of that year before he lost them, as he often did with accessories such as cell phones and keys. Another feature that became a hallmark of Molina's appearance were his thick eyebrows, which inched inward to meet one another, forming a uni-brow. Unlike anyone more image obsessed, Molina wore it with pride and refused any suggestion of waxing, shaving, or plucking it. "He thought it was awesome and hilarious," Darcie said. "He fully owned it."

Molina listened to and adored just about anything Darcie said or did at this point, eyebrow grooming recommendations notwithstanding. This was especially true after an incident at the local quarries, where townies and students snuck off to swim. "Jason never mentioned it before we went, or even on the way there, but as it turned out, he couldn't swim," Darcie said. Still, he hurled himself off the giant rocks and landed smack in the middle of the water next to Darcie. She noticed that he was struggling to stay afloat, so she grabbed his arm and swam him back to shore. "I don't know if any-one else even noticed that this happened, but from that day forward, Jason would swear that I saved his life," she said.

This is her earliest memory of Molina's mythologizing of her. Like the persona he cultivated at Oberlin and the stories of his Spanish ancestors, she, too, was the subject of exaggerations and half-truths that catapulted her from the ranks of mere mortal. From then forward Molina believed Darcie had the power to save him, but only he truly knew how much

trouble he was in that day. The biggest problem with the tale of the heroic
rescue was that Molina spent much of his childhood swimming in Lake
Erie and in the family swimming pool when he visited kinfolk in West
Virginia.

When questioned about the veracity of the events, he'd swear to it. "I
wouldn't say that about all of his stories," Darcie explained. "He believed
many of them to a point, but if pressed it was clear he knew he'd taken some
liberties with the truth for the sake of a good story. Not this one, though.
I'd often refute the severity of the situation that day, but he was insistent.
True or not, he believed it." Like many facets of Molina's personality, his
power to will something that might not be true into the ranks of truth was
something Darcie and many of his family members and friends accepted
about him. After all, this was a man who saw ghosts his entire life, who lived
vicariously through the moon, and who believed in ringing bells as a way
to convene with spirits and express his inexpressible thoughts and feelings.
Though Molina passionately championed authenticity, he cultivated many
personal truths that could in no way be proven. It was at once incredibly
frustrating and incredibly alluring to the people around him.

After the summer sublet ran out, Molina moved into a wood-paneled
apartment on 10th Street in the fall of 1998. There he, along with Ben
Swanson and Jonathan Cargill from the label, recorded a self-titled Songs:
Ohia 7" single for Western Vinyl, a brand-new folk-leaning indie label
founded by Brian Sampson, a friend of the Secretly Canadian family whose
label is now distributed by SC. Ben Swanson and Molina had become
friends via their roommate status and through spontaneous musical collaboration. The pair often took long walks together, sometimes for hours at
an time, until Molina would abruptly stop, say, "Adios!" and walk away, an
illustration of his cryptic and quirky personality.

Cargill and Molina had become fast friends through the label, but also
via casual jam sessions outside of business hours. "When Jason needed a
drummer or a bass player, I was the closest person within reach," Cargill
explained. "And then we found that we kind of meshed well not only musically but as friends too." The single's A-side "7th Street Wonderland"
recounts a winter stroll Molina and Darcie took along 7th Street in Bloomington, early on in their romance:

> The sky was full with a gray winter light
> And each freezing degree made its target that night
> And the pulse of the snow was the pulse of twilight
> The pulse of the snow was the pulse of diamonds

And you wear it in your hair like a constellation
And we both swear by the size of that moon that
The sky will sink tonight

Swanson and Cargill both recalled that Molina wasn't easy to get close with. He was the type of person who had a lot of acquaintances, but not very many close friends. "That was a sort of peculiar thing about him," Cargill explained. He preferred to write at a feverish clip, often crafting love songs for Darcie or songs steeped in the hard work of love, art, or the everyday.

Molina played the BAM festival in Barcelona in September of '98, which footed the bill for Darcie to come along. It was the only time she'd go on tour with him, though throughout their lives she'd often drive to regional gigs with Molina if he was playing solo. Will Oldham, Belle and Sebastian, the Silver Jews, the Magnetic Fields, and Mark Kozelek were all on the bill at the Spanish festival. It was the biggest event Molina had played up to that point, and Darcie thought he was a rock star.

Unlike in America, there were innumerable indie rock–centric festivals popping up throughout Western Europe, which became Molina's early experiences in festival settings. The notion of such an indie-rock jubilee had not crept over to the States beyond CMJ and South by Southwest, and largely wouldn't for some time, outside of college campuses. Lollapalooza, Coachella, and other behemoths were focused on big-name alternative acts, leaving indies to fend for themselves.

After Geof Comings and Molina finished their set at BAM, they stood backstage watching the other acts and chatting with the promoter, who remarked, "Songs: Ohia is good, but it will never be as big as these other bands because Jason doesn't have a good story." The dig was a fairly astute observation on the dichotomy of Molina's stage presence and life presence, favoring the image of a plain and simple songsmith over the David Berman-esque poet-madman or Will Oldham's mercurial howling.

In life, Molina constantly crafted stories, often playing into a larger-than-life persona. But onstage, he was just a guy who played songs. He didn't even want to be considered a guy who played a certain type of song or with a certain type of band. "Will Oldham has an obvious character that he played to a degree," Comings remarked. "Jason was kind of working class, stick your head down and go forward. It wasn't about a frilly character." At the festival, a friend of Mark Kozelek's told him about a guy he might like named Jason Molina, "who kind of sounded like Will Oldham."

After the gig in Barcelona, Molina and Comings took off for a pair of dates in London. During this tour overseas, Molina carried a two of hearts playing card in his guitar case, which at every show he removed and taped somewhere where he could see it. It acted as an extension of the cover of *Axxess & Ace*, one heart representing Darcie and the other himself. Despite newfound love, walking around London's streets, he felt sentimental for the time he'd studied abroad. He sent a postcard to Anne Grady, with whom he'd fallen in love at the city's museums and royal parks:

Made it back to London. Went to some old places, Regent's Park, Waterloo Bridge. Miss you over here. It's cold as all hell and rainy whenever possible. Ran out of money but made it all back at a London show last night. Hope you are doing well, looking forward to seeing you soon + some more great art.[15]

After rounding the club bases in London, Molina and Comings drove north to Manchester and linked up with caustic Scottish indie-rock act Arab Strap, whose core was the two-piece of vocalist Aidan Moffat and multi-instrumentalist Malcolm Middleton, and who were riding a hype wave after their remix of producer David Holmes's "Don't Die Just Yet" broke into the UK charts. Songs: Ohia had played a couple of shows in the States with the two Scots and happily agreed to join them for the string of five dates.

Their initial U.S. tour dates together had come as a welcome surprise after it was booked through Arab Strap's agent. It was Moffat's first time in the United States, and it proved to be a rather arduous jaunt, though the couple of dates with Molina really lightened his mood. Moffat had purchased Molina's very first single on Palace Records when it came out, and the *Black Album*, too. "The two-piece guitar and drums setup is pretty common these days but seemed unusual back then, and it really worked for me. I loved them," Moffat said. He added that he saw a lot of himself in Molina. "He was really good fun, too. Like a lot of folk who write about darker feelings, he often seemed very much the opposite of the Jason in his songs."

Molina had been writing about the rapture and complexities of new love, but also the hard work of the everyman. And, occasionally, about how the two meet. Nine of the songs would eventually comprise the album he called *The Lioness*, an apropos image conjured by Darcie's crimson locks and canyon-deep love of cats. After the tour, Molina and Comings decamped to Scottish comrade Alasdair Roberts's empty apartment in Glasgow—he was away visiting a girlfriend in Denmark—to wait out a five-day stint before they had to leave for a festival in Amsterdam. Moffat, having fallen in love with the new songs Molina had been playing on the road, invited the pair to his parents' house in Falkirk, about twenty miles northeast of Glasgow, which was currently sitting empty on the sales market.

Molina, Comings, and Moffat played fast and loose on Arab Strap's Tascam four-track recorder in Moffat's parents' garage before he suggested that the group book some studio time at Arab Strap's home studio, Chem 19. At Peacock Cross Industrial Estate, about twenty minutes south of Hamilton, Molina taped his two of hearts playing card within eyeshot on the window of the studio's control room. "We were little more than an audience," Moffat said, explaining that their drummer David Gow added scant keyboards. Moffat also convinced Molina to allow him to add a drum machine on the song "Being in Love." Moffat particularly loved watching Molina write the song "Baby Take a Look," which the group then performed off the cuff without any rehearsal. For the most part, though, the dream team of Molina and Comings steered the session. When they were done, in his packing haste, Molina forgot the two of hearts.

Back in the States, after several spins of the recording he'd just done in Scotland, Molina was dissatisfied with the result. He'd been sick during the session and thought his voice sounded weak. He also wasn't happy with the Marshall amp he played on in the studio, as he was a Fender man all the way. Regardless, after returning to Bloomington, he submitted the tapes to Secretly Canadian with a handwritten note that read,

To Secretly Canadian

I am hereby submitting to Secretly Canadian Records first, the new Songs: Ohia + Arab Strap recordings for consideration.

Respectfully,
Jason Molina

After taking a spin through the recordings, Chris Swanson of SC largely echoed Molina's dissatisfaction, but for different reasons. "The lyrical content was relying too heavily on workingman tropes," he explained. "The poetry felt more like a lecture series, and the music was more rhythmic and punchy than graceful and musical."

Molina invited Jonathan Cargill and Swanson to set off with him and Geof Comings for a June–July 1999 jaunt through Europe. After playing a handful of gigs, the pair realized that many of the songs Molina was playing live would be better suited for the suite of heartworn material Molina wanted to package for his new album. To Swanson, a re-record seemed like a huge ask. But much to his surprise, Molina went for it. The foursome of Comings, Molina, Cargill, and Swanson booked additional time at Chem 19 near Glasgow. When they entered the studio, Molina's two of hearts stood on the control room window, where he had left it months earlier.

Molina, Comings, and Cargill recorded along with friends Alasdair Roberts and Richard Youngs. Feeling a tremendous responsibility to play his part correctly, during the intro track, "The Black Crow," Roberts can be heard faintly whispering at the fifty-second mark, "Is it out of tune?" "One of the best things about working with Jason was that he gave the other players total freedom to express themselves," Cargill explained. "It's the dynamics of the songs and other musicians that dictate what one should play, so as long as you can sense the vibe, and play within that, then more than likely it will sound good."[16]

At the session's end, Molina packed up his guitar and headed off, his two of hearts intact and in tow. On the tour the trio of Molina, Comings, and Cargill also captured many of the live and improvised tracks that would appear on Molina's 2000 tour-only release *Protection Spells*, Molina's tiny, beloved Pignose travel amp delivering the sounds for the homespun recordings, which Chris Swanson also contributed to from the road.

In the first *Lioness* session with Arab Strap, fourteen songs were recorded, but only "Lioness," "Baby Take a Look," and "Nervous Bride" made the final cut. The remaining six tracks were essentially Molina and Comings, with assists by Cargill on bass and Roberts, though that became largely lost in the early Internet PR cycle of misinformation.

The presence of Scottish songwriters gave the press something to latch on to other than overwrought Will Oldham comparisons. This was likely because Molina gave them a "thank you" shout on the album's credits, and their name appeared on the press release. As such, *The Lioness* was widely touted as a joint venture between Songs: Ohia and Arab Strap. "I guess it was a more interesting story than 'Just Geof Again,'" Comings remarked. Despite the overstated presence of Scots, *The Lioness* marked the only time that anyone, especially someone from the label, ever convinced Molina of a reworking or self-edit that massive. "Molina is a very binary person," Chris Swanson explained. "He's either immediately embracing what you're saying, or he's immediately rejecting you. There were ecstatic truths with him and you couldn't get caught trying too hard to strategize. He'd immediately shut it down."

Though Molina would grow increasingly weary of album-related details and corresponding marketing and PR—he found mixing, choosing album

artwork, and doing interviews particularly daunting—*The Lioness* proved
to be a clean synthesis of his and Secretly Canadian's visions. "It felt like a
major give from Jason," Ben Swanson said. "But he was obviously satisfied
as he used the entire [second] session."

The Lioness was released just after the hoax of Y2K ran its course. *CMJ*
remarked, "Although it's musically modest and somewhat heartrending,
The Lioness manages to let out a quiet roar." The album's title track deftly
illustrates Molina's new source of passion—the act of being in love—and
the conflicting emotional goulash intrinsic to his entering into a new partnership. In its lyrics he explains that if even Darcie, his Lioness, is to break
his heart, he would welcome the pain.

> It is for me the eventual truth
> Of that look of the lioness to her man across the Nile
> It is that look of the lioness to her man across the Nile
>
> Want to feel my heart break if it must break in your jaws
> Want you to lick my blood off your paws
>
> If you can't get here fast enough
> I will swim to you
>
> Whether you save me
> Whether you savage me
> Want my last look to be the moon in your eyes
> Want my heart to break if it must break in your jaws
> Want you to lick my blood off your paws
>
> It is for me the eventual truth
> It is that look of the lioness to her man across the Nile
> And if you can't get here fast enough
> I will swim to you

The song was an instant classic and remains a fan favorite. Though the
episode at the Bloomington quarries provides a literal explanation of the
swimming lyrics, it speaks also to the steadfastness of the commitment
between him and Darcie and the mélange of mixed emotions commensurate with such a deep connection. The lyrical theme of love and romance
remained, but the tonal shift of the music on *The Lioness* is markedly shad-
owy. It's as if Molina eclipsed the sunny warmth of *Axxess & Ace* with a cold
glowing moon. Seven-plus-minute opener "The Black Crow" laments, "I'm
getting weaker / I'm getting thin / I hate how obvious I have been," while

in "Being in Love" he explains, "Being in love / Means you are completely broken," over a drum machine's taps. The tempos are slower. The electric guitar he strummed with sparsity was metallic and cutting. The space between the words weighted them with palpable intensity and immediacy.

Molina's first album of love songs, *Axxess & Ace*, crisscrossed the hope and adoration associated with new love in a sunny tapestry of romantic violin and pastoral harmonies. In contrast, *The Lioness* traded in love's pain and anxiety, a sparse and glacial landscape steamed by lover's breath and fiery hearts. The crux of "Being in Love" says it all: "We are proof that the heart is a risky fuel to burn."

6

IRELAND

Jason and Darcie moved in together in the spring of 1999, sharing the main floor of her rented bungalow in Bloomington, while two other roommates shared the basement. In the house, Molina hung one of his most precious belongings: the red, white, and blue flag representing the state of Ohio. Schoenman described their first run in Bloomington as their happiest period, though they did get into one minor kerfuffle just after the new year. To rectify the situation, Molina wrote her a check for "one million kisses." In the memo section he noted "No More Fite." He also penned piles and piles of letters from the road. "Now that I look back on it, I think Jason was obsessed with me, in an unhealthy way," she said. "But at the time it seemed very romantic and sweet."

Molina spent nearly three straight months on tour in 1999. He welcomed the 1998–1999 winter with a pair of Bloomington shows, one at CD Exchange where he used to work. At that show he played an old tune from the *Black Album*, "Gauley Bridge," which he had written for Anne Grady. He explained, "It's old and hard to play. It's classic rock."[1] The more Molina wrote, the more the older material comprising the *Black Album* and *Hecla & Griper* faded into the distance. Always forward looking, he'd grow to loathe playing older material, and in part it's easy to see why. Artistic evolution aside, for Molina the emotional attachment of his songs loomed too strong overhead and inside of himself. As he focused on his *Lioness*, he let go of *Waltham*.

He zigzagged across the United States with Geof Comings and his friends in the band DRUNK in March of '99. On the tour he toted a home-recorded album, *The Ghost*, which was limited to five hundred copies and which sold out its run on that tour. He came home to Bloomington to a pair of shows in late April and early May, when Schoenman graduated from Indiana University. In July, while Molina was on the European tour where he rerecorded *The Lioness*, Schoenman secured an apartment for the couple in Chicago's Uptown neighborhood, on the north side and a stone's throw from Lake Michigan. They moved in August 1999.

Shortly after the couple headed northwest on I-65 to the Windy City, a letter from Ireland arrived at Secretly Canadian's post office box addressed to Molina. "I did something I've never done before or since," musician Glen Hansard of the Frames and the Swell Season explained. "I wrote a fan letter." He explained that the *Black Album* had become a sort of religious refuge for him, something he enjoyed musically but also craved emotionally, much in the vein of Joni Mitchell's *Blue* or *Five Leaves Left* by Nick Drake. The budding Irish rock star had scooped up the album in a record store in Birmingham, Alabama, while on tour with the Frames. "I was looking for an Incredible String Band record," Hansard said. "But I remember seeing this cover that was just a hare jumping through a hoop on this beautiful black paper. For the rest of the tour, two or three weeks, that album never stopped playing. It was so captivating and so deep. His voice was coming straight out of another time."

This was before the onslaught of interconnectivity associated with broadband Internet, and Hansard explained that due to the nature of the *Black Album*'s historic themes and homespun quality, he had no way of knowing whether Molina was alive, currently touring, or even if the record was new or from thirty years ago. "I thought maybe he was a Nick Drake–style character," he added. In the letter, Hansard introduced himself and explained that if Molina ever wanted to play in Ireland, his band would be honored to open and host him overnight. "He got straight back," Hansard said. "I can't tell you what that meant. This was like writing to Elvis and getting a reply."

Now officially a Chicago resident, Molina extended a somewhat cryptic invitation to his friends from Crosshair, Jeff Panall and Dan Sullivan, that fall. He explained that some sort of Irish rock star had gotten in touch and wanted Songs: Ohia to travel to the Emerald Isle for a couple of shows. Molina seemed completely nonplussed about the situation. In turn, the pair wrote it off as a Sparky tall tale, typical of their days in Oberlin together.

A few weeks later Molina and Dan Sullivan paired up for a Songs: Ohia show at beloved Chicago watering hole the Empty Bottle, a staple of the city's independent rock scene since 1993. Molina and Jeff Panall hand screened the fliers for the gig.

Having nearly forgotten about the Ireland thing, Sullivan and Panall were shocked when the photographer Zoran Orlic, a close friend of Glen Hansard, hand delivered plane tickets to Dublin inked with their names.

The trio arrived in Dublin in February 2000, and they couldn't believe the packed house for the Frames. "We'd definitely never played a show like that before," Panall recalled. "Glen was a certified rock star, but so down to earth." Molina explained to Hansard that he hadn't prepared anything specific for the two-show run and that the trio would largely be working in the spirit of improvisation, with some general guidelines they'd worked out. "The gigs were really weird, but brilliant," Hansard remembered, adding that he didn't get to hear the songs he loved from the *Black Album*, which was somewhat disappointing. However, he soon realized that Molina had released many more records beyond that debut. "He gave me a copy of *The Lioness*, which I fell in love with," he said. "And from then on he always sent me cassettes of his records from the masters, with beautiful artwork and a lovely letter."

After returning from Ireland, on April 11, 2000, Molina booked his first session at Electrical Audio, the famed Chicago recording house responsible for iconic records by alternative acts Nirvana, the Pixies, and PJ Harvey, as well as countless punk, post-punk, folk, and indie acts. Its outspoken figurehead and head engineer Steve Albini is perhaps as known for his biting opinions on the commercial music industry as he is for his chops as an engineer and producer and survives as a beloved figurehead of independently made music. To Molina, Albini was a god. The chance to record with him was a dream come true.

That day Molina played solo and recorded eight songs. He had just test-driven the slow burners "Are We Getting Any Closer," "Break the Young Men" (aka "Railroad Song"), and "Vision of Death" (aka "In the Deeper Shade") in Cork, Ireland, with Glen Hansard. "Vision of Death's" fourth line, where Molina sings the phrase "in the deep shade," became the 2001 title of a mega-popular instrumental track by Hansard's band, the Frames, though Hansard cites it as a coincidence.

Most of Molina's debut session at Electrical was never released, falling to the depths of obscurity courtesy of a head cold, the same fate as much of the first pass on *The Lioness*. A few songs made it to wax, though. "Hawk + Fog" became the A side of a 2002 Songs: Ohia single, under the new name "Keep It Steady," while "United or Lost Alone" comprised the B side. Re-recordings of a few tracks popped up on later releases, too. For example,

Molina brought "Be Your Own Guide" to the table at a future session with friends and colleagues Alasdair Roberts and Will Oldham and released it on a split single with Louisville-based indie upstart My Morning Jacket.

This pattern of rerecording and renaming songs is uniquely Molina, largely due to his prolific pace and faulty memory. His tendency to anecdotally rename his songs was almost always unintentional. He often introduced songs, even more popular or well-known tracks from his albums, by different names. This was especially true in live settings or on the radio, but also informally in practices or during off-the-cuff jam sessions with friends. Subsequently, Molina unintentionally designed a very convoluted road map for the tape-trading journeymen that traveled his musical highways, sharing and swapping their live records from his gigs across the United States and Europe. Cross-referencing the various names of the songs became something of a comical hobby to fans, as illustrated by the many parentheticals that accompany their track listings.

After their two-show run in Ireland, Glen Hansard was so fond of Molina and his Songs: Ohia personnel that he wanted to book more time with them. During his next solo tour of the States in the spring of 2000, Hansard came to Chicago to test-drive Electrical Audio and invited them to play. "Jason was fundamental in changing the direction of the Frames' career, because he suggested that I work with Steve Albini," Hansard explained. "Jason booked the session and offered to play in the band with the Songs: Ohia guys." At the time Glen was a huge name in Ireland and Europe but relatively unknown in the States—his independent hit film *Once* wouldn't be released for seven more years, and 1991's *The Commitments* hovered steadily in the realm of cult status. Ahead of their session with Hansard, Jeff Panall, Dan Sullivan, his brother Rob, and Molina watched Hansard play solo at now-shuttered Irish pub Gunther Murphy's. After the set, Hansard asked them if it was normal in the United States to be paid just $150 for a gig, a foreign concept to the Irishman but no surprise to the indie-rock-bred friends in his midst. They explained that wages made on the road in the United States, for indie-rock bands, were quite often negated by the cost of gasoline.

Hansard, Molina, Jeff Panall, and brothers Dan and Rob Sullivan assembled on May 23 for a session that resulted in six tracks under the engineering guidance of Electrical Audio's Rob Bochnik, who helped hand build the studio Electrical Audio with Steve Albini, laying the adobe bricks they special ordered from New Mexico. During the session, Albini was booked in the next studio over, working with Cheap Trick. "We were beside ourselves and giddy," Panall explained. "I grew up listening to Cheap Trick and AC/DC at my friend's house in grade school."

Molina was a quieter version of himself during the session, the product of a personality that preferred to write alone on a guitar with weird tunings, which made it difficult to follow someone else. He wasn't someone who liked to get together and jam in the traditional sense. He also didn't have the same formal training, which might have also served as a point of insecurity. Still, Hansard remembered Molina as being his usual, generous self with both his time and his talents. "The songs were just ideas, they weren't really formed," Hansard explained. "And one of them was really influenced by Jason, so it was kind of funny for me to be playing it."

At this point Molina was focused on a Danelectro baritone guitar, which emitted sounds often associated with surf music or spaghetti westerns. It also marked his transitions to playing the full suite of six strings after having spent time removing one or two on his earlier recordings. The deeper register of the Danelectro suited his heavy metal bass player sensibilities, too.

Molina's contribution on the group's "A Caution to the Birds"—the song Hansard wrote, which was inspired by Molina—was so beautiful that they chose it for a split 7" Hansard released with Molina in December 2000. After Molina and Hansard's first pass in the studio, Dan Sullivan, a masterful, classically trained guitarist, and Hansard sat in the control room to review the playback. "That's so good!" they proclaimed when Jason's guitar kicked in during the intro. "You guys should just stand back so I can play," Molina jokingly replied as he sipped on a Heineken, before suggesting that they add a piano part, which made it onto the final recording.

Hansard and Molina labored a bit during the song's second take, as Molina struggled to learn the three parts of the song. "I think this is the first time I've learned to play a song in the studio," Molina joked.[2] Once they dove in, though, the low register of Jason's baritone Danelectro guitar frolicked against Hansard's higher-range vocals and guitar in something of a romantic duet. It was sort of magic. "I guess most people wouldn't call it a solo, but for Jason it was," Panall explained. "This was probably the first time he played a solo on a recording, and I think he was embracing his inner rock star, even if a bit tongue and cheek."

After the palpably great take, they celebrated momentarily, Molina proclaiming, "I knew all three parts that time!"[3] As they walked away Molina explained to Hansard his preference for first takes. He explained that while it might not be the best for the lyrics or singing, the first take is the "most true" version of the song. He carried this philosophy for the rest of his life and through his most iconic recordings.

During the session, the group also laid down an amped-up version of the Frames' song "Early Bird," Panall's drums booming from Studio B's live room, a signature mark of the Albini sound on rock albums, sort of like if the drums had been hooked up to their own amplifier. They also captured a similarly rocking version of "Precarious Aiming," with Dan Sullivan echoing each of Hansard's words in the chorus: "I can't go back to that place I've been / The world has lost its faith in me." They followed it with "The Cost" and a solo version of "Disappointed," which sounds very similar to the version on the Frames' 2001 LP *For the Birds*. Dan Sullivan and Hansard also cut a textural acoustic guitar instrumental that remains unreleased in any form, as do the remaining tracks from this session at Electrical.

The day cemented a lifelong bond between the Chicago core of Songs: Ohia and Glen Hansard. It also prompted the engineer of that session, Rob Bochnik, to leave Electrical Audio and join up with the Frames full-time, as well as contributing to Hansard's band the Swell Season, formed with his *Once* costar and former flame Markéta Irglová. Though Hansard never felt deeply connected to Jason on a personal level—Molina made a habit of keeping people at arm's length—his music left a lasting imprint on the famed Irish musician.

7

CHICAGO

When he wasn't working the children's section of a local Border's Books or in the library at the Art Institute of Chicago, Jason Molina was writing in his dedicated space at his Northside home, or playing and rehearsing with his Oberlin friends at the Butchershop loft in the West Loop. He was often seen catching shows at local clubs the Hideout and the Empty Bottle, too, especially when Oberlin-related acts like Trans Am rolled through town. Molina kept his home life and his band life separate and rarely invited his friends to his apartment and vice versa. His then-girlfriend Darcie Schoenman admitted that she was somewhat intimidated by Molina's hip artist friends living and working in a fringe art gallery loft, as she toiled away at her nine-to-five job.

Foodies before the current foodie explosion, Molina and Schoenman loved exploring the many new dining options available to them in Chicago, from Italian bakeries to cheese shops. The pair loved cheese so much that they often kept a running list of their favorites taped inside a cabinet door or in a notebook Jason dubbed "Jason and Darcie's Cheese Journal." Molina adored any bar or restaurant that felt historic and frequented spots in the city's downtown Loop such as the Berghoff, a German restaurant and brewery open since 1898, and Miller's Pub, a 1950s supper club dishing American classics since 1935. Molina especially loved the no-frills burger-and-fries shack across the street from the Butchershop called the Peoria Lunchbox, which sat in the parking lot of the Peoria Packing Company. He frequented it so much that it became the namesake of the sixth track on the Songs: Ohia album *The Magnolia Electric Co.*, sung by his friend Scout Niblett.

In Chicago, Molina and Schoenman adopted their first and only pet, a black-and-white tuxedo cat they found at Harmony House for Cats, a local no-kill shelter. Molina grew up in the company of canines, but Schoenman was solidly a cat person and won out in the couple's pet negotiations. Their shy guy with voluminous whiskers earned the name Bhaji after Molina sent a series of e-mails from the road in Europe from Nordic keyboards, which butchered the cat's original name. It morphed from Maurice to Bhajrice to finally Bhaji.

Molina wrote hundreds and hundreds of silly songs about Bhaji, more than were ever released in his real-life musical outlets. Bhaji became their de facto child, as the couple chose not to procreate, though they both liked kids. Because of Bhaji, Molina became such a cat lady that he often e-mailed Darcie pictures of other people's cats from the road . . . but never their owners. "He [Bhaji] followed us around from room to room, preferring to be as close as possible, preferably on a lap if it was an option," Schoenman explained. "I've had three other cats in my life, but never one more outwardly loving." Molina also penned hundreds of silly songs that would surprise anyone familiar only with his public persona, that of a gut-wrenching balladeer or the leader of a whip-sharp roots-rock outfit who'd have your head for yelling out a request. In addition to love, loss, moons, stars, wolves, lions, and wars, Molina penned rock anthems about his favorite food, pumpkin pie. In the midst of a household cooking frenzy, he sang a song he called "Too Many Things Are Happening at Once," with nods to pork chops, potatoes, corn, and tea. One of his favorite self-penned silly songs was also about food, one he'd sing to lift his mood:

> If you wake up in the morning
> And your life's looking like it's shit
> Eat some chocolate
> Eat some fucking chocolate

Soon after the couple moved to Chicago, singer-songwriter Alasdair Roberts flew in from Glasgow, Scotland, in the spring of 2000 to record a concept album with Molina. Roberts knew only that Molina had been inspired by an image his mind had conjured, centered on the idea of tropical ghosts—an extension of Molina's increasing interest in mysticism. After touching down in Chicago, the pair of friends hopped in a rented car and drove to Lincoln, Nebraska, to record at the home studio of Mike Mogis, an MVP in that state's early emo scene, who produced and played with acts such as Conor Oberst's Bright Eyes and Cursive from the Saddle Creek label, which Mogis also helped to cofound.

Molina had become attached to the Danelectro baritone guitar he played in the session with Glen Hansard and used it throughout the session for the record he'd soon title *Ghost Tropic*. Roberts played acoustic guitar and keyboards, while Mogis's friend Shane Asperegen of Lincoln's Lullaby for the Working Class helmed drums and other wooden percussion, with additional embellishment assists by Mogis. At the session's onset, Mike Mogis had the idea to record the drums separately, which Molina swiftly rejected, leading to tension between the two of them up front. After it dissipated, though, the performers recorded live over a weekend, largely under the spirit of improvisation. Instead of providing finished songs, Molina instead pointed to the lower pitches emitted from his Danelectro as inspiration for the mood of the record and allowed his friends and studio personnel to contribute based on their intuition.

The finished product, *Ghost Tropic*, embodied a deep dive into Molina's meditative, mystical side, during an era in which he became palpably attached to ghosts, both in life and as a lyrical motif. Molina regularly constructed altarpieces and iconography he called protection spells and affixed a cross made from white medical tape to all of his guitars, guitar cases, and other equipment. In the Molina home hung a Brigid's Cross, a four-sided Irish symbol of pre-Christian origins, which Molina had purchased to help ward off evil spirits. He also carried essential oils, tarot decks, and other ephemera related to mysticism or the supernatural. He took great pride in the way in which he organized his mystical wares and sometimes told friends and family that he self-identified as a witch. "I think he believed in Wicca," his brother Aaron explained. "He read a lot about spells and magic."

Ghost Tropic opened with Tom Waitsesque clacking percussion and Roberts's acoustic guitar and dynamic keyboards cutting through Molina's vocals. The album was divided by two tracks bearing the LP's title, at the four-song and seven-song mark. Both were about three-minute long ambient pieces accessorized with birdcalls the group recorded in Mogis's yard, which demarcated the movements within the symphony of the album.

With a pace even more glacial than *The Lioness*, Molina's vocals on *Ghost Tropic* were an exercise in restraint. He sang no more than two notes, and the space between the words outnumbered the words. The words that did come out of him were almost always warbled with sorrow. They were sung deeper than his normal tenor, with no wailing and no whispering. It was as if he was standing alone, staring into a bathroom mirror and into himself, plucking the words out with his mouth as they slowly bubbled up through his throat. The act hurt, but it was worth it for the physical and emotional reprieve.

The twelve-and-a-half-minute track "Not Just a Ghost's Heart" was lost on nearly everyone, including writers, who panned *Ghost Tropic* almost unanimously, if not unfairly, given that the album's production quality and thematic unity were an artful pivot in Molina's vision and execution. Music rags snubbed the record with lazily recycled comparisons to Will Oldham, with *Pitchfork* offering the only semi-studious observation that *Ghost Tropic* was an evolution for Molina—not a lineup of trad-inspired folk tunes or un-veiled love songs as was largely Molina's previous inclination. Molina's musical worldview was becoming as binary as his personality. There were dirging contemplations, in the case of *Ghost Tropic*, and bootstrapped everyman anthems, in the case of a new, not-yet-recorded album he'd begun to write.

When Molina returned to Chicago and told his friends at Crosshair about the record he'd just made, they were flummoxed. They'd already played in the studio with Molina during the session with Glen Hansard and had no idea Molina had been writing a record outside of what they'd been play-ing with him at live shows and in scant rehearsals. *Ghost Tropic*'s Alasdair Roberts, on the other hand, had no idea Molina had been playing with a new band regularly. Molina never mentioned it. "I always got the sense that Jason was into collaborating, playing with different people, and sort of treated each record as a discrete entity," Roberts added. Up until this point, Roberts's observation had been the case, the sturdy support beam Molina found in former Songs: Ohia drummer Geof Comings notwithstanding. But at this point the Chicago core of Songs: Ohia felt that they were Molina's new band and had been groomed as such by frequent road excursions and local gigs. They took great pride in Molina's inclusion of their talents and ideas, which is why Molina's secret record making stung.

A general observation among friends and loved ones during this time was how dark Molina's tune had turned. Schoenman saw it bleed into their re-lationship. Whereas Molina once worshipped her, almost to near obsession, in Chicago Schoenman described an environment that led to her "fall" in Molina's mind, when he realized that she was human and could be cranky, selfish, moody, or any other affliction all humans are occasionally faced with. He didn't handle her plummeting to mere mortal well. Molina was deeply disappointed that she chose to pursue a straitlaced nine-to-five job instead of theater. He grew increasingly frustrated about it the further she moved up the corporate ladder. During their first memorable argument,

Molina shouted at Schoenman about selfishness and how he could "walk you from here to Kansas with how selfish you are."[1] It obviously wasn't a breaking point, as the two would marry in 2003, but it did illustrate a shift in her position, from "goddess on golden pedestal" to "girlfriend who could tread on his nerves."

Molina's maturity as a songwriter began to fully reveal itself in Chicago via his frenetic writing and releasing pace. Much of his long-playing catalog up to this point was centered on his loves, and the loss of those loves, dotted with his interests in history and art. His lyrics largely took the form of cryptic poetry instead of standard A-B song structures. But that began to change in the Windy City. He even admitted that he didn't know how to write songs in his earlier days. "I just would get ten words and a chord, and say 'record it,'" he explained. "That resulted in a lot of half great, half shit songs, now that I look back on them."[2]

Molina dove deeper into his contemplative, downtrodden sides via albums such as *The Ghost, Protection Spells, Ghost Tropic,* and later *Pyramid Electric Co.* These albums were all more meditations than rock songs. But as he crawled inside himself he also displayed a dual desire to ditch the trappings of Solo Balladeer of Heartbreak. This shone through in his forthcoming albums *Didn't It Rain* and *The Magnolia Electric Co.,* as well as the new band he'd eventually form under the name Magnolia Electric Co.

Before that band came to life, though, Molina strengthened the Chicago-based core of Songs: Ohia in the summer of 2000, after Oberlin-based drummer Geof Comings left the band to go back to school and begin a life of his own. "Jason had hit a new formula where his vocal lines were very similar and the songs were becoming kind of monotonous, and I thought maybe that was it for him," Comings said. "I thought maybe he'd blown his songwriting wad."

Chicago-based drummer Jeff Panall stepped in to replace Comings, having roomed with Molina at House of Boys in Oberlin. Dan Sullivan, brother of Molina's redheaded friend Rob Sullivan, stepped in on added guitar duties. He had his own solo project, too, where he performed under the name Nad Navillus. Dan MacAdam, the second of Molina's redheaded friends from Oberlin, who ran the screen-printing shop Crosshair on Lake Street, played bass. In the fall of 2000 the quartet left for their first-ever tour of Europe. They played about thirty dates with Songs: Ohia label mates Swearing at Motorists, a two-piece rock band centered on the songwriting of Dayton, Ohio, native Dave Doughman, and Parker Paul, an enigmatic piano balladeer signed to Secretly Canadian's sister label Jagjaguwar.

On the European tour, the new Chicago core of Songs: Ohia largely stuck to a twelve-song set comprised of songs from *The Lioness*. They also wrote a song onstage that never received a title, which they now anecdotally call "Wha Nah Nah Nah," a sort of onomatopoeia of its introductory notes. Molina sold the *Protection Spells* live album he had recorded the last time he was in Europe, as well as corresponding T-shirts. At this point he found designing and screen printing album covers and corresponding merch like T-shirts so tedious that he once wrote a Post-It note that simply said, "You fuckers figure it out." MacAdam later memorialized the note on a t-shirt he screen printed and distributed to friends and family, a reminder of his friend Molina.

In the UK the new lineup of Songs: Ohia met a young misfit songwriter who introduced herself as Emma and who eventually performed under the name Scout Niblett. A fan of Songs: Ohia, she handed Molina a demo tape in Leeds, which the band fell in love with. In a 2001 interview Molina recounted,

> There are stacks and stacks of demos that people have given to me and sent to me recently, and I am in the middle of separating them by the ones I've heard and the ones I have to get to. One that I received in Holland is by a songwriter calling himself Lion. I think it's fucking amazing.[3]

Figure 7.1.   The Songs: Ohia lineup of Jeff Panall, Dan Sullivan, Dan Mac-Adam, and Molina on tour in Europe. *Photo courtesy of Dan MacAdam*

Chalk the misplaced pronoun as a typo on the interviewer's behalf and you have the very sincere feelings Molina had about the artist that would become known and adored on the underground circuit as Scout Niblett. She attended a number of Songs: Ohia shows during that European tour. "We all loved her tape, and we listened to it a lot in the van," Jeff Panall said. "It was one of the tapes in the van we would all agree to listen to without going into ridiculous debates." On the tape was her scorcher "Miss My Lion," which in 2001 Secretly Canadian paired with Songs: Ohia's "Lioness." Molina's A side featured his friend Jennie Benford from Oberlin, who added harmonies to the burning love song.

In Modena, Italy, the Chicago-based Songs: Ohia quartet captured what would become its 2001 live album, *Mi Sei Apparso Come un Fantasma*—in English: *You Came to Me as a Ghost*. It's Molina's first true swapping of his solo artist brand for a rock band. A loud rock band. The eight-song album was unique in that it didn't act as a "greatest hits" collection or a line up of fan favorite songs. Rather, it captured the quartet's live lightning in a bottle, circa reimagined entries from Molina's songbook, spanning from his first LP the *Black Album* to *The Lioness* and new songs like seven-minute slower burner "She Came to Me as a Ghost," in which Molina solemnly howls over the crashing of Panall's booming drums and Sullivan's skittering guitar, as if they were closing in and all he could do was plead for his lover.

A classically trained guitarist, Dan Sullivan helped steer Molina's newfound interest in four-part crescendo and guitar texturing and began acting as musical director of the band. This was in part to help quell Molina's frustrations with rehearsing and having to explain his vision. The pair developed a unique musical language with one another, an almost telepathic understanding of the other's sonic needs. Of all of the members of the Chicago-based band, Dan Sullivan spent the most alone time with Molina on the road, often touring in a two-piece guitar format. For Sullivan, working with Molina became both a blessing and a curse.

Once Molina trusted him, Sullivan had carte blanche to spread out and add or withhold as he liked during Songs: Ohia performances. However, this was often achieved with few or no rehearsals, and with as much feedback from Molina. Jason's writing clip and commensurate catalog of song sketches had become so vast that he never thought to edit or hold back, in what he viewed as a deep commitment to authenticity. His goal was always to lay as many songs to tape as possible and then move on, which often didn't sit well with his less poetic or less autodidactic musician friends, like

Dan Sullivan. It also didn't help hurt feelings when Molina left town to make albums without telling his new band.

After returning from Europe, in the late fall of 2000, Molina headed out on a twenty-two-date tour, which included a fortuitous stop in Philadelphia. There he played an otherwise unassuming house show where he was reintroduced to a fan named Edan Cohen. Molina had stayed with Cohen with in the late '90s in Rochester, New York, while on tour as Songs: Ohia. In the years since that slumber party, Cohen had moved to Philadelphia, opened a recording studio, and became a locally recognized, go-to engineer for indie-rock acts in the City of Brotherly Love. He and Molina shared a deep-seated love of roots rock and Southern gospel and soul music. Given that he was a huge Songs: Ohia fan, Cohen invited Molina to his studio space that night after the show, around 2:30 a.m., to lay down a track for a Muscle Shoals tribute album he was producing. He figured that the invitation was a stretch and that Molina would be too tired, too busy, or both.

Much to Cohen's surprise, Molina agreed to do a cover for the compilation, and excitedly. Given the option of almost any track recorded at the famed Muscle Shoals Sound Studio in Alabama, Molina chose the tune "Sweet Release" by blue-eyed soul figurehead Boz Scaggs. It was a perfect fit for Molina, its southern-fried balladry a nod to current evolution in his home songwriting and recording. Cohen rounded up a group of local friends to accompany Molina on the seven-minute slow burner—a sort of American answer to what Van Morrison did with *Astral Weeks* in 1968— which they captured in a single take. Cohen had no way of knowing that this spontaneous way of working appealed very deeply to Molina, or that a follow-up phone call soon after would result in one of Songs: Ohia's most iconic works.

A week after he returned home to Chicago from Philadelphia, Molina got face time with the mysterious act Cat Power he'd inquired to Edith Frost about so many years ago in Oberlin. Molina opened for Chan Marshall's songwriting vehicle during a two-show run at Schuba's on the city's north side, a notoriously warm bubble of a room perfect for the pair's acoustic leanings. On December 17, Molina's beloved Fender Vibrolux Reverb amplifier was christened the "Cat Power Amp" after Marshall borrowed it from Molina for her headlining performance.

The Chicago crew of Songs: Ohia played in various formations at U.S. dates with Molina throughout the winter of 2001, strengthening their sound and work habits. A show in St. Louis with Milwaukee-based emocore group the Promise Ring stands out in particular to the band. On the campus of Washington University, Molina let his perplexing disdain for all sound engineers get the better of him when he became inconsolably frustrated with the amateur student board setup and its inexperienced driver. What transpired is what the group now jokingly calls "Songs: I'll Fire Ya." After becoming deeply embarrassed by Molina's berating of the student sound-man in front of hundreds of his peers, bassist Dan MacAdam stood up for the kid by *strongly* encouraging Molina to back off. Given MacAdam's sharp and at times biting humor and Molina's general hardheadedness, it's not difficult to imagine that Molina became incredibly defensive by the suggestion. Things went downhill from there. After the show, MacAdam was Songs: Fired. The band drove home and MacAdam and Molina didn't speak for a period of months.

After the disastrous St. Louis gig, Molina and Dan Sullivan returned to Ireland to join Glen Hansard and Americana artist Josh Ritter for five dates. Each singer-songwriter performed a short solo set. Sullivan names the experience as a turning point in his solo career under the name Nad Navil-lus, and an example of Molina's generosity. Sullivan wouldn't have been included on the invite had it not been for a forcible nudge from Molina.

In Ireland the four musicians convened over Molina's four track, the same one he'd use to record his tour-only releases *Protection Spells* and *The Ghost*. Hansard remembered that as a group they captured the spirit of the individual sets they each played over the tour's five days, which Molina was ready to release without a second thought, as was his style. "He was like, 'This is it, this is an album,'" Hansard said. What Hansard didn't have to say was that no one else agreed with Molina, only that the recordings now sit unreleased in his possession. But Hansard loved observing Molina's dedicated working methods, when he'd rise at five o'clock in the morning and write lyrics until eight or nine. "He [Molina] loved music as work, and I loved that about him," he added.

After returning to the States from Ireland, Molina arranged for a re-cording session with Edan Cohen in Philadelphia, who'd captured his Boz Scaggs cover for the Muscle Shoals tribute album *Burlap Palace*. Prior to the session, Molina told Cohen over the phone that he'd like to record a full-length record he'd been working on, inspired by American blues and gospel traditions, and in particular a song covered by Chicago's Queen of Gospel, Mahalia Jackson. He thought Cohen's knowledge and fandom of the Muscle Shoals Sound Studio and its recording techniques would align nicely with the pivot in his personal sound, something less dirgey-indie and more roots rock. Molina had been reading a lot of Studs Terkel, Chicago's voice of the common man, which practically seeps through the pores of that album's namesake, *Didn't It Rain*:

No matter how dark the storm gets overhead
They say someone's watching from the calm at the edge
What about us when we're down here in it
We gotta watch our own backs
But if you do see that golden light
That it shines in its fiery eye
Go on and catch it while you can
Go on and catch it if you can
Let it course through you
And let it burn through you
If it's the light of truth
If they think you got it they're going to beat it out of you
Through work and debt whatever all else there is
You got to watch your own back
Try to see the light of goodness burning down the track
Through the blinding rain through the swaying wires
If I see you struggle I will not turn my back
I've seen a good man and a bad man down the same path
I've seen the light of truth keeping out of it and told them to watch their own backs
If I see you struggle and givin all that you got
I see you work all night burning your light to the last of its dim watts
I'm gonna help you how I can, if you see me struggle all night and
Give me a hand cause I'm in need I'll call you friend indeed
But I'm going to watch my own back
Didn't it rain

Inspired by historical struggles of the Rust Belt workingman and sounds of blues and gospel traditions, and armed with the words of Studs Terkel and Gwendolyn Brooks, both of whom he'd been reading obsessively, Molina rolled up to Soundgun Studios in Philadelphia in what engineer Edan Cohen remembers as a rented, jet-black cop car, something like a Ford Crown Victoria, looking pleased with himself as Sade blared from its speakers. It was in this North Philly industrial moor, commonly referred to as the "Badlands," which was controlled by a pack of roaming feral dogs, that the songwriter and engineer crafted what many consider Molina's first perfect record, a nod to the gospel, blues, and roots traditions that inspired Molina, released under the namesake of the traditional tune popularized by Sister Rosetta Tharpe: "Didn't It Rain."

In a 2002 interview, Molina explained, "I try to do as little editing as I possibly can in my songwriting, even now. That's just a way of keeping things free and spontaneous, which is, pretty much, just keeping to a sort of blues tradition. The blues singers, the great ones, they start out on an idea, and they advance on that idea for five minutes, singing in sort of a circle about the same five things they want to get across. I think that free, circular, abstract kind of songwriting can be a very complete form of storytelling, and it's something we all can do when we're not so self-conscious."

This couldn't be more true of *Didn't It Rain*, in which subtle instrumentation conceived and executed by a cast of musicians who'd never played together before, and would mostly never play together again, including Molina's friend Jennie Benford from Oberlin and her Pinetops bandmate Jim Krewson, helped create a work dominated by lyrical themes of desolate landscapes and downtrodden moods. Molina was very specific about his atmospheric goals for the record and filled the room with physical manifestations of the album's aura in the form of posters of iconic Chicago blues musicians hung on handmade wheeled bevels. Next to each image lived an oversized sheet of white paper—ubiquitous accessories of corporate conference rooms—with a song's lyrics scrawled in Molina's distinctive, romantic script. "He'd write in red, 'Jim sing here' or 'Jim and Jennie sing here,'" Benford recalled. They started each recording after sundown and dimmed the lighting so that the words were barely visible, allowing near darkness to envelop the room and drive a spectral and contemplative posture. Benford recalled Molina asking her to listen to Neil Young's *After the Gold Rush* ahead of the session, for tonal reference, which inspired her to play the piano.

Molina and Cohen had discussed the record a bit over the phone prior to the session, where the singer insisted that everything be recorded live, with a minimal studio cast. Having a self-described hard head, one perhaps as stony as Molina's, Cohen pretended to acquiesce and then immediately prepared himself for battle. He wanted lush instrumentation and had a strong hunch that live vocals just wouldn't work in his sprawling studio space, a former factory.

Once Molina hit town, Cohen was particularly adamant about the inclusion of lap steel player Mike Brenner, a local whose homemade "lap bass"—a bass guitar he rigged up so it could be played slide style on his lap—added the eerie, cello-like sounds heard throughout the record. After a few verbal rounds, Molina relented after hearing a number of recordings of Brenner's session work. Cohen also managed to call in friends Greg Castano, Matthew Schwed, and John Popovics to help flesh out the tracks, though the three were largely uncredited after the album's release.

Molina's voice was as doleful and commanding as ever, and he placed great trust in his players, who'd quickly work out parts and run through a song just once or twice before they'd hit RECORD. Every track was captured in one or two takes. "I have nothing but happy memories of that time," Benford said. "But sometimes it wasn't so easy to roll with." She explained that for most of the songs she and Molina stood at a single mic together—two tiny mice huddled together in Cohen's seemingly endless studio field—as Molina played guitar. Given his faulty memory, he had trouble sticking to the lyrical script. "He would suddenly change up a word in a lyric and I'd still be singing the old version," Benford said. "In those cases we'd have to do the song again." Throughout his career, Molina insisted on capturing songs as unrehearsed and as live as possible and then released them with blemishes and all. The most recognized and beloved example from this session lives at the 6:57 mark of *Didn't It Rain*'s namesake, when Molina audibly whispers to Benford, "Let's bring it back, we can sing one more." This first track sets the lovingly homespun nature of the album, an authentic tribute to the self-taughtedness of the Muscle Shoals, Alabama-based studios that inspired Molina and Cohen.

Despite Molina's binary personality, which throughout his life straddled extreme solacement and extreme silliness, everyone in the studio that week remembered him as pleasant and generous, with just a few exceptions. "Mike, who's a professional session guy, initially said things like, 'Throw up one more track because I have a harmony for that part,' and Jason got mad and insisted, 'No! No overdubs!'" Cohen explained. "I could tell that Mike, who'd never heard of Jason before, was thinking, 'Who is this little dude?'" It took more than a little coaxing for Molina to relax as Brenner recorded harmony parts for his lap bass in separate tracks.

"I think he just expected me to do the initial parts and walk, but I had some ideas," Brenner said. "So we did the overdubs anyway. He could have erased them if he didn't like it. Edan and I were used to working together, so we were being a bit mischievous." Cohen also remembered conversations about music turning from casual to confrontational, when a deadpan Molina would deride some of Cohen's favorite artists. "Richard Buckner? Gram Parsons? They're hacks!" Molina would proclaim. "I think he was just messing with me, but it was always hard to tell with him," Cohen added.

Molina also managed to work in a few half-truths and exaggerations about the album. In a 2002 interview, he explained, "I've studied with a guy who worked at the Muscle Shoals studio for a long time [Edan Cohen], who made *Didn't It Rain*, was the guy who dug up all the original Muscle Shoals engineers and learned a lot of great recording techniques for live recordings. And a lot of that shows on this record."

While it's true that the spirit of live recording practically seeps through each groove of *Didn't It Rain*, in reality Cohen spent just one week with one figure associated with Muscle Shoals Sound Studio, guitarist Jimmy Johnson, who flew to Philly to hang out at Cohen's studio while he recorded some of the bands for the *Burlap Palace* compilation. He wasn't there during Molina's take, however. And Cohen insists he never spent any time in the actual Muscle Shoals Sound Studio space in Alabama. "I went down to mix for three days in his [Johnson's] studio, which had nothing to do with Muscle Shoals Sound, which at that point was totally empty," he added. "It's a cool story for Jason, but none of it is true." Cohen also recalls reading interviews where Molina boasted of a magical studio in Philly filled to the brim with vintage gear, when in reality he had just two vintage mics.

To many who worked with Molina, the compromises he made with Cohen and Brenner in the *Didn't It Rain* session were miraculous. "He definitely wanted to be the guy who made great work that was self-evident," Chris Swanson said. "He was committed to first drafts, sort of like the Kerouac method. Revision was not the type of work he wanted to do." This stubbornness nearly sent Cohen through the roof when Molina attempted to abscond with the recordings without mixing them. After another kerfuffle in which Cohen pleaded for Molina to give him just a few hours with what he had captured, to make subtle adjustments to the levels, Molina relented. "The record had to have at least a little compression before I turned it over to the mastering guy," Cohen added with a laugh.

Despite the uncharacteristic compromises he made in the studio, *Didn't It Rain* remains a testament to a vision that could only have been spun by Molina's mind, with its meditations on images from the banks of Lake Erie in "Blue Factory Flame" and romantic observations of Northwest Indiana's steel factories and industrial open graves on "Steve Albini's Blues," the product of Molina's having recently relocated to Carl Sandburg's "City of the Big Shoulders" and having two sessions with its most heralded recording engineer on the books.

It was a conscious move away from the territory occupied by Will Oldham, more Studs Terkel than Bonnie "Prince" Billy, with sweeping relatable themes of the heartland replacing arcane equivocation or dripping love songs. In "Blue Chicago Moon," there's an early, unmistakable confession of Molina's emotional state, a sort of foreshadowing of depression's fog that would eventually envelop the singer:

> Out of the ruins
> blood grown heavy from his past
> his wings stripped by thunder
> but those storms keep coming back

> singing birds in sickness
> sing the same blues songs
> when they fell out of the emptiness
> they must have brought along
> space's loneliness
> space's loneliness
> gotten so good at hiding it
> even he does not admit it
> that glittering flash in his eyes
> makes it look like he might be alright
> but if the blues are your hunter
> then you will come face to face
> with that darkness and desolation
> and the endless depression
> but you are not helpless
> and you are not helpless
> try to beat it
> try to beat it
> and live through space's loneliness
> and live through space's loneliness
> you are not helpless
> you are not helpless
> I'll help you to try to beat it

The sprawling compositions conjured a supernatural portal that transported Molina's words from earthly to ethereal. The record laid the foundation for the sound that was to become his signature: sweet and sorrowful crackles, pastoral sparseness, all evolving into a contemporary roots-rock revival. Molina's voice was at its strongest—no longer a cherubic Oberlin virgin, and no longer a sinewy tenor confined by two-note vocal meditations.

The *Didn't It Rain* session also cemented a relationship with lap steel player Mike Brenner, who'd go on to record and tour with Molina for years to come. And ultimately, Molina didn't make every concession. He ended up winning what was perhaps the biggest battle. "All the vocals were recorded live," Cohen admitted. "While I was originally upset at having to do this, I am confident he made the right call, and I'm glad he pushed me out of my comfort zone."

Pitchfork bestowed an 8.4 rating on the album, noting, "In the process of recording another incredible album, he's discovered that light is most visible when it's flickering alone in the dark." The blog *Dusted Magazine* remarked that any Will Oldham comparison at this point was moot, as Molina had fully come into his own. *CMJ* awarded the album its "Best New Music" tag. "I thought I'd make the genius move of the century to pick that point in 1999 to move on," former drummer Geof Comings explained. "*Ghost Tropic* came out and I thought 'Yep, I'm a genius. I don't like that record. If I'm giving up my life and that's what he's doing, I played my cards right. Then *Didn't It Rain* came out, and I thought, 'I'm an idiot. What did I do?'"

8

LIGHTNING IN A BOTTLE

Back in Chicago, Rob Sullivan from the Chicago-based Oberlin friend group picked up Songs: Ohia bass duties in fired Dan MacAdam's stead, and the group headed to South by Southwest on March 16, 2001. Upon their departure, Molina casually hopped in the van with a hand-dubbed cassette, totally nonplussed. "He was like, 'Check out this record I just made,'" Rob Sullivan remembered, laughing. Given the recent *Ghost Tropic* bomb, the act wasn't terribly shocking. But the band's collective chin hit the floor when they heard the recording. They couldn't believe that the rust-worn slice of indie roots rock had come from Molina, not because they didn't believe in his talent, but because the material they'd been rehearsing with him, a series of rock 'n' roll dirges with sharp guitar texturing and metronomic drumming, was so different from the blues-steeped song cycle that comprised the cassette.

"When he went and recorded *Didn't It Rain*, some of us had been playing with him for years," drummer Jeff Panall said. "And we had been playing a completely different set of material. I think the drummer and the bass player on *Didn't It Rain* had never played with him before, and they probably only did one or two takes and probably never played with him again." Duped again by their mysterious friend-bandleader, they tried not to let their disappointment get the best of them as they headed to Austin for the biggest indie-rock showcase west of the Mississippi, with Molina's new, and very good, album on repeat.

The Songs: Ohia van also blasted Peaches, the Canadian electro-feminist performer whom Molina adored and evangelized to the band. Imagine a van full of skinny, Dungeon and Dragons–playing indie-rock dudes singing and dancing along to "Diddle My Skittle" and arrive at their collective silliness. Now imagine Molina's rendition, in his high-pitched, Meatwadesque "Mr. Squirty" voice, and arrive at his utterly charming absurdity.

When the group pulled up to Austin's 6th Street confines to register for the festival and grab their credentials, they were shocked to see Peaches in the van in front of them. Throwing boundaries out the van window, they freaked out, piled out, handed her Songs: Ohia records, and then jetted back to their own vehicle giddy as schoolgirls. Her set with Chicago-based avant-gardist Bobby Conn served as a perfect prefestival performance warm-up for the four friends, who couldn't have imagined a better pre-show lubricant. During their performance, Molina introduced Panall as the "future girlfriend of Peaches," after proclaiming that "Songs: Oheea is in the house!"

Molina and his two drummers, Jeff Panall and Geof Comings, played student radio station WOBC's fiftieth-anniversary concert in Oberlin in May, revisiting the site that had started Molina's recorded career as a solo artist. Panall helmed the kit for newer material, while Comings took over for a few older songs that he and Molina regularly played in their years touring together. Jeff Panall and Molina then returned to Chicago for a show with Glen Hansard, who'd become a friend in music but not quite in life, given the cross-continental divide and Molina's general caginess with anyone who tried to get too close. Still, their relationship proved to be a sturdy tent pole throughout Molina's last days, even after Hansard's profile shot northward, propelled by the success of the 2007 film *Once*. "I got a letter from him after we won the Oscar saying how proud he was, how he was telling all of his friends that he knows me, and how his parents were proud," Hansard said. "It was like, 'Fuck, man, good on ya.'"

After the shows with Hansard, the full version of Songs: Ohia took off for a short tour with, for the first time on the road, Jim Grabowski on keys. Molina and Grabowski had become chummy during a practice session for the friend group's annual holiday band, Dave LaCrone and the Mistletones, which performed at a Christmas party each year at Crosshair. "He had volunteered to sing 'All I Want for Christmas is My Two Front Teeth,'" Grabowski explained.

Before hitting the road, Grabowski played a couple of local Chicago shows with Songs: Ohia and enjoyed the spirit of improvisation and the camaraderie among the band members. On the tour he proved to be a great match for the hijinks that the band enjoyed.

One night on the tour, there weren't enough beds for the entire band between the two hotel rooms Molina had secured. Instead of drawing straws, band newcomer Grabowski placed two nickels under three cups and said, "Two nickels share a bed." After he shuffled them, Jeff Panall picked first and got a nickel. Then Molina picked and got a nickel, leaving Grabowski spread out solo. After the display, Molina pointed out that they never looked under the third cup and was convinced that Grabowski had tricked them, which earned him the name "Three Nickel Jim."

The group played a show at the Knitting Factory in Manhattan where Molina adopted a larger-than-life persona. He excitedly told his friend Jennie Benford, who was living in New York at the time, that he was learning all of the Carter Family songs. "That's hundreds of songs," she said with a dubious laugh. In New York, Molina also met up with his former flame Anne Grady. Over dinner they lamented how far apart they'd grown, and Molina cried to her over dinner, something that wasn't out of character for him in the context of their relationship but which also seemed unusual to her. He told her that he later captured the spirit of their encounter that night in his song "Bowery," named for the street that runs the southern

Figure 8.1.   The Songs: Ohia lineup of Dan Sullivan, Molina, Rob Sullivan, Jim "Three Nickel" Grabowski, and Jeff Panall. *Photo courtesy of Jim Grabowski*

portion of Manhattan. It wouldn't be released until 2007 on the album *Nashville Moon*:

> While the wolf had her fangs
> Deep in my heart
> Who's been writing the songs
> Who's been singing
> And who's been listening
> Blue eyes while you've been gone
> And that two dollar hat and them old black stockings
> Down on the Bowery
> Hand in hand the full moon went walking
> With blue eyes without me
> And now tears used to write 'em
> And the cold wind would blow 'em
> Down on the Bowery
> Broken hearts were the only things listening
> And blue eyes, I heard everything
> And that two dollar hat and them old black stockings
> Down on the Bowery
> Hand in hand the full moon went walking
> With blue eyes without me
> With blue eyes without me

Molina joined Alasdair Roberts for a house show in Bloomington in September before the pair headed south to the Oldham family farm in Shelbyville, Kentucky, to convene under what would become the project Amalgamated Sons of Rest. For the collaboration, Will Oldham, Molina, and Roberts each contributed an original song or two, in addition to performances of Scottish folk tunes like "My Donal" and "Maa Bonny Lad." The project was proposed and championed by Molina, a curious move for a guy who hated Oldham comparisons and worked to skirt them. Still, he jumped at the chance to join his old friends under the watchful studio ears of Will's brother Paul Oldham.

The resulting album was a contemporary nod to British folk music traditions, a sound that would become increasingly fashionable in the indie landscape as the 2000s pushed forward into the 2010s. Roberts's gentle rhotic accent blended beautifully in trade-offs with Oldham's light warble and Molina's stronger tenor. The plucked guitar lines and vocal harmonies recalled the folk sounds that echoed from the shorelines of Roberts's Scotland, without outright aping them. The warm fidelity of the recording acted as a fuzzy sweater, enveloping each player's parts in a familiar coziness. Perhaps too early for its time, the album received lukewarm reception by critics, panned as a disc that sounded too much like a display of each songwriter's individual traits.

Perhaps more affecting than the album that resulted from their stay was what transpired the morning of September 11, 2001. "I was still in bed at about ten in the morning and Jason came upstairs and said, 'Ali, you'd better come downstairs, something terrible is happening,'" Roberts explained. He initially thought the Oldham brothers were having one of their notorious squabbles. After wandering downstairs, he joined Molina on the sofa. Looking up at the television, Roberts asked, "Aren't there two towers?" "Not anymore," Molina replied.[1]

The musician friends spent the morning watching the news before Oldham's mother and father stopped by and prepared a meal for the group. Later that night they recorded a song Molina extemporaneously composed, a sort of prayer or incantation they eventually titled, quite simply, "September 11." "It was a spontaneous response from Jason's soul to the unimaginably terrible events of that day," Roberts explained.[2] Molina sang of ringing bells and tempests over Roberts's bowed dulcimer and Oldham's soft piano playing. Molina felt as if the world was returning to its origins, a darkness falling over the light of civilization.

When Molina returned to Chicago, he fashioned an altarpiece to the victims of the 9/11 attacks and placed it in his living room. He often engaged in spiritual or ritualistic practices such as burning sage, ringing a bell in a dedicated tone or pattern, or mixing herbs and oils into a brass pot before burning them—all attempts to clear or convene with the energy and spirits that surrounded him. Having been already uneasy with the practice of flying, the cyclically broadcast images of the World Trade Center towers crumbling to the ground propelled Molina's fear of flying from "manageable" to "nonnegotiable." The nerves Molina had once eased with tiny bottles of wine now haunted every cranny of his consciousness.

Before Molina's sojourn to the Oldham family farm, the members of Songs: Ohia plotted and booked a two-week tour of the Netherlands and Belgium for late September 2001. After the events of 9/11, Molina canceled the tour, swearing he'd never fly again. The band was particularly disappointed because they had meticulously planned the jaunt overseas and scheduled stops that required very little driving time between cities at venues where Molina was especially popular at the time. It would have been a great moneymaker and a fun and somewhat relaxing trip for the band of brothers. Crafting lemonade from Molina's lemons, Dan Sullivan, Jeff Panall, and Rob Sullivan instead used their plane tickets to Amsterdam for Rob's bachelor party.

East Coast indie-rock record label Jade Tree approached Louisville, Kentucky–based rock band My Morning Jacket in late 2001 about doing a split EP with Molina for its new—and short-lived—"Split Series." It consisted of bands with similar aesthetics contributing tracks to a joint, short album. Other artists in the series included punk acts the Alkaline Trio and Hot Water Music. My Morning Jacket frontman Jim James had seen Molina play in Bloomington a handful of times, and the two struck up a casual friendship over e-mail. "I loved his spirit, and he had a sweet smile paired perfectly with those lost eyes and longing velvet voice," James explained. "I considered him a 'creature' more than human, undefined by any natural laws, which is the highest compliment I can give any living being."

My Morning Jacket contributed four songs to Molina's one, including "O Is This the One That Is Real," which provided a stylistic teaser for the band's forthcoming, widely heralded LP *It Still Moves*. The song made steady rounds on CD-R mixes in indie-rock fan circuits upon its release. Though the number of songs the two artists contributed to the split differed, they weren't that far off in total playing time. The track Molina submitted was the ten-minute slow burner from the Amalgamated Sons of Rest session in Shelbyville, which he titled "Translation" and attributed to "A. S. of R." In the song his vocals steered sparse acoustic guitar, drums, bass, and auxiliary percussion elements. It was a vastly different version from what had appeared on the *Me Sei Apparso Come un Fantasma* live album with his Chicago rock band.

Aligning with his flummoxing and often unpredictable behavior, after having just vowed to never fly again, Molina went to Europe with label mates Scout Niblett and June Panic. On January 26, 2002, the trio had a particularly transcendent experience, where the crowd in the packed club circled around the players, leaving only a small space between them and the fans. "Every word and every note seemed like a climax, or some kind of new beginning," Panic explained. "Everybody in the room seemed to be falling in love."[3]

About ten days after returning from Europe, Molina left for Australia for the longest flight he'd taken in his life thus far. He played six solo dates. Afterward, during an April 6 stop in Harrisonburg, Virginia, for the Mid-Atlantic College Radio Conference known as MacRock, the local fire marshal shut down the show due to overcrowding. Instead of kowtowing to authority, Molina stomped across the street with his Gibson SG and played solo on the steps of the courthouse. Molina smirked as he played the song "Ring the Bell" from *Didn't It Rain*, particularly as he sang the line, "They're always close, they're always so close," as the police circled around the display. At an August 2 show at the 40 Watt Club in Athens, Georgia, Molina snarled at the chatty crowd, "If I wanted to play for fucking assholes, I would have played in New York City."

Fellow singer-songwriter Damien Jurado, who had recently signed with Molina's label Secretly Canadian after a split from Seattle grunge behemoth Sub Pop, flew to Wisconsin to join Molina for a string of solo dates. Molina had rented a boat-sized car very similar to the one he'd driven to Philadelphia to record *Didn't It Rain*. "I don't know how he got this car—I believe it was a Lincoln Continental," Jurado explained.[4] Molina almost immediately inquired if Jurado knew German experimental act Kraftwerk's 1975 album *Radio-Activity*, which had lyrics sung in English and German. After Jurado admitted that he didn't know the record, Molina screeched the car to the side of the highway. "There's semis going full-speed, right by our car, and every time they pass our car is moving to the left and to the right," Jurado recalled.[5] Molina then reached into a duffle bag, pulled out a copy, and gave it to Jurado explaining that he had to own it. "But he said it almost like someone would say, 'Take this pill, it will save your life,'" Jurado continued.[6] "We listened to it, from front to back. We listened to it maybe twice. And I still have that CD to this day. It became one of my favorite albums of all time."[7]

After a couple of years of out-of-town album sessions and mysteriously lifted flying embargoes, Molina's Chicago-based band no longer questioned his rhyme or reason. Mostly because they sensed there weren't any. Instead, they began to accept the idea that their time spent playing with him might be reaching an end, mostly because he had been packing up solo or with Secretly Canadian artists so often. Though they feigned nonchalance, the feeling of being slowly dismissed especially stung drummer Jeff Panall and guitarist Dan Sullivan, who had spent the most time on the road and in rehearsal with Molina. In fact, the band had come to respect Dan Sullivan as the de facto musical director, as Molina often grew frustrated with such minutia and instead preferred that people just pick up in a song and move forward, never looking back.

The band's confidence was boosted, though, when Molina invited both Dans—Sullivan and MacAdam—Rob Sullivan, Jeff Panall, and Jim "Three Nickel" Grabowski for a session at Electrical Audio on July 1 to perform a new set of material that he described as rock songs. It was the first time they'd perform songs written by Molina that already had multiple chords and parts planned out. Grabowski recalled Molina explaining that he had written new songs that were more like country songs or songs that you'd hear on the radio.

Molina had recorded the set of demos to cassette in his home music room, using an Audio Technica AT4047/SV mic that Electrical Audio figurehead Steve Albini recommended to him during the session with Glen Hansard. Outside of distributing copies to the band, Molina mailed a cassette of some of the songs to his friend William Schaff in Providence, Rhode Island. On the j-card of the demo he sent to Schaff, Molina dedicated the track he called "Magnolia" to the Chicago-based cartoonist Chris Ware, perhaps best known for his character *Jimmy Corrigan*, a lonely and misunderstood thirty-six-year-old man with a complicated relationship with his father—no doubt feelings Molina could relate to. Ware explained that he was unaware of the dedication until recently but was touched by it all the same, particularly given the tragic arc of Molina's life.

Schaff, a visual artist best known at the time for his album cover designs for the Austin, Texas–based Okkervil Band, met Molina at a Songs: Ohia gig in

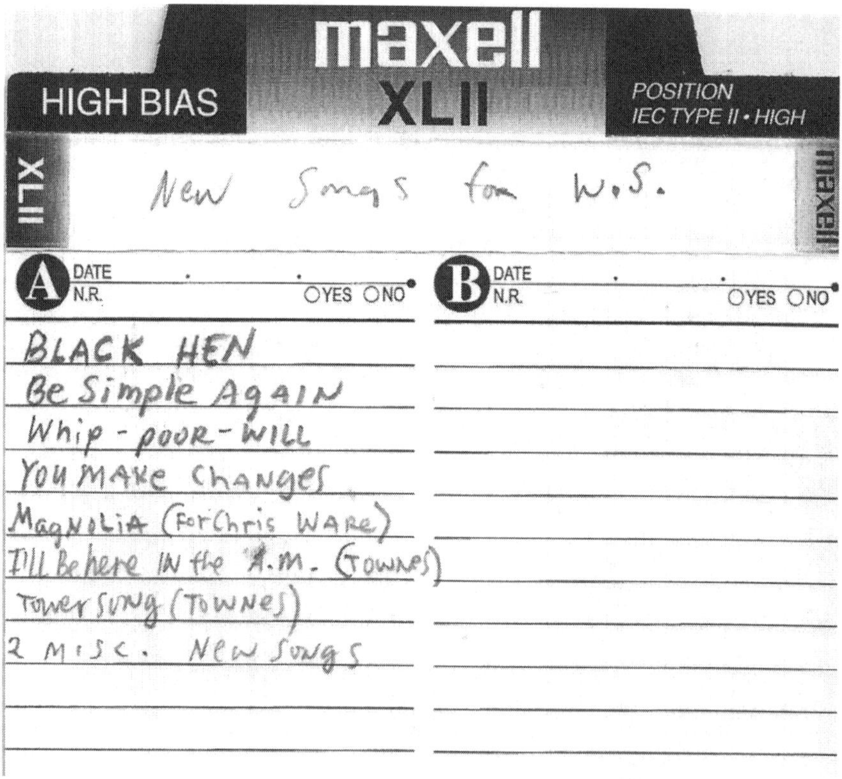

Figure 8.2. The j-card from the demo Molina sent to William Schaff. *Image courtesy of William Schaff*

the early aughts, and the two struck up a pen-pal friendship, trading art and letters. Their communication through letters and images drew them closer than Molina often allowed in his face-to-face relationships, when he'd come off as awkward or cagey. They spoke in a visual medium, something Molina had been craving since graduating from Oberlin.

In the demo he sent to Schaff, Molina also included a pair of Townes Van Zandt covers, the ballads "I'll Be Here in the Morning" and "Tower Song." He also tucked a Polaroid of his headphones, a four track, his Pignose amp, and his white Jerry Jones guitar signed by Link Wray, which he called "Molly," into the package.

In exchange, Schaff sent a drawing, which depicted Molina as one of his signature, skull-headed creatures. Molina liked it so much that he asked Schaff to contribute cover art for his new album of rock songs. He provided only a few parameters. "All he said was, 'When I was making this album, I was thinking a lot about owls, pyramids, and magnolias. You take it from there,'" Schaff explained. "It cracks me up to think how simple it was, and I use it as an example to this day when letting people know how I work if they are going to commission me."

Songs: Ohia played a pair of local Chicago shows as an act of rehearsing Molina's demo of rock songs. Jeff Panall listened to Neil Young's *Harvest* on repeat ahead of the session and became inspired by drummer Kenny Buttrey's chops. Having played with Molina at Electrical once prior, Panall knew that Steve Albini had a stellar collection of drums.

On day one of the session, Panall chose a six-lug brass Ludwig model from the 1920s, which he used for most of the songs, playing from the dead room of Electrical's Studio B. Molina brought his white guitar Molly, a black Gibson SG marked with his Southern Cross insignia in white medical tape, his beloved tiny Pignose amp, and the "Cat Power Amp," which he'd lent to Chan Marshall at Chicago rock club Schuba's. Finally, after years of playing together, the Chicago core of Songs: Ohia—Jeff Panall, Dan Sullivan, Rob Sullivan, Jim Grabowski, and Dan MacAdam—met at 2621 W. Belmont Avenue for what many describe as lightning in a bottle, a mystical conjuring of sonic spirits in Electrical Audio's Studio B. *The Magnolia Electric Co.* sessions included guest vocalists Jennie Benford, from Molina's Oberlin days, who appeared on *Didn't It Rain*; Lawrence Peters, a Chicago country singer and friend of Molina; Scout Niblett, the misfit British auteur whom Molina had just toured with; and lap steel player Mike Brenner from the *Didn't It Rain* session.

There was a palpable buzz in the studio, but not everyone was excited about the new material. "Molina was casually like, 'Here's the record we're making,'" Dan Sullivan explained. "I became frustrated because it was so

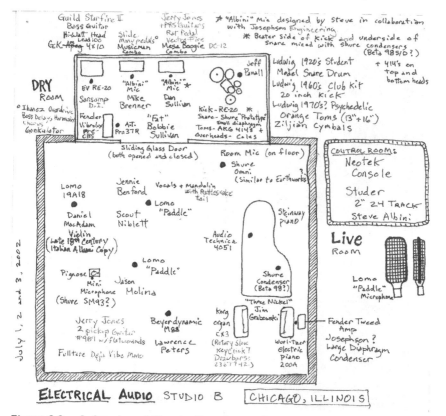

Figure 8.3. A drawing of the studio setup and gear used during the recording session for *The Magnolia Electric Co.* "Jason was very proud to write down the serial number of his Jerry Jones guitar that he played on the session because it was an original," Panall said. *Drawing courtesy of Jeff Panall*

far from what I had become comfortable playing with him, and at that point I sort of knew that he and I were done." Still, Sullivan showed up for the session, hoping the spirit of brotherhood with his friends and brother Rob would offset his dissatisfaction with the demos.

Lawrence Peters recalled that Molina had the posture of an Olympic athlete, as if his whole life's work was coming down to this one moment. Others remembered him buzzing around the studio at a hummingbird's pace, intent on getting every song in one or two takes, observing and playing with a watchful eye, while injecting spontaneity into the songs with last-minute personnel and instrumental shuffling.

Mike Brenner held the title of True Outsider, having met Molina for only a couple of hours during the *Didn't It Rain* session in Philadelphia. Molina invited him to the session in the eleventh hour, giving him very little time to practice and work out his lap steel parts. As a professional session player, this was not the way he was accustomed to working. Still, the greatness he heard in the demos Molina mailed to him were more alluring than his fears about not having enough time to rehearse.

Brenner flew to Chicago from Philadelphia on Molina's dime, receiving a meager sum for his time. "I took the position of session musician, where you just kind of have to take the temperature of the room," Brenner explained. And he received very little direction or feedback from Molina or the large studio cast the bandleader had assembled. "The funniest part is that after the sessions wrapped, the only other person staying at the studio was Scout Niblett, and she went out with friends," Brenner explained. "It went from this huge troupe of people collaborating, playing music all day, and kind of being on top of each other, to me sitting in this studio by myself watching videos until 3 a.m. It highlighted my outsider status." One night when he was watching ESPN solo, Steve Albini slipped into the room quietly and the pair watched baseball highlights in silence.

Exacerbating any tension that might have been in the room due to Brenner's presence was the fact that Dan Sullivan had been working on a lot of slide guitar parts to add to the songs, blissfully unaware until a few days before the session that Molina had planned to fly in Brenner, a professional slide player. Dan took it as a personal affront to his vision and contributions, while Brenner was blissfully unaware that any of this was going on. "We were in the same [isolation] booth, and I could tell he was frustrated about something, but I didn't know what," Brenner remembered.

"I showed up expecting to play a couple of violin parts and then leave," Dan MacAdam remembered. Molina had invited him to the session after "firing" him from Songs: Ohia months earlier. "But Jason was like, 'We're recording a song. Go step up to the mic with Lawrence and sing.'" The song was "Farewell Transmission," counted among the album's most iconic tracks, and that's MacAdam and Peters cooing the line "long dark blues" off the cuff. The biggest surprise was when Molina asked MacAdam to handle guitar duties, which was Dan Sullivan's domain.

"We were recording 'John Henry Split My Heart,' and I was playing violin and Jason said, 'Hey Dan, why don't you play guitar?'" MacAdam said. What MacAdam didn't know was that Dan Sullivan had not shown up for the third day of the session. "I didn't have a part, but I went to the basement where Steve Albini's guitars are, and I was like, 'I'm going to play the Rapeman guitar!'" he added. The same thing happened with "Almost Was Good Enough."

"What I really didn't want to do was fuck up the session," Dan Sullivan said. "We all knew we were making a great album. There was this big cast of characters and everyone was bringing their best, myself included, even though I was frustrated. There had been some intense moments of me feeling humiliated because my input had been shot down, whereas before I had had such an open dialogue with him. And it was his right! It was his record, and it turned out beautifully. I tried my best to just be a bit player and do what I was told. But I was pissed off and feeling like a hypocrite, so I played the first two days and then left." Some players thought Molina had instituted one of his famous firings, à la Dan MacAdam—Songs: I'll Fire Ya.

Dan Sullivan said his departure from the Magnolia session was voluntary. "I actually showed up the morning of the third day, but he wasn't there. I was ready to talk to him about it, about how I wasn't happy," Sullivan recalled. "He called me later and chewed me out. I was wrecked because my brother and all my friends were there, and we had made this great thing. But my experience making this record was terrible. It just took a time to get over that. It was obviously the end. I loved it so much, and when I couldn't be a part of it anymore, it just broke my heart."

Sullivan's departure wasn't even the biggest shake-up that Songs: Ohia experienced during that session. It was then, too, that Molina announced, casually, that he had decided to move back to Bloomington. "I didn't appreciate how shocking it was because I wasn't really there for these other bombs that he would drop," Jim Grabowski said. "I thought, 'That's too bad,' and assumed these other guys had heard about it before because of the way Jason had said it."

As they were driving away from Electrical Audio after mixing the record, drummer Jeff Panall remembered that he and Molina agreed that *The Magnolia Electric Co.* was their crowning achievement, the most important thing either of them had ever done. What he didn't know, however, was that Molina said that every time he finished a record. "He'd say this is the best thing I've done and I'll never do anything better," Darcie remembered. "He was always convinced that he'd never do anything better than what he'd just done." But he'd recount in a 2012 e-mail to Panall, "Putting a bunch of sweaty Oberlin people in a room together has usually turned out some very interesting and magic things, those sessions were for sure that and a lot more."

Ben Swanson from Secretly Canadian said Molina returned to Bloomington with the two-inch tapes from the *Magnolia Electric Co.* session labeled NOT SONGS: OHIA, and that he was dying to start a more traditional band with consistent players. "I don't think it was only because of the Sullivan experience, but it was informative," Ben Swanson explained, adding that "Jason and Dan could both be fiery, which is the reason they had chemistry, but also the reason they infuriated one another. I think Jason had this idea of the recording process in his brain and Dan encroached on that, and probably went a little too far and Jason overreacted a little too much. Part of it, too, was that Jason knew he had created a really unique record, different from what he had done in the past, and he saw the power of a truly great band."

Molina included a handwritten note that gave credit to the personnel not featured on the gatefold photo of Grabowski, Rob Sullivan, Molina, Jeff Panall, and Dan Sullivan that appeared on the inside of the original vinyl release. It read:

> Dan MacAdam: Hard Assigned Transcender
> Jennie Benford: Magic Forever
> Lawrence Peters: Set Down The Revelation
> Scout Niblett: Out Past The Dark
> Mike Brenner: Set The Lightning Down
> Steve Albini: Everything Did Work
>
> Someone used to say to me: If the only two words you ever say are thank you, then that will be enough. Thank you.

Below the credits Molina wrote the names Pyramid Electric Co. and Magnolia Electric Co. side by side.

An extension of the introspective folk balladeer meets roots-rock revivalist dichotomy Molina exhibited during this time was his return to Nebraska, where he'd recorded *Ghost Tropic*. There he recorded what would become his solo album *Pyramid Electric Co.* It was his darkest, most spectral song cycle yet. Molina originally wanted to package the *Magnolia* and *Pyramid* records as a double-album release, representing the two sides of his conjoined songwriting face. The label released them separately, about a year apart from one another.

Molina had been writing the two sets of material at about the same time and viewed them as equally important, though sales and celebration would come to belie that belief in his fans' collective consciousness. And then there was the issue of the band name, which Molina hadn't provided for either album. He instead insisted that one record simply be called *Magnolia Electric Co.* and the other *Pyramid Electric Co.*, without an attribution. The cover of *Magnolia* holds true to this aesthetic, too, without any mention of Songs: Ohia or Jason Molina being included on the record's cover or spine. The label contextualized the release with stickers on the shrink-wrap and track listings on the inside of the album. "He was the first artist I had worked with who took to the image so much that no text was anywhere on the sleeve of the original release," William Schaff explained. "Nothing on the spine, front or back. No label name or number, no band name . . . nothing. I was blown away he was willing to put it out like that."

Molina had threatened to change the Songs: Ohia name since he began making records under the peculiar moniker recommended by Will Oldham. He reveled in a certain level of anxiety among his collaborators, Secretly Canadian included. Rob Sullivan remembered Molina telling him that he planned to change the name of the band after the release of *The Magnolia Electric Co.* "He was kind of opaque about it, and I didn't really believe him, until he did it," he said. "But that was like many Jason Molina things." Molina was never business minded—it was always about the craft—which aligned with his Luddite tendencies and fascination with maintaining the persona of a salt-of-the-earth workingman. He treated songwriting like a shift with a punch card, and his only personal measure of success was his sustained ability to crank out songs and records.

To this day *The Magnolia Electric Co.* remains Molina's best-selling and most anecdotally heralded album. Songs such as "Farewell Transmission," "Riding with the Ghost," "Just Be Simple," "Hold on Magnolia," and "Whip-Poor-Will" stand as classics in the ten-song lineup and have been covered by numerous artists ranging from Grammy-nominated Seattle rock act Band of Horses to Molina's Oscar-winning friend Glen Hansard. On the album there's a marked pivot in Molina's lyrical themes and vocal delivery, inspired by the increased channeling of his idols such as Neil Young, Warren Zevon, and Boz Scaggs. This is particularly true in the opening track "Farewell Transmission," in which he speak-sings the introductory lines, channeling Zevon's style. Jeff Panall's precise hits and rich drum tone, and potent harmonizing by Jennie Benford, Lawrence Peters, and Scout Niblett, flesh out the heartland effect as Molina sings:

> The whole place is dark
> Every light on this side of the town
> Suddenly it all went down
> Now we'll all be brothers of the fossil fire of the sun
> Now we will all be sisters of the fossil blood of the moon
> Someone must have set 'em up
> Now they'll be working in the cold grey rock,
> in the hot mill steam . . . in the concrete
> In the sirens and the silences now
> All the great set up hearts
> All at once start to beat
> After tonight if you don't want this to be
> A secret out of the past

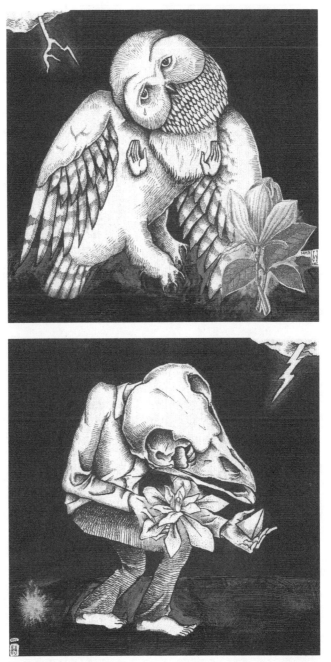

Figures 8.4. and 8.5. The original artwork William Schaff created for the front and back covers of the Magnolia Electric Co. His SAMA moniker was removed from the front cover during production. *Courtesy of William Schaff*

I will resurrect it, I'll have a good go at it
I'll streak his blood across my beak
dust my feathers with his ash
Feel his ghost breathing down my back
I will try and know whatever I try,
I will be gone but not forever
Real truth about it is
No one gets it right
Real truth about it is
We're all supposed to try
There ain't no end to the sands
I've been trying to cross
Real truth about it is my kind of life's no better off
If it's got the map or if it's lost
We will try and know whatever we try,
We will be gone but not forever
The real truth about it is there ain't no end to the desert I'll cross
I've really known it all along
Mama here comes midnight
With the dead moon in its jaws
Must be the big star about to fall
Mama here comes midnight
With the dead moon in its jaws
Must be the big star about to fall
Long dark blues
Will o the wisp
Long dark blues
The big star is falling
Long dark blues
Will o the wisp
The big star is falling
Long dark blues
Through the static and distance
Long dark blues
A farewell transmission
Long dark blues
Listen
Long dark blues
Listen
Long dark blues
Listen
Long dark blues
Listen

"I've Been Riding with the Ghost" serves as a lyrical manifestation of the very real phantoms Molina traveled with throughout his life and his pained attempts to see beyond them: the disconnect from his mother, depression, lost love, alcohol, the passing of friends and family, and of course the very real ghosts he convened with via hand-constructed altarpieces and protection spells. "Old Black Hen" country vocalist Lawrence Peters remarked that as a fellow songwriter, it was one of Molina's most genius observations about the struggle of the human condition.

> While you was gone you must have done a lot of favors
> You've got a whole lot of things I don't think
> That you could ever have paid for
> While you've been busy crying
> About my past mistakes
> I've been busy trying to make a change
> And now I made a change
> I've been riding with the ghost
> I've been doing whatever he told me
> I've been looking door to door to see
> if there was someone who'd hold me
> I never met a single one who didn't see through me
> None of them would love me if they thought they might lose me
> Unless I made a change
> See I ain't getting better. I am only getting behind
> I am standing on a crossroad trying to make up my mind
> I'm trying to remember how it got so late
> Why every night pain comes from a different place
> Now something's got to change
> I put my foot to the floor
> To make up for the miles I've been losing
> I've been running out of things
> I didn't even know I was using
> And while you've been busy
> Learning how to complain
> I've been busy learning
> How to make a change
> Now I made a change

In contrast, "Hold on Magnolia" serves as a lighthouse steering heart ships in from murky waters, Molina's insisting that things not only have the ability to get better, but that they will. Through the steadfast image of an ancient flowering plant, he insists, "Hold on Magnolia / To that great highway moon / No one has to be that strong / But if you're stubborn like me / I know what you're trying to be."

Molina had found his voice, channeling the trailer park shores of his youth and the industrial confines of his adoptive home Chicago, the struggles of the common man and the laboring of love. Rather than lions or tropical ghosts, Molina steeped himself in the most authentic and relatable themes he could bear witness to. He was the shores of Lake Erie. He wanted to be simple, as hard as that seemed.

Pyramid Electric Co. didn't fare as well sales-wise, or in the eyes of the critics, though *Pitchfork* noted, "'Honey, Watch Your Ass' is one of the best Molina compositions ever, *ever*, and it convicts its neighbors of slightness." The fact that Molina slept solo overnight in the studio as he wrote in his notebooks and practiced parts practically seeps through the record's grooves, which reek of solitude and introspection. The sparse guitar-and-vocal incantations were accented with just an occasional piano tickle.

Molina's time in Chicago had run its course, largely due to his and Darcie's frustrations with big-city hassles such as traffic and expensive everything. In the throes of urban frenzy, they longed for their simpler life in Bloomington, the ease of the pace and the tight-knit community there. She left her job. He packed up his gear. The couple returned from whence they came, four hours south down I-65.

9

THE ELECTRICIANS

Like in many college towns, the beating heart of creativity in Bloomington lived outside its campus's confines. A small, left-leaning incubator plopped in the midst of an overwhelmingly red state, "the Region" east of the border of Chicago notwithstanding, the network of underground bands, art spaces, and art makers was very much alive and thriving throughout its tiny downtown streets and prototypical midwestern ranch homes that dotted the periphery of the university. The figureheads of said art scenes convened over strong coffee at favored cafe Soma near the city's center at Grant and Kirkwood, or over cheap beers at the beloved dive the Video Saloon, where mulleted "Mike the Doorman" stood post on a stool for more than two decades.

A couple of days after Jason and Darcie returned to the town where they met, Molina saw ghosts. It was nothing new for him, as he'd seen them since childhood and accepted the relationship. But an incident involving their tuxedo cat Bhaji shook the couple. In the middle of the night they were jarred awake by a crashing sound from their closet. Inside, Bhaji hung from the curtain rod with a paw caught through his collar, surrounded by detritus that had fallen. From that day Molina was convinced that their new place was haunted. What Darcie didn't realize at the time was that Molina was frequently carousing with a different kind of spirit.

Bloomington, Indiana, in 2002 differed only slightly from when Molina had lived there before in the late '90s. Many of his old friends had graduated from

Indiana University and were now in graduate school, running art galleries or working at the ever-swelling offices of Secretly Canadian, at its distribution arm SC Distribution, or at Bellwether Manufacturing, the label's product design and fabrication operation. Around this time Molina began dreaming up his imaginary root beer stand, the Frosty Nickel. His plan was to open it in the tiny shack that still stands mysteriously empty across the street from Secretly Canadian's headquarters at 1499 West 2nd Street. Though the idea never became a reality, Molina told a fan in 2004, "the old Frosty Nickel is our root beer bar in southern Indiana. It is hidden but we're doing fine. The old boxer Magpie Mac came in and gave us an autographed pair of boxing gloves."[1] There is no way any of that could have been true.

Once touted as the new Seattle in the late '90s by *Billboard*, Bloomington's ever-swelling basement punk scene had shifted from the driving force of Secretly Canadian's roster back to that of a truly DIY enterprise, operating largely outside the pocketbooks and pressing-plant relationships of the homegrown label. Since signing Molina, whom they considered the label's flagship artist, Secretly Canadian had merged operations with fledgling indie label Jagjaguwar, run by Virginia native Darius Van Arman, who'd moved to Bloomington in 1999 to solidify his bond with SC. Though Secretly Canadian continued its focus on Songs: Ohia, it had also turned its attention to newer signees such as the shambolic folk-twee act the Danielson Family, singer-songwriter Damien Jurado, and Sweden's contemporary answer to Jonathan Richman, Jens Lekman. Lekman's satiric pop songs would soon sweep up Swedish Grammy nominations and receive national airplay in the United States.

In 2005 the combined labels scored their greatest sales and marketing coups in their signing of two acts that couldn't be more different. Jagjaguwar rode a wave of *Pitchfork*-enabled buzz courtesy of Canadian stoner-rock band Black Mountain, whose self-titled album was awarded the music review website's highest honor, a "Best New Music" tag. The band's second album, *In The Future*, was nominated for a Polaris Music Prize. Black Mountain's album sales were the highest Jagjaguwar had seen to date, in no small part due to the increasingly wide information funnel of the Internet—with streaming services, bloggers, and news outlets increasingly focusing attentions and affections on the growing swath of indie-rock labels and bands. The sea change of "indie rock" from that of a DIY movement to that of an aesthetic tag meaning such things as "guitar driven" or "bearded," was mounting from ripples to riptides.

Meanwhile, at Secretly Canadian, high art conceptualists Antony and the Johnsons came aboard after two years of courting by the Swanson brothers. Steered by the vocal and songwriting prowess of ANHONI, the artist formerly known as Antony Hegarty, the group's second album, *I Am a Bird Now*, blew the doors off the label's DIY-rooted operations after winning Britain's coveted Mercury Prize. It forced Secretly Canadian onto the global music scene and led to a massive marketing, public relations, and distribution expansion on the U.S. coasts and overseas. Soon, sister label Jagjaguwar signed fledging singer-songwriter Justin Vernon's unknown vehicle Bon Iver, who'd self-released a little folk album *For Emma, Forever Ago*. The label reissued it in 2008. Vernon's next album, *Bon Iver, Bon Iver*, netted him two Grammy awards in 2012.

In the midst of the sea change, the label's founders shifted into actual leadership roles, amassing a growing staff underneath them. In the late '90s, the Swanson brothers were incredibly hands-on with Molina, but as their business grew they became increasingly preoccupied with running their various appointed departments. Eventually, Jonathan Cargill was delegated the job of primary label contact for Molina, Songs: Ohia, and Magnolia Electric Co. "I acted as sort of a liaison between Jason and the world, and because of that I developed a little closer relationship with him than the other people at the label," he explained.

Though Molina hated that his friends in Ativin, Early Day Miners, Scout Niblett, Swearing at Motorists, and Parker Paul were getting lost in the swelling popularity of newer Secretly Canadian and Jagjaguwar acts, and that he was no longer the center of the Swansons' attention and affection, he was happy to work with Cargill. "He wouldn't have picked anyone else," Darcie said. In the midst of Antony and the Johnsons' popularity, Molina talked a lot about famous musicians who'd been ripped off or ignored by their labels. He was generally hesitant to sign contracts, but he was not motivated enough to go anywhere else.

By the time Molina's album *The Magnolia Electric Co.* was released, alternative country momentum had been pulsating through the music scenes in the Midwest and in southern states since the '90s, via labels such as Chicago's Bloodshot Records and bands ranging from Jeff Tweedy's Wilco and Ryan Adams's Whiskeytown to solo artists like Neko Case, whom Molina adored. It was by no means dying out, with newer, folk-influenced bands such as Iron & Wine growing and affecting music's collective consciousness. But the idea of electrified country in the new millennium wasn't exactly innovative. Though the label supported Molina's new direction, Secretly Canadian was keenly aware that alternative country was on its way out of vogue, shrinking from an entire continent to a mere statehood on the landscape of independent music.

Some of the band members believed Secretly Canadian released *Magnolia* under the Songs: Ohia band name for marketing purposes and to sell records, but according to Chris Swanson, Molina didn't have a new name for the band. "He probably had the idea for a band named Magnolia Electric Co., and then he decided to name the record that," Swanson said. "And sometimes he'd say that it was the first Magnolia Electric Co. record, but that's an act of convenience. He was being whimsical with the truth there." It wasn't until Molina made the distinction that he wanted to start an actual band, rather than soldier on as a lone wolf with a rotating cast of characters, that the label got on board with the name change. "We were very excited and very proud that he chose a Bloomington band," Swanson added. "We were proud that he chose to live in Bloomington. It legitimized something about our relationship." Now that he was back in his former home and musical community, Molina needed a band.

Pete Schreiner played in iterations of Secretly Canadian–signed bands Panoply Academy and Intro to Airlift. In the early more fledgling days of SC, the label encouraged its artists to commune with each other's music and offered free copies of albums to anyone signed to the label. The first Songs: Ohia record Schreiner heard was *The Lioness*, and he met Jason Molina through playing label showcases. Ultimately, though, he connected with *Didn't It Rain*. "The album gave voice to heavy humid rust belt regret, burnt realization and hinted suspiciously at a foggy hope," Schreiner explained. "The narrator spoke to me emotionally but geographically, too. I grew up near Chicago's rusty steel industry and Jason, Cleveland's."[2]

Jason Groth and Mark Rice were musicians on the local underground scene, playing guitar and drums in the Impossible Shapes, an Elephant 6–inspired band that signed with Secretly Canadian for its fifth record, *We Like It Wild*. The pair also played guitar and drums, respectively, in midwestern white boy R&B outfit John Wilkes Booze—a sort of clone of Washington D.C.'s the Make Up, with a scruffier aesthetic.

Groth remembered meeting Molina for the first time a few years prior at Roadworthy Guitar in Bloomington, where Molina was unusually open about his life. "I was buying a weird heavy metal guitar and he suddenly told me all about his entire guitar collection and which rock stars played them," Groth said. "Then he mentioned that he was about to go record an album with Arab Strap." This openness struck Groth as a contradiction to Molina's music and stage presence, but it also came to underline Molina's unique brand of social ineptitude, where he would sort of get to know someone immediately, without cause, but then later hide things or tell wild stories in order to skirt any depth of conversation. "He wasn't as cryptic. He was a lot more goofy, and wasn't dark or depressing at all," Groth said. "He was just like a talkative kid."

Jason Molina was keenly aware of the public's perception of him, but he often explained that he didn't believe he was making funeral music, but that he found a lot of hope in his songs. He eventually grew to hate it when his music was described as depressing or even mournful. It was clear to Jason Groth, Mark Rice, and Pete Schreiner that Molina had a strong desire to fit in with a band instead of continuing to be tagged as a solo bastion of depressive strumming. He was seeking true brotherhood with like-minded folks from a DIY background and saw himself in the community of friends and bands that Pete, Jason, and Mark entangled themselves in. "I got the sense that he wanted a band of brothers as much as he wanted a band," Rice said.

As with his friends in Oberlin, Molina couldn't have convened with a more genuine, less pretentious group of people—solely focused on the community of making music and art, and not at all the cliques, fashion, or gossip that are often associated with said music and art-making circles. The guys who'd form Molina's new band couldn't know a stranger and also couldn't say no to an opportunity to make music with friends, their over-scheduled lives being perhaps their only point of critique. The new band would become so close that they even adopted unspoken band uniforms, which evolved naturally over time. In their early stages they wore black T-shirts, and in their later stages Western-inspired wear such as suits, cowboy hats, and bolo ties.

Jason Groth, Mark Rice, and Pete Schreiner together also comprised a three-piece punk band they dubbed the Coke Dares. Famous for sets that surpassed the fifty-song mark, the trio played three-second to three-minute fire drills centered on trips to the emergency room, meth-head neighbors, Juicy Fruit gum, and anything and everything that could be laughed and/or soloed about. The band's "Fuck You I Quit," pairs just that four-word phrase with four seconds of explosive drums, guitar, and bass. They were sort of the ultimate rock 'n' roll party band, totally unpretentious with a collective tongue planted firmly in cheek.

Molina was also particularly enamored by Jason Groth and Pete Schreiner's Neil Young cover band, the Cinnamon Girls, after seeing them play *Tonight's the Night* in its entirety on September 4, 2002, at local pub grub–cum–rock venue Bear's Place Ale House & Eatery. Molina liked the set so much that he expressed disappointment when he wasn't able to attend the gig where they played *Zuma* by Neil Young and Crazy Horse.

The man behind Songs: Ohia asked Groth, Schreiner, and Rice to join up with him in his new band during a very nonchalant conversation at a gig by local folk act the Decanters on November 14, 2002. Jason Groth and Pete Schreiner got on board immediately. But Mark Rice, the youngest of the group, had another year of school to finish. He remembered that at the show Molina seemed particularly interested in his studies in printmaking. "He asked something like, 'What does art mean to you?'" Rice explained. "And I remember being totally tongue tied and pretty intimidated." He couldn't join the band until later in 2003, but he and Molina's mutual interests in architecture and visual art helped quickly create a unique dialogue between the two of them.

The Decanters gig also led to a chance co-billing on November 15 at beloved local club Second Story. The Coke Dares were set to play with Molina's friends in Oneida, whose van broke down suddenly. One of the Swanson brothers delivered the news to Schreiner, Groth, and Rice during the Decanters gig as they were talking to Molina. "He was like immediately, 'I'll play!'" Groth remembered. The next night at the show, Molina and the Coke Dares took up a collection for Oneida so that their van's transmission could be fixed. The gesture became memorialized in a photo on the inside of the Coke Dare's first CD.

Always one to attach sentiment to a seemingly meaningless and casual situation, Molina invited Groth and Schreiner to lunch at Bloomington pub the Irish Lion for their first band meeting. There, he gave each of them a pocketknife as a symbol of brotherhood.

The trio of Molina, Schreiner, and Groth practiced only one or two times before playing a couple of shows as a three piece, centered on the *Magnolia* album material and under the Songs: Ohia name. Both Jasons played guitar, and Schreiner sat behind the drums. The trio's first gig together was December 8 at the Southgate House in Newport, Kentucky.

Molina soon recruited friend and Indiana University music school graduate Michael "Mikey" Kapinus to play bass after chatting with him regularly during his shifts at local coffee shop Soma and seeing him play multiple instruments in the Decanters. "Molina always told us that the guys from the Magnolia record couldn't tour, so we didn't think there were any hard feelings," Schreiner said. "Maybe those guys felt differently at the time, but we had no idea."

The guys from the *Magnolia* record did feel a bit differently. In August 2002, shortly after Jason moved back to Bloomington, Songs: Ohia drummer Jeff Panall traveled to see Molina play a solo Songs: Ohia set during the town's annual music celebration, Bloomington Fest. Mark Kozelek also played the festival where he remembered being wholly impressed by Molina, "The little guy with the big voice." "I generally got a bad vibe from him regarding Chicago, which really caught me off guard," Panall explained. Later, after a few drinks at the Molina household, Molina told Panall that he was growing increasingly weary of working with drummers. And he didn't say it in a nice way. Panall took this to be their official breakup, though neither verbalized it as such.

"I was pretty bummed out when we were replaced by the new guys, certainly it was sour grapes for me to see them play," he said. "I always thought that the ten-person lineup on the *Magnolia Electric Co.* record would have killed it if we were put on tour and played the right venues." Knowing how unpredictable Molina was, and despite the fact that they were hurt, the Chicago core of Songs: Ohia say they didn't begrudge the new Bloomington-based lineup. In fact, the two groups would become incredibly close in the years to come, but for reasons that were yet unseen.

As the pick-up guy peering in from the outside, both in the studio and on tour, lap steel player Mike Brenner got the sense that there was always a sort of friction between the former Songs: Ohia members and Bloomington-based Magnolia Electric Co. camps. "It seemed like there was this underlying bit of tension, sort of like a proprietary thing," he explained. "The Chicago guys were with Jason early and did a lot of touring and played on the record that got the most amounts of attention, and yet the Bloomington folks got the lion's share of publicity."

In addition to the *Magnolia Electric Co.* material, the new Bloomington-based band learned by fire a new set of songs that Molina had written. They also learned quickly how much Molina hated to rehearse, and so they often convened without him, or with him for no longer than thirty minutes. They got in about ten shaky practices before they left for a spring 2003 European tour, though admitting that many of the arrangements were worked out on-stage. "Before our first European tour he sent us all a message, the last line of which was 'If you have any fears or miscellanious anxiety, shove it. We know what we're hear for. Ax me any questions,'" Groth said. Though they would eventually convince Molina to write out set lists, in the first year they flew by the seat of their thrift-store pants. Encores were always a point of contention. Molina occasionally fired Jason Groth for suggesting that they honor fans' requests for encores.

A show at Brussels club Ancienne Belgique on April 14, 2003, became immortalized in vinyl grooves as the aptly named live album *Trials & Errors*. It was released in January 2005 under the band name Magnolia Electric Co., though when the set was recorded the quartet toured under the Songs: Ohia namesake. Its songs are quite literally a new band working out songs onstage and a clear testament to Molina's increasing demand for first takes and the commensurate authenticity he associated with that moment when a new and unrehearsed band tips from chaos to harmony.

The Belgian venue had a built-in recording system, which the band happily took advantage of, trading the sparsity and negative space of Songs: Ohia for filled-to-the-brim electrified country. The inclusion of three fragments of Neil Young songs, including the refrain from "Tonight's the Night," cemented a Crazy Horse comparison in the press that would follow the band for the rest of its tenure, though it clearly wasn't unwanted to the same degree of the Will Oldham likening during Molina's Songs: Ohia term. Molina chose to cover Neil Young and release it on a record, after all. In the album insert, Molina wrote:

Electricians Tonight
Jason Groth: Guitar
Pete Schreiner: Drums
Mike Kapinus: Bass, Trumpet
Jason Molina: Guitar, Singing
Jochem Schouten: Sound, Driving
Songs written by J. M. and there are ones that clearly have not, they're included here respectfully. Thank you. Back in the van and Johnny strike up the band.

That last bit was a nod to Warren Zevon, another artist Molina held a torch for. They'd eventually do a straightforward cover of Zevon's biggest hit, "Werewolves of London," which was included in the band's live show and on the Magnolia Electric Co. EP *Hard to Love a Man*.

The *Trials & Errors* set included songs that would appear on Magnolia Electric Co.'s studio debut, *What Comes after the Blues*, as well as the label's ambitious compiling of multiple studio sessions in the box set dubbed *Sojourner*. "Almost Was Good Enough" from the *Magnolia* album session was also played, but in line with Molina's tendencies to eschew the material from his most recently released album, he was reticent to include anything else from it. Molina never acquiesced to playing the song "Lioness," even though so many people wanted to hear it. Once when the band requested to rehearse it, Molina broke down crying, explaining that he'd lived the song, and it was too hard for him to play.

Perhaps the most telling composition from the new batch of songs captured during the live recording is "North Star," which plays out as a roots-rock-style jammer, something that became Magnolia's signature sound. Jason Groth's guitar soloing lived front and center, lacing the songs with a southern drawl. However, a solo radio session Molina did for the "Duyster" show in Brussels in April 2003 turned the tune on its head. His voice-and-guitar rendition cut through the live act fat, straight to the lyrical heart. It's a foretelling that is as beautiful as it is unnerving. On the show, after performing a solo acoustic version of his song "Leave the City," in which he lamented moving away from Chicago, Molina sang "North Star":

> You used to say I had what it takes
> I think I did if you meant too little too late
> By the looks that I'm getting, I made some big mistakes
> But I thought you said I was great
>
> I shoot straight and give it my best try
> I made my heart as hard as nails
> That might be the way you live your life
> But it's almost got me killed
>
> Darling, I'm not giving in
> That happened miles ago
> I heard the North Star saying,
> Kid you're so lost even I can't bring you home
>
> Now did you think that we was gonna last
> Well honey, you know you don't have to answer that
> Half of that was my kind of joke
> But I don't remember which half
>
> I didn't know how blue I'd get
> I didn't know how I'd get blamed for it
> I didn't choose to go down this road
> No one chooses to be sick
>
> I'm saying everything is fine
> By the look in my eye
> But you know darling
> Half of what a man says is a lie
>
> It's your last chance to forget me now
> And then it's done for good
> You always said I'd make it out
> Somehow darling I knew I never would

In Chicago his interest in introspective meditations and sweeping themes from the heartland diverted into two strains of records, leading to the recording on *Magnolia Electric Co.* At the onset of Magnolia the band, they increasingly merged, though delivered through a roots-rock filter. The Belgian radio session, anecdotally christened the "North Star Blues" session, reveals Molina's lyrical thought in an unadulterated form, and it's easy to see that at this time his psyche, which had struggled with depression his entire existence, was increasingly tipping the scale in melancholy's favor. That in this song he basically predicts the next ten years of his life is uncanny.

In May 2003 Jason and Darcie tied the knot in Brown County State Park, Indiana's largest park, named for General Jacob Brown who fought in the War of 1812—an ideal synthesis of nature and history for Molina, who'd proposed in Chicago over a near nightly ritual for the couple, in which they'd prepare, pour, and commiserate over a cup of hot tea at home. At this point they'd been together nearly six years and loved each other deeply. They did everything together and to Molina's friends seemed like the perfect illustration of the thing between people who say they're "marrying their best friend." Even though life with Molina would grow increasingly difficult after the couple left Chicago, and Darcie knew of Molina's struggles with depression, she had no way to be prepared for what would come.

At the wedding reception, Molina told Magnolia Electric Co. guitarist Jason Groth that he wanted to record a series of 7" records using the Electric Co. moniker, much in the same way he used a different adjective behind Songs: in the past. In interviews he explained that he intended to release material under his own name, too. So far he had the albums *Magnolia Electric Co.* and *Pyramid Electric Co.* under his belt, and he wanted to explore other concepts he sought to electrify. It made sense, then, that on *Trials & Errors* his band became the "Electricians"—those conductors invigorating Jason's midwestern contemplations with unpretentious electrified rock 'n' roll.

By summer Darcie had grown weary of her commute back and forth from Indianapolis. She had accepted a position from the company she worked for in Chicago, which she felt she couldn't refuse for financial reasons. To help alleviate his new wife's road fatigue, Molina agreed to move to Indianapolis, where the couple bought their first house. At first they were energized by the idea of owning a home together and making it theirs. But soon after they relocated Molina became depressed and only focused on

Figure 9.1. Darcie and Jason tie the knot in Brown County State Park.
Photo courtesy of Darcie Molina

the isolation he felt living in a suburban setting without a car and without any local friends or collaborators. Though Bloomington was just a forty-five-minute jaunt down IN-37, Molina felt as if he was alone on an island devoid of culture and camaraderie. In its stead he began to find kinship with the bottle, stowing away in his music room to drink or disappearing into the nearby wooded lot.

Darcie had never seen Jason drunk before, and hindsight revealed the problem. What was actually going on at the time didn't click, especially because he hid the act extremely well and drank in strange and sporadic patterns. In Chicago the couple purchased the occasional four pack of Hoegaarden, what they considered a "fancy" beer, and it would sit in the refrigerator for weeks. But in Indianapolis Darcie first began to encounter what she thought was Jason being weird or a complete jerk. He'd crawl around on the floor or be mean or defensive without cause. She knew he was unhappy in Indianapolis and thought the behavior corresponded with the bouts of depression he'd dealt with for most of his life. She thought it would pass.

Molina's brother Aaron visited shortly after the couple moved to Indy and was alarmed by the new behavior he witnessed. Not only had Aaron never really seen Jason drink; he'd never seen him drink to the extent that he was, like when he downed a six pack at lunch or drank two large bottles of Chimay in succession, a high-alcohol Belgian Trappist beer.

Around this time, too, Molina's friend Henry Owings began to receive phone calls from Molina that seemed wildly out of character from the person he knew. Since the late '90s, Owings, founder of the snark-first music zine *Chunklet*, had helped Molina book shows in the Georgia area where he lived—both in Athens and in Atlanta—when the Songs: Ohia strummer called him from the road about two or three weeks out looking for an extra gig. Over the years, Owings had offered his home to Molina as a crash pad, and the two maintained a long-distance friendship during which they talked on the phone about music and art.

Owings recalled that mid-2003 introduced a pattern of strange phone calls. "It was like words that didn't even go together, just this freestyle nonsense," he explained. "It was this really suspicious behavior from someone I'd known for so long." Still, Owings invited Molina and the Magnolia Electric Co. band to play at the 40 Watt Club in Athens, along with Scout Niblett and Swearing at Motorists, for his August 14 wedding celebration. "He asked for me to come up and sing with him," Owings remembered. "It was like, wow, I get to sing a song with one of my favorite bands ever."

To counteract his loneliness, Molina spent most of September on tour with Mike Brenner and Pete Schreiner as a three piece, a time which Brenner recalls fondly, saying the stripped-down format really allowed Molina's voice and lyrics to take center stage. He recalled a somewhat unnerving encounter with Molina when they returned from the tour, though. He stayed at Molina's home in Indianapolis in between touring stints in the United States and Europe. Mourning Warren Zevon's untimely passing on September 7, 2003, Molina made a regular habit of getting up early to drink whiskey, rendering him intoxicated for much of the day.

By the time the band was ready to hit the skies for a fifteen-date jaunt in October through Spain, Molina instituted a last-minute shuffling of personnel, adding Mark Rice, who'd just wrapped up his undergraduate studies. He called the new band the Magnolia Electric Co., a decision he never verbally communicated but instead something they read about on *Pitchfork*. "It was just days before we were getting ready to leave and all of a sudden Mark Rice is on drums, Jason Groth is on guitar, Mikey moved to keyboards and Pete moves to bass and I'm like, 'Really?'" Brenner explained. "We had one day to rehearse with two people I'd never met, and the two people I had been playing with switching instruments." The fact that Molina had a renowned distaste for rehearsal only compounded Brenner's anxiety. "We ran through one tune and it sounded like shit, but he wanted to move on," Brenner said. "And his withering look at me when I wanted to try it again said it all. We didn't really get it together until about a week into the Spain shows, but that was just kind of how Molina was."

After that initial hurdle the quintet synthesized into the solid band that would release four LPs, one box set, two EPs, and a single in its six years together. Jason Groth recalled the conversation he'd had with Molina about the 7" series, in which he wanted to title each single an adjective followed by "Electric Co." But no one ever knew how or why the band name was chosen.

In November they cut across the East Coast and headed west to Chicago, where they played Northside club Schuba's and then holed up at Electrical Audio. It was their first studio session as a band. The new group felt a lot of pressure in the wake of the success of the album *Magnolia Electric Co.*, which more than any other record of Molina's had captivated audiences and sold copies. On the way in, they swung through the western 'burbs so Jason could buy a custom-made Victoria amplifier, which he hooked up to a 1949 Oahu Hawaiian steel amplifier for the session.

There, they cut the album that became *What Comes after the Blues*, with Songs: Ohia alumnus Jennie Benford, Dan MacAdam, and Jim "Three Nickel" Grabowski stepping in for backup vocals and auxiliary instrumentation. Mikey Kapinus and Benford acted as the musical directors at Molina's behest, pointing various personnel to their posts when it was time to record their parts. Groth, Schreiner, and Brenner huddled in an isolation booth, while Rice helmed the kit in the dead room. Molina and Benford stood singing together in the large room of Studio A. Everyone felt a palpable urgency in Molina and stridently worked to not mess up the live band takes, armed with the knowledge that Molina would scrap it if anyone messed up. Editing and overdubs were not allowed.

As a result, the session was swift, and all of the full band songs were tracked in about two days, with the Benford-led "The Night Shift Lullaby" being the only memorable sticking point due to Molina's unpredictable guitar soloing and Benford missing her vocal cues. The group had a considerable amount of downtime, and the newcomers felt completely surreal just hanging out at Electrical Audio.

It was their first time staying overnight in the studio's lounges, which they could rent for somewhere in the ballpark of $100 a night—much cheaper than a couple of Chicago hotel rooms. As was his way, Molina woke up early to walk and clear his mind and write. On the last day of the three-day session he returned to the studio after an airing with the words to "Hammer Down." He recorded it impromptu solo with Steve Albini and played it later for the band. They were blown away by its neogospel throwback intoning. "I really like that he did that on just two tracks," Rice added. "I thought that was incredible." The song acts as a sort of companion piece to Molina's solo acoustic version of "North Star," its melancholia lamenting:

> Hammer down, heaven bound
> Hammer down, heaven bound
> I saw the light
> On the old gray town
> Sometimes I forget that I've always been sick
> And I don't have the will to keep fighting
> Hammer down, heaven bound
> Hammer down, heaven bound
> Hammer down, heaven bound
> Hammer down, heaven bound
> When it's been my ghost and the empty road
> I think the stars are just the neon lights
> Shining through the dance floor

> Shining through the dance floor
> Of heaven on a Saturday night
> And I saw the light
> I saw the light
> Hammer down, heaven bound
> Hammer down, heaven bound

On the album there's also an early lament to Darcie about his behavior in their relationship, using a device he employed through his writing career—writing from another's perspective of him, often a woman. "It was hard to love a man like you / Goodbye was half the words you knew," he sings of himself from Darcie's perspective. "While you was waiting for me not to call / I sent my love, I sent my love," he responds to Darcie from his own perspective, Benford coming in for "I sent my love." It's in reference to the many times Darcie pleaded with Molina to call or send her more than just a four-word e-mail from the road.

The record has a strong alt-country undercurrent, acting as a sort of continuation of the sound Molina was building on *Magnolia Electric Co.*, but with a deeper dive into southern rock–inspired guitar solos, fiddle parts, and slide guitar. New to the mix: trumpet, courtesy of multi-instrumentalist Mikey Kapinus, the driving force of track 3, "Leave the City."

In line with Molina's newfound commitment to a solid band, he began cutting Groth, Schreiner, Rice, and Kapinus in on the sales of the records. Molina received 60 percent of the royalties, while his four bandmates took in 10 percent each, and it was this way through their last album together, *Josephine.* It was a monetary example of Molina's generosity with the band, as oftentimes he'd come home from a tour with less than he had during his days as a solo or two-man act under the Songs: Ohia banner. And much like his college days, when Molina had money, he spent it almost immediately, often on things like antique lanterns or four star hotel rooms. He once dropped fifty British pounds into the hand of a London street musician.

In the session the band also recorded a number of songs they'd been playing on tour, which didn't make the final eight songs included on *What Comes after the Blues*. Versions of "Don't This Look Like the Dark," "Whip-Poor-Will," and "North Star" remain in the vaults as does that session's "Nashville Moon," particularly memorable as Molina berated the band for being a bunch of idiots after they collectively could not decipher his cryptic instructions for the take.

The band did about fifty U.S. tour dates in 2004, playing much of the material from *What Comes after the Blues*, which wasn't released until

April 2005. By the time the album had come out, the band had decamped to Paul Mahern's Echo Park recording studio in Bloomington to lay down their EP *Hard to Love a Man*, which was released in December of the same year. The seemingly inauspicious recording session with their hometown acquaintance ended up being more memorable than the blur of their first run with Albini.

It's because of what happened on day three. Schreiner, Groth, Rice, Kapinus, and Molina showed up in the morning rehearsed and ready to go and recorded the songs "Bowery," "Doing Something Wrong," and "31 Seasons in the Minor Leagues." The recorded versions of "Lonesome Valley" and "Montgomery" didn't make the final cut for the EP. At midday the band stepped outside for a short lunch break. When they returned, Molina was a completely different person.

"It was the first time that we experienced Jason getting fucked up on something and then lying to us about it," Groth said. "It was really, really weird," Rice added. "It was the first time that Jason couldn't sing, and that was sort of the point of the band." Molina told Schreiner that it was anti-anxiety medication that caused the odd behavior. Schreiner called Darcie to ask about it, and she said Molina wasn't on any medication that she knew of. The band shrugged it off as a onetime thing as there wasn't any evidence of alcohol or prescription pill bottles in the bathroom or the trash cans. Mike Brenner was headed into town from Philadelphia, and then the band was leaving for about three and a half months of touring across the United States, Canada, and Europe. They hoped it was an isolated incident—the product of nerves or poor sleep.

"We couldn't understand how he was getting obliterated so quickly," Groth reflected. Molina always drank in secret and very quickly—he'd go from sober to completely wasted in twenty minutes or less. There had been a couple of incidents prior to the recording session in Bloomington, one at a show in October 2004 in Montreal at La Sala Rossa during the Pop Montreal Festival. There, Brenner saw Molina chug almost an entire bottle of whiskey before the show, rendering him totally incapable of standing, not to mention playing his guitar or singing. During the set Molina crawled around on the floor stacking monitors and talking about how sad he was as the band played through the set more embarrassed than they collectively had ever been in their lives, fluctuating between Groth's guitar solos and Brenner's lap steel solos. Groth also remembered Molina chugging half a bottle of Eagle Rare bourbon at his house when he and Darcie stopped by on Thanksgiving of 2004. "We didn't know that he was doing this so frequently, though, and that it was a problem," Groth added. "He hid it really well."

During the 2005 summer tour, Molina nose-dove semiregularly. The band had been told by Secretly Canadian that Molina had a penchant for self-sabotage, particularly when faced with increased pressure to do interviews, or when the volume of press surrounding his records increased. They assumed he might have been trying to sink the tour because of the sustained attention from the *Magnolia* album and increasing demands from audiences to play songs from that album. Molina was also doing more interviews and radio appearances. After a rough encounter with Canadian Border Patrol on May 5, Molina got drunk and ruined that night's show in Victoria. By the time they met up with a crew for the filming of their documentary *The Road Becomes What You Leave*, Molina was drunk regularly. In Saskatoon, Mike Brenner saw Molina crouched behind a car in a parking lot chugging mini-bottles of airplane booze.

By the time they reached Europe in the summer of 2005, Molina had displayed a semiregular pattern of absconding with some form of hard liquor and returning barely able to walk, let alone tune or play his guitar. At a show in Serbia on June 20, a fan gave the band a bottle of traditional slivovitz, a kind of plum brandy. Two days later at their show in Vienna, Molina downed the entire bottle before they took the stage, rendering him incapable of remembering any of the songs. The only thing more mortifying than Molina's demeanor was hearing their tour manager maniacally laughing at the display as they eked out a shaky rendition of "Bowery."

These patterns caused a palpable strain on the group, but particularly on Brenner. He didn't as strongly hold on to or identify with the brotherhood or community connection to Molina that the rest of the band did. Being a session guy from Philly who wasn't involved or attuned to the socialization, mutual friends, and history of friendship that the Bloomington crew had with one another, he grew increasingly impatient with Molina's drunken displays, and he urged the band to work together to stop it. To finish out the tour, they employed three methods for managing their leader:

1. Hide the bottle
2. Throw away the bottle
3. Drink the bottle (when Molina wasn't present)

It worked about 75 percent of the time. Brenner recalled a particularly triumphant moment in London, where Molina hadn't played with a full band in years. The Magnolia Electric Co. show at Bush Hall in the Shepherd's Bush neighborhood—a room that held five hundred people—had been sold out for months. The group was collectively amped to put on a great performance and could almost smell the anticipation by concertgoers queuing outside the venue. "We did a sound check, and it was glorious," Brenner recalled. When they were hanging out backstage waiting for the show to start, a crew member walked into their dressing room with a fifth of Jack Daniels, explaining that Molina had requested it. "So we hid the bottle," Brenner said, which visibly annoyed Molina when he came backstage to retrieve it. "He didn't say what he was looking for, but we all knew what he was looking for," he added. Instead of asking his band and thus admitting his intent to imbibe, Molina sent the crew member back to inquire about the liquor's whereabouts. The band pulled him aside to explain that they didn't want Molina's mitts on the thing or the performance would be ruined. "The show was triumphant," Brenner said. "We did three encores. Scout Niblett was onstage with us. We just crushed it."

"In my mind I felt like every show should be like that," Brenner lamented. But unfortunately Molina had other plans. Brenner, perhaps the least tolerant of the destructive behavior, especially given his background playing with the turbulent Philly rock 'n' roll outfit Marah, couldn't roll with the punches as easily as the rest of the band, which was less experienced and aware of the pernicious patterns of alcoholism. "In a similar way to Magnolia, I was on the first Marah record and probably played on more of their records than anyone else," Brenner said. "But again, I was sort of on the outside. [Marah] didn't blow shows, but the alcohol abuse was really difficult and destructive." He grew increasingly weary of the babysitting aspect of his touring gig and felt defeated when the music suffered at the hands of Molina's wavering sobriety. "It just seemed like the ground was giving way," he added.

Brenner's perfectionism stood in contrast to the more DIY and community-driven aspect of the rest of the band, some of whom don't remember the tour being as awful as all that. "Mike is a professional musician, and he approaches things in a very studio, perfection sort of way," Rice explained. "And that's awesome, and Jason really liked him because of that. But they also had lots of problems getting along because of that." Though Jason was drunk during a number of the gigs, Rice remembered it not being very noticeable and not very frequent. "I remember having a lot of fun," he added.

When they got back from Europe, the band played the first incarnation of *Pitchfork*'s annual summer festival, called Intonation, on July 16, 2005. By the mid-aughts, independent music festivals, and corporately produced fetes filled with indie acts, were popping up throughout the country—from Austin's Austin City Limits Festival, the Bonaroo Music and Arts Festival in Tennessee, and the Sasquatch! Music Festival in Washington State, to the smaller potatoes of the electronically focused Moogfest or the Central

Figure 9.2. Molina plays a piano backstage at Bush Hall, London. *Photo courtesy Mikey Kapinus*

Illinois–based Pygmalion Music Festival. For fans of indie rock, there was no shortage of options for catching long lineups of emerging acts, forcing behemoths like Lollapalooza to reconsider their own bookings.

Jason and Darcie had moved back to Chicago from Indianapolis in the summer of 2005 after Molina's nonstop mourning for the Second City and his general malaise and sporadic inebriation in Indianapolis. Molina's patterns of depression and self-medication had begun to strain their relationship, and Darcie agreed with Molina that a return to Chicago, where he could be close to his friends, might be good for him. She took the position that his band would soon adopt, that of support beam and role model, believing that Molina might benefit from a steadying presence who didn't drink to excess. Around this time Molina began actively formulating cycles of misinformation to Darcie and the band in an attempt to pit the two parties against one another. He told Darcie that his bandmates were cokeheads and scoundrels who cheated on their wives and girlfriends, and the band that Darcie was a nagging shrew whom he couldn't please.

In the days between returning from Europe and playing the festival, Magnolia Electric Co.—anecdotally nicknamed MECo by fans and the label—stopped at Electrical Audio to record another album of country-rock songs Molina had written, which he called *Nashville Moon*. Despite his semi-regular drunken episodes, Molina still wrote and recorded demos at a breakneck pace. He had so much material under his belt that he and Secretly Canadian came up with the concept of packaging a series of Magnolia albums, which Molina would record in different studios across the country with varied personnel. They called it *Sojourner*.

"With the tear Jason was on, he'd have another eight records done in the two years it would have taken to release each of those [albums] properly, not to mention those records cannibalizing themselves both from an artistic and marketing perspective," Ben Swanson explained. "It's just a lot for any fan to absorb." When the idea for the set synthesized, Molina was excited and actively contributed to the design of its components—a custom wooden box, not terribly dissimilar from the cigar boxes he collected; a medallion in the spirit of the many historical medals and coins he actively collected; and custom art for each CD. He even wanted to put chicken bones in each box, a nod to the hundreds of pounds of fried chicken he consumed during his numerous road dog sojourns, his favorite being Gus's World Famous Fried Chicken in Memphis. By this time MP3 downloading was taking over the CD's former dominance in the realm of music consumption, and the resurgence of the vinyl record was in full swing. Because of this, a CD box set seemed a bit of an odd choice. But Molina was never tuned in to trends or modern demands anyway.

The band had no idea that *Nashville Moon*, the first full-length they'd record together as a band with any confidence, would be packaged as a CD box set, which was produced to just five thousand copies. "I think the label thought that Jason was communicating all of this to us," Groth explained.

Regardless of their varied disappointment over the release, they were all extremely pleased with the session where they rerecorded songs left off from the *What Comes after the Blues* and the *Hard to Love a Man* sessions, as well as a few others they'd been playing on tour. "We were a much better band by that point," Schreiner explained. Molina remained sober around Steve Albini, for whom he had a significant amount of deference, which helped the productivity of the session. And given their months of rehearsing on the road, they played like a band that had been playing together for years. "We sounded like we knew what we were doing," Schreiner added.

After finishing the *Nashville Moon* session and a few U.S. tour dates, lap steel player Mike Brenner took a hiatus from Magnolia Electric Co. "I'd had it, and [Molina] had probably had it with me," he said. "I certainly voiced my opinions, which started out as concern and probably ended up with me being miserable and extremely frustrated, which is too bad. I have really good memories from my early experience touring with Jason and those guys." Similar to his time in Marah, Brenner mourned the loss of the amazing songs Molina had written—the thing that drew him in during *Didn't It Rain* and kept him going through *Nashville Moon*—as much as or maybe more so than he mourned the loss of his time with the band. "He was a lot less naive about everything than we were," Groth added. They would invite him to their last session together, but in Brenner's mind he had cashed in his Molina chips.

In April 2006 at a show in Memphis, Molina was given a three-hour session at the city's iconic Sun Studio, the historic recording home base of Elvis Presley, blues icon Howlin' Wolf, Johnny Cash, and Jerry Lee Lewis, which now spends its days flooded with droves of cotton-topped retirees pouring from chartered tour buses. Sherman Willmott, owner of Memphis-centric record shop Shangri-La, was a Molina superfan and offered to put Magnolia in the studio ahead of its show at the Hi-Tone. The band happily obliged and took to the tiny room with Sun house engineer James Lott. They ran through a new version of "Hold on Magnolia" and learned "East St. Louis Blues" and "Memphis Moon" in the studio. The latter song was yet another personification of Molina and his wife as stars, with a nod to his proposal in the first line: "Tea for two stars falling from the Memphis sky." The four songs recorded in the session became the third record in the *Sojourner* box set, an EP which Molina simply titled "Sun Session."

After finishing some dates in Texas, Florida, and Georgia with the band, Molina took off solo for Richmond, Virginia, to meet up with musician and producer David Lowery of the bands Camper Van Beethoven and Cracker, whom he'd met through the touring network in Athens, Georgia. Lowery's

Figure 9.3. Magnolia Electric Co., in its black t-shirt phase, during the session at Sun Studio in Memphis. From left to right: Jason Molina, Jason Groth, Pete Schreiner, Mark Rice, and Mikey Kapinus. *Photo courtesy of Pete Schreiner*

wife booked the 40 Watt Club in Athens, and the pair had become friendly through the relationship, a bond that was solidified when Lowery and Camper Van Beethoven borrowed some gear from Molina after theirs was pinched on the road.

Knowing that Molina was headed to Virginia to make a record without them, the guys in Magnolia wondered if their time with him was up. Given the inconsistencies of the performances and Molina's wavering sobriety, they needed a break from the road. They headed home sans Molina wondering if they'd ever play with him again.

Molina was a fan of the songs iconic indie singer-songwriter Eric Bachmann had done with Crooked Fingers and Archers of Loaf at Lowery's studio, and he arranged to have many of the same personnel work on his session, including Alan Weatherhead, who acted as guitarist, engineer, and auxiliary instrumentalist, and drummer Miguel Urbiztondo. David Lowery played the role of producer and decided to helm bass duties live in the room with Molina to set a vibe for the songs, which were largely sketches rather than finished products. Molina told Lowery the songs were inspired by ghosts. "There were a lot of quirks and anomalies in what he was doing, so I wanted to be on bass out in the room so I could understand that a bit better," Lowery said. "We were trying to create a big open space around his voice, which required us playing a little bit less." Joining for backing vocals and a few classical guitar parts were Sound of Music studio personnel Molly Blackbird and Rick Alverson. Chicago-based folk hero Andrew Bird's famous whistling was overdubbed on a few tracks by special request from Molina.

Soon after they began the session, Molina's mother Karen suffered a brain aneurysm. He put the get-together on hold, and he and Darcie returned to Lorain, Ohio, for the first time in a dog's age. In the process he canceled an appearance he was to make during a group show of his artwork at Fireproof Gallery in Brooklyn on November 18. The installation, which he titled *Ghost Songs*, lived in the gallery alongside the work of David Berman of the Silver Jews, John Darnielle of the Mountain Goats, Archer Prewitt of the Sea and Cake, and Pall Jenkins of the Black Heart Procession. His work was comprised of twelve wooden cigar boxes filled with found objects like bones, fossils, coins, torn paper, drawings, collages, and handscrawled lyrics, which provided a teaser for the spirit of the *Sojourner* box set to come. Visitors were allowed to sift through the boxes and examine their contents, a tactile way to connect to Molina, where he had been and where he was going.

Complications from surgery related to the aneurysm took Karen Molina's life on February 15, and Jason and Darcie made what would be their final trip to Lorain, Ohio, for the funeral. Karen died in an assisted-living facility on the same grounds as the trailer park where Jason was raised, overlooking Lake Erie. Despite their strained relationship, Jason carried his mother's ashes with him for the rest of his own life.

After the funeral, Molina returned to Richmond to pick up where he and the Sound of Music crew left off. The work was spontaneous. The studio cast composed their parts live in the studio, in a sort of spectral aura that was very hushed and private. There were no added friends or fans hanging out in the studio or control room, which was empty save for their small cast of characters. Close friends of Lowery's had recently been murdered in a brutal home invasion in Richmond, leaving him in a sustained fog of PTSD. Between Karen's passing and the loss of Lowery's friends, the pair felt that they were certainly among ghosts.

In this session, Molina wrote the lyrics after finishing the music. He overdubbed his vocals later, which was an unusual practice for him. "We'd get the skeleton of the song together, and then generally he'd get the words and vocal melodies together overnight," Lowery said. They worked with as few tracks as possible for a minimalist effect, adding just enough to make the song cross into the threshold of sounding finished. Molina didn't drink when the other players were in the studio, largely out of respect for Lowery's sobriety. But they knew that he was drinking, and heavily, at night.

When he was done in Richmond, Molina reached out to the Bloomington band asking if they wanted to go on tour with Canadian prog balladeer Destroyer in the spring of 2006. When they linked up in March, Molina was undeniably excited to share the *Black Ram* session with the band, which had just come back from mixing. He played the recording for Groth, Kapinus, Rice, and Schreiner in the van a number of times on that tour. And uncharacteristically for Molina, he saved the material from the record for the live show until it arrived on shelves with the *Sojourner* box set in 2007.

During the spring tour with Destroyer, the band made a stop at Emo's in Austin, Texas, for a performance at South by Southwest during Secretly Canadian's label showcase. There Molina had the good fortune of meeting one of his idols—Oberlin alumnus Chris Brokaw, who'd led one of Jason's favorite bands, indie-rock slowcore pioneer Codeine. Brokaw was walking down Austin's 6th Street with a friend who spotted Molina and suggested the pair say hello. Molina nearly had a heart attack after Brokaw introduced himself. His behavior nearly gave Brokaw a coronary in return. "He punched me in the chest, right in the heart," Brokaw said. "I was so taken aback and so uncertain whether or not I was going to be able to breathe. It was a huge shock to the system." Molina, notoriously awkward when he was nervous or the center of attention, played off the ill-advised how do you do as a prototypical midwestern hello. "I'd lived in Oberlin for four years and had never experienced anything like that," Brokaw said. "I was tempted to punch him in the face and say, 'That's a Boston way of saying hello.'" After catching his breath, Brokaw said a quick good-bye and walked away with his friend, who explained that Molina could be all thumbs socially. "I thought, 'That guy's going to fucking kill someone one day,'" he laughed.

After having about four months off from Molina, the Magnolia Electric Co. collective felt revived and reinvented on the spring 2006 tour and had a new plan for combating Molina's dangerous dance with alcohol. They'd continue to hide bottles but also to lead by example, often instituting sober tours or physically voicing their support for him, explaining that they were a band of brothers who'd help him in any way possible. And sometimes it worked. "We thought we could get it under control," Rice explained. "It wasn't bad for years and years and years, at least not for me."

In the fall, Secretly Canadian released a single LP compilation of Magnolia Electric Co.'s recent recordings, titled *Fading Trails*. It came as a shock to the band, who'd expected a box set. Jason Groth learned of it shortly before its release date during a racquetball game with Jonathan Cargill from the label, who'd again assumed that Molina had been filling the band in on what he was up to. "We never wanted to be creatively stifling to Jason," Ben Swanson explained. "But I think it's a lot to ask of any fan to buy multiple records of yours in a year."

"I just didn't understand why they would put out such a stupid record like *Fading Trails* when we had all of these other records ready to go," Groth said. The cover art featured a topless woman in underwear, under a graphic treatment of blue and white. It was particularly uncharacteristic of Molina and the band, who tended to prefer illustrated images of birds and moons and old-timey fonts. As head scratching as the cover art seemed, it was actually Molina who provided the image of the woman to Henry Owings. He requested that his friend complete the cover using the image, and after providing it he left the rest up to Owings without providing any input or feedback, which was not uncharacteristic. After designing what felt like hundreds of album covers for Molina, Ben Swanson—and his limited design abilities—felt lucky to be off the hook for this one and didn't protest when the finished product came back, even if it didn't feel quite right.

Despite the band's dissatisfactions with the *Fading Trails* compilation, it was widely heralded in the press as a return to form for Molina. The nine tracks chosen represented the essence of each recording session where they were captured and harkened back to the days when Molina's songs were less concerned with being overstuffed and electrified, focusing instead on the space between the chords and words. It felt drifting and cinematic, not dense and dirty, and sated both fans longing for Songs: Ohia and also those increasingly captivated by Molina's new, post-Newport '65 Dylan leanings.

It was a seamless synthesis of the old Molina and the new, with moons, stars, ghosts, and horizons filling in the gaps. In the songs, he increasingly lamented the hardships of depression and how it affected his relationships, penning lyrical heartbreak and regret and a general malaise at nearly every turn. In "A Little at a Time," he sings, "Maybe if I send back the blues / Her broken heart / He'll send back mine / A little at a time." In "Don't Fade on Me" he sings about himself but from Darcie's perspective: "Don't fade on me / You come out of the blues all them times by yourself / Nothing lives for nothing / And that goes for pain and goes for everything else / But you faded on me / You faded on me." The most haunting track on *Fading Trails* is "The Old Horizon," which counts as Molina's closest nod to plaintive *Boatman's*

Call–era Nick Cave, waxing introspective over sparse piano, Alan Weather-head's ambient flourishes a swap for Warren Ellis's violin melancholia. In the song, he mediates,

> Moon above the raging sea
> Lightning to firefly
> I built my life out of what was left of me
> And a map of an old horizon
> Arrow find my chesnut heart
> Shadow for conjuring
> Big black eyes to hide my secrets in
> And the map of the old horizon
> With this flag I surrender the crescent moon
> With this death's head I hold the tear
> And two black eyes to hide my secrets in
> And the map of the old horizon

Molina leaned on repetitive imagery, too, using the devices in quite literal contexts to describe his current mood on marriage, music making, and touring. It was a very Dylanesque melding of fantasy and reality. The song "The Old Horizon" set the stage for an entire album of introspection that Molina would release under his own name in August 2006, titled *Let Me Go, Let Me Go, Let Me Go*.

The nine-song album aligned with 2004's *Pyramid Electric Co.* and the more plaintive meditations of Songs: Ohia, the space between the words as important as the words themselves. Though he was increasingly interested in the electrified version of himself, *Let Me Go* reveals that the solemn poet inside him still demanded, and commanded, an audience.

He recorded the album in "The Garage," his friend Jim Zespy's Project Studio in Bloomington, over the course of three mornings before he moved back to Chicago in 2005. He wrote and recorded more than two dozen songs in the room illuminated only by a lantern rigged inside an old kick drum, a few candles, and the occasional silent film projection. "The place screamed doom as far as atmosphere goes," Molina explained in the press release for the record. "I put myself to the task of writing about what is human about that particular feeling; the concrete and tactile nature of depression and actually writing or working yourself out of that." If there were any question that in Indianapolis he was struggling and was on an internally downward trajectory, his very straightforward explanation of the depression muse of this record left no room for interpretation, making it clearer than any crystal he might have held in his arsenal of protection spells and cigar-box collages.

When the album was released in August 2006, Molina was on a touring tear with the classic Magnolia lineup, sans lap steel player Mike Brenner. The shows ranged from spirited and magical to embarrassing and ordinary, depending on the amount of liquor Molina poured down his throat. But the band remained optimistic in their approach—to not allow Molina to recoil too far into himself, to be supportive yet firm, and to hide booze in an attempt to divert his attention from wanting it. They had only limited glimpses into his struggles, confined to their time awake and together on tour, which allowed Molina to shelter them from the full breadth and depth of the problem. He didn't share his feelings of isolation or loneliness and was not the type of person to say he was sad. He was also not the type of person to call his friends on the phone from home when they weren't on tour. "He'd say, 'They're my brothers, we don't have to talk on the phone,'" Darcie explained.

Ever bearing a hard head, Molina became resistant to the demands commensurate with such an intense touring schedule. He often said that he didn't want to be a hugely popular artist and deal with the personnel that came with that—like a manager. He wanted full control over the music and the way it was put into the world. He refused to participate in social media for his band and was reluctant with interviewers who still focused on the *Magnolia Electric Co.* album. One of his only concessions was that he agreed to work with European and U.S. booking agents, who helped to wrangle the many months of road excursions he embarked upon each year, as well as the occasional European tour manager. In July 2006 he began working with Bas Flesseman for MECo and solo tours through Europe. Flesseman was a big Molina fan and answered "How high?" to any request from Molina to jump.

"He was sloppy and forgetful and inconsistent and messy," Flesseman remembered. "But he also had a very strong will and good sense of direction in that he wasn't to be distracted. He had a perfect sense to surround himself with people that both loved him and took care of him and were very organized." Though Molina was more chatty than any human being Flesseman had ever encountered, and he rarely got a word in edgewise, he loved Molina dearly.

On European tours the band always requested packs of fresh black socks each night on their rider—the list of supplies bands provide to venues, which usually consist of snacks and drinks. At a 2007 show in Germany, the promoter took the black socks request to mean hashish, and when the band arrived that's what they found. They explained they actually wanted black socks because theirs got filthy on the road and they rarely had time to do laundry. So the promoter got those, too, and the quintet thoroughly enjoyed the real and the metaphorical black socks.

At this point, the band felt that their stage show and bond was getting too tight to let it fall apart. Molina's songwriting still flowed from inside him, though in the months bridging 2006 and 2007 his pace slowed. "We'd be on these long tours and Jason would say that he was going to write, and then he wouldn't," Rice explained. "We all noticed, but we didn't know about some of the other things there going on with him."

They'd established a great routine in the van, too. Mark Rice and Molina generally holed up in the back, while Pete Schreiner, Jason Groth, and Mikey Kapinus took turns up front and behind the wheel. Like the big shared houses Molina inhabited at Oberlin, there were plenty of hijinks. This often came to life in Molina's crude drawings—many involving penises or scrotums—and a particular character he drew repeatedly. The cartoon man he crafted from a simple black line featured a distended stomach and commensurate stomach problems proudly on display. It wasn't far off from the shape Molina shifted to and from, his once diminutive frame swelling and deflating depending on his intake of beer and fried chicken and the number of times he'd forgotten that he'd already eaten. There were innumerable inside jokes and quirks along the way, too. Molina often crawled into small spaces and declared, "This is my house now!"

In the back of the van, Molina often constructed a "dog bed" out of newspapers, where he took naps. He decorated his confines in cigars, trinkets, and torn bits of paper. Always the first one awake in the morning, he continued his regular habit of taking early morning walks, and to mess with him, Molina often tagged Rice's name on walls and fliers he knew Rice would pass by later. He'd also prank the band by putting weird notes and trinkets in their guitar cases.

In his own guitar case he carried bottles of frankincense essential oil, which always spilled out and stank up the van. It was a part of his protection spells but also a way to mess with his brothers in Magnolia. "He was like a bratty little brother," Groth said. Molina also had a habit of taking the jokes and his incessant talking too far, leaving his bandmates to pretend to sleep or to hide in their headphones in order to disengage. When they had longer breaks, Molina and Rice took their sketchpad drawings to Kinko's and crafted little zines to trade. "Repetitive humor was a big thing with us," Rice added. It wasn't all booze and sadness.

⑩

LONDON

By the time Magnolia Electric Co.'s box set *Sojourner* filed onto record store shelves in August 2007, Jason and Darcie had made yet another move, this time to London. She'd been offered the chance to relocate through her job, and the pair decided that it'd be an energizing adventure, as Molina was again dissatisfied with Chicago. He remembered how enthralled he'd been with London's access to art and architecture when he was a student there in 1995, a nostalgia that fueled his desire to hop across the pond.

That all seemed like a great idea in theory, but in reality, Molina felt more lonely overseas than he ever had. Instead of being energized or inspired, he crawled further inside himself. He didn't make an effort to form friendships and spent as much time at home writing by himself as he could, when he wasn't out taking long walks to admire the city's streets and museums, the only thing he did love about being in London. In a 2010 interview he explained, "No, I don't have any friends . . . I don't really want them."[1] He added that in London playing music with people was a logistical nightmare. "It's not like the Midwest where people are prepared to play music anytime day or night," he said. "If you live here [Chicago], you can throw a rock and hit a great musician. Just don't throw it too hard, you don't want to hurt anyone."[2]

Contrary to his road dog nature in the States, Molina increasingly dreaded going on tour, even if it meant that he got to see his friends. The only thing that motivated him was that he needed the extra income that touring provided, especially because he was extremely popular in certain European countries like Norway, the Netherlands, the UK, and Spain. Emotionally, it was tough. "I would basically have to push him out the door and he would be crying," Darcie explained. "Psychologically he didn't want to do it, because seeing the guys again made him really sad. It was bitter-sweet, but the bitter took over."

He also grew to hate the drudgery of touring, and the fact that laptops, DVD players, and iPods played an increasingly present role in the van. "It really bothered him that the band sat there on their devices, because I think he wanted that to be bro time," Darcie said. And as much as he expressed his thoughts and feelings through moon and wolf metaphors in his songs, he wasn't someone who'd talk about the way he was feeling to his friends.

He never expressed his sadness and loneliness to the band, who only picked up on it through context clues, such as his marked downheartedness and social withdrawal since moving to London. Molina kept his drinking very private. The band got the sense that the shift from completely being isolated in London to playing music and living in a van with his old friends was incredibly hard for him. "It made it easier for him to go back to London and have this secret problem with alcohol," Rice explained.

Shortly after the move to London in 2007, Molina embarked on a winter tour of solo dates in the Netherlands, England, Germany, and the Nordic north before meeting up with the band for nearly three months of touring across the United States and Europe. In the spring they joined up with Jay Farrar's alt-country engine Son Volt for twelve U.S. dates, a tour that had been offered to Mark Kozelek but that he'd turned down. Still, Kozelek convened with Molina and Farrar—cofounder of the alt-country act Uncle Tupelo with Wilco's Jeff Tweedy—backstage at the Fillmore on March 30 in his hometown of San Francisco. "He was his typical, upbeat, gracious self," Kozelek remembered. "I don't drink, so I didn't notice how much alcohol was around or anything," he said. "But after he died, my friend said, 'Yeah, we were drinking a lot of his beer that night.'" Molina's voice blast-ing across the room left a lasting impression on him, who compared him to Gregory Peck's line in *To Kill a Mockingbird*. "Kill all of the blue jays you want," Kozelek said. "But it is a sin to kill a mockingbird, because all they do is sing their hearts out for us."

Pete Schreiner couldn't join a fall 2007 U.S. tour, and in his stead Bloomington-based musician and friend Evan Farrell stepped in. A multi-instrumentalist who'd played in indie-rock act Rogue Wave, countless Bloomington-based projects, and his own shambolic gypsy-punk collective the Japonize Elephants, Farrell was a beloved force in the local scene—

and, much like the rest of the Magnolia crew, an extrovert who did not know a stranger. Like Molina, he had his own struggles with alcohol. "I don't know if they talked about drinking," Schreiner said. "But I suspect that went on because Evan was really open and could talk about how his addictions would affect his relationships."

Farrell toured with the group for 42 dates stretching from August 23 in Bloomington to October 6 in Detroit. He fit in immediately, and Molina took to him—almost to an obsessive degree, like a crush. On the tour, Molina pulled himself together, as he often did with those he admired, and the shows with Farrell were some of the strongest the band had played in the last year.

The third annual "Campout" hosted by David Lowery's bands Cracker and Camper Van Beethoven at Pappy and Harriet's in Pioneertown, California, near Joshua Tree National Park, was the first time Molina's friend and *Black Ram* recording engineer ever saw him drunk. He played the festival solo, sans Farrell, on September 8, with mixed results. "I knew he was

Figure 10.1. Magnolia Electric Co. meets up with Molina's old friend Glen Hansard at the airport while on tour in Australia. *Photo courtesy of Jason Groth*

Figure 10.2. Mark Rice and Evan Farrell in the Magnolia Electric Co. van.
Photo courtesy of Jason Groth

buzzed because he'd been staying in a house with us, and he was certainly up all night," Lowery explained.

The next night the full band with Farrell on bass played a triumphant show at Emo's in Austin, Texas. They were in great spirits, and it showed through the music onstage. Texas-based musician proliferant Will Johnson of Denton-originated indie-rock band Centro-Matic and alt-country leaning South San Gabriel was in the audience. Johnson had met Molina a handful of times at festivals and through friends and approached him at the merch table after the show. There, the pair revealed their Mutual Appreciation Society membership cards. They bonded over everything from their favorite kinds of hats to wear onstage to their favorite songwriters and songs of each other's. "The lights in the club were going up and they're closing the whole place down, but we're still standing there talking," Johnson remembered. "We were about to say our farewells and he blurted out, 'We should make a record together!'"

Soon after Molina returned home to London, tragedy struck in the States. In December, Evan Farrell died of smoke inhalation in Oakland, California, after an outdated gas-powered floor furnace in the apartment where he was staying with friends caught on fire. Molina and his bandmates were devastated, and on the Magnolia Electric Co. website they wrote a tribute:

> All of us are tremendously saddened by the sudden and tragic death of our good friend and collaborator, Evan Farrell. Evan, who played bass and pedal steel with us during our fall tour this year, was caught in a fire caused by a faulty furnace in an apartment in Oakland, CA late last week. He died due to massive smoke inhalation.
>
> Evan was an incredible musician and a dear, dear friend. He was a member of Japonize Elephants, Rogue Wave, The Hollows, Mega Mousse, Kentucky Nightmare, and countless other projects and collaborations. He was funny, kind, generous, and supremely talented—he will be missed terribly.
>
> Evan was also a husband and a father, and a memorial fund has been set up in his honor. If you find it in your heart, please donate.
>
> We love you, Evan, and we are better people for having known you.

Two months after the tragedy, a still-shaken Molina flew from London to Texas to meet up with Will Johnson to make a record. Molina had written to Johnson about it only forty-eight hours after he'd proposed the idea. "He said, 'We'll make a record together near the night of the first full moon,'" Johnson remembered. "That was just one of those crystallizing moments that reinforced my love for that guy."

The pair decamped to the Echo Lab recording studio near Denton, Texas, home recording base for Johnson's band Centro-Matic. There the pair wrote, recorded, and mixed twenty-two songs in ten days. They enlisted the help of a handful of friends for auxiliary instrumentation, including Mikey Kapinus from Magnolia Electric Co., Texas-based multi-instrumentalist Howard Draper, and Denton singer-songwriter Sarah Jaffe. Famously prolific with an intense focus on his craft, Johnson knew he'd met his match in Molina, whose quick ways of working and intuition in the studio setting seemed something of a force of nature. "He came all the way from London and still beat me to the studio," Johnson laughed. "The thing that I really loved about it was that he didn't know me but he immediately trusted me, and I trusted him." Kapinus explained that Molina was actually more nervous about the situation than he let on to Johnson, but was comforted by his Magnolia brother's presence.

After making a trip to buy essentials—Molina's preferred Mirado Black Warrior pencils, which Molina often sharpened with a knife, Pink Pearl erasers, notepads, a thesaurus, a BB gun, and a case of Lone Star beer—the cast dove in, often heading to their respective corners to write. After scrawling ideas separately for a few hours, Molina and Johnson workshopped what they'd produced later in the evening or the next day. Molina was very opinionated, but so was Johnson. In the end they managed to arrive in the middle for a suite of songs that made as much sense logically as they did romantically, steeped in each writer's sonic signature, road-worn auspices and a poet's lexicon. In "The Lily and the Brakeman," which refers to the lilies the couple chose for their wedding, Molina sings to Darcie:

> Whose heart is that on the Allegheny
> With the lily in her autumn hair
> That chestnut-eyed one with the broken heart
> Whose sorrow and whose tears
> Rhododendron waits in the shadow's time
> Mountain whisperin
> Let the moon be the next shore you find
> Leave the boy behind
> Who does the whistle of the #8
> Remind of the way
> The twilight wind rolled through the pines
> And the first lily that he gave
> You took his name, he brought you just sorrow
> The brakeman with the stargaze in his eyes
> Has lost you now, his only love
> Leave the lily behind
> Leave the lily behind

Over the ten-day creative retreat that Texas winter, the pair drank. They smoked cigarettes. They shot BB guns. And they wrote volumes of lyrics. A friendship formed. It couldn't have been a more idyllic troubadour version of Boy Scout camp. "He was incredibly functional," Johnson said. "There was never a point where I felt like we needed to stop the session early or that there were any sort of diminishing returns." Molina did occasionally mention that he was unhappy in London. He found the soccer hooligans particularly unamusing, and even signed a few of his e-mail correspondences to Johnson, London: Sink It.

After returning to London, on July 1, 2008, Molina hammered out a thoughtful series of exercises for songwriting practice to his friend Matthew J. Barnhart, who played in the Denton, Texas–based rock band Tre Orsi. The pair became acquainted in Molina's Songs: Ohia days, and in October they would embark with their bands on what they dubbed the Bourbon and BBQ Tour, eight days stretching from Texas, through Oklahoma, Kansas, and Missouri, and up to Chicago.

Barnhart had written to Molina, explaining that he was having trouble finishing a couple of new songs, and asked for advice. Typing from his Blackberry because his computer was broken, after chastising London ("It is a huge joke that the west virginian coal mining town hillbilly trailer park songwriter has moved here. Fuck this towne Downward mobility I'm lovin it."), he recommended the following methodologies to Barnhart. These techniques stretched as far back as Molina's Oberlin days, when he woke at 5 a.m. to write on the shared front porch of his college flophouse:

1. Wake up one hour earlier than usual. Don't fuck around with this hour. Have a glass of water and go to the toilet and sit down at a desk and write. One hour and not on a computer. Set a kitchen timer. Better to hear it ring from another room than to keep watching your watch. You ain't writing a song or a poem or a masterpiece. Just write. It helps to have a good dictionary and one around 1950 is best since it has all you need and is prior to the gutting of so many important things. Pick a page. Just find a word you like not really random. Then write something like the opposite of the definition. Or write

Figure 10.3. Molina in his favorite Gus's Fried Chicken shirt, on the "BBQ and Bourbon Tour." *Photo courtesy of Howard Draper*

a short eight liner about two random things out of the page in front of you. Pile of drugs and Mark E. Smith and you got a Fall song. Personally I think it's dangerous.

2. A good book. Get a good and not cheap copy. Read about three pages prior to number one. Read it fast and reread and since it's only a few pages take notes. Also don't listen to music at this time. Just mining for ideas. Make your own lists and notes and hey you have these pieces and you will see how you can go from here. During that hour in number one exploit that good diction-ary. Let it take you all over the place. In about an hour you will have great words and nothing academic and you will easily put your own personal lan-guage and matter material in the midst of such hard fought and won writing. The music will be next. That one is another chapter. Take care. Yours in the good fight. Hugs.

The Bourbon and BBQ Tour of 2008 concluded in Chicago, where Mag-nolia Electric Co. played a show at the Abbey Pub on the city's northwest side. At this point the band had fully adopted a western-wear look, follow-ing Molina's lead, after he'd taken a black thrift store suit to a high end tailor, who included custom blue stitching on its lapel and on its sleeves.

After the Abbey Pub show, the Magnolia Electric Co. quintet made its way to Chicago for a third recording round with famed engineer Steve Albini at Electrical Audio. Adding to the excitement buzz associated with recording, the session began November 4, 2008, the same day Chicago resi-dent and U.S. senator Barack Obama was elected president of the United States. At this point the band had been playing together for five years, and the musical chemistry between them was as fluid and effortless as an Al Green tune. They were also uniquely attuned to the cues of Molina's sobri-ety, which ebbed and flowed throughout the session. He remained sober largely for the up-front recording, but then wavered between manageably drunk and out of control during overdubs and mixing. Still, his tenor voice rang out stronger and clearer than ever, like the many bells he'd glorified in song.

"When you're listening to the record you should be getting the impres-sion of what the band sounds like as an organic unit, rather than listening to the record and getting sort of a Spielberg CGI presentation of the music that happened to originate with the band," engineer Steve Albini explained. "The personality of the band, the performance characteristics of the band and the live interaction of the players is the focus of the sound." He added that Magnolia's—Jason's, really—method of working was incredibly effi-cient in that they only recorded one take of each song. By the time they'd recorded eleven songs, they'd use half of the amount of two-inch tape that other bands might normally use. "Jason, when he makes decisions, they're pretty solid decisions," Albini added.

This wasn't the case when Molina had a large Chicago-style pizza delivered to the studio—a regional bastardization of the form, its greasy depths dense as an actual pie, slathered and drenched in mozzarella and marinara. "This is my second lunch," Molina announced with pride.[3] "He's going to eat that whole pizza by himself?" Rice asked with a laugh.[4] After realizing he wasn't actually hungry, Molina pushed the pizza aside.

Evan Farrel's death had cut deep in Molina, perhaps because he could too clearly see himself in the meta-narrative of tragedy. "Seeing an extreme drinker and a super incredible musician fall, there were some parallels there," Schreiner said. Molina used his grief as a channel for the record the band crafted during their final run with Albini. They didn't know it at the time, but it would be the final Magnolia Electric Co. record, which Molina titled *Josephine*.

Though the press release touted the album as a tribute to Farrell, most likely because that's the information Molina provided in the press release for the record, it was actually a mix of new songs written in the studio and songs that Molina had written and delivered to the band via demos as early as 2003. They'd performed many of them live. "Shiloh" appeared in the 2007 *Sojourner* box set, and Molina had written a demo and recorded a version of "Whip-Poor-Will" for the album *Magnolia Electric Co.* way back in 2002. For most of the new songs, Molina brought lyrical sketches to the table, and the band fleshed out the sound as a unit in the studio, playing live in the same room for the first time, instead of being divided into different rooms or in isolation booths. Mike Brenner even flew in from Philadelphia to add lap steel parts.

Though they'd worked out many of the songs on tour, the band had to pivot from the way they played live. A band that played loud rock music, contained in one room, was privy to sound bleed and not being able to hear their respective instruments. Instead of playing on full blast, the hushed versions of the Electricians that appear on *Josephine* worked greatly to the album's advantage. Rice played the drums primarily with brushes, anchoring the songs with a whispered beat. Schreiner's dark, fuzzed-out bass lines steered the melancholic undercurrents of the tunes, while Kapinus's bright piano and organ wove in threads of hopefulness. Jason Groth even got to put his childhood saxophone lesson to use, adding a lengthy solo to the album's opener, "O! Grace." He was so proud of the moment that he teared up in the control room during playback. And despite his varied mental and emotional states, and commensurate intake of whiskey, Molina's voice rang out front and center and was as strong as ever, which had shrunken considerably from previous periods of drinking-related weight gain. A bottle of Wild Turkey was passed around the control room, the band taking bigger swings to temper Molina's intake.

In the studio, Molina crafted an altar in tribute to Farrell and penned lyrics that spoke to the recent tragedy. In tandem, he spoke at length about his failures in his marriage, which he also viewed as a tragedy. In the song "The Handing Down," he weaves imagery of Darcie (three rivers, in reference to her hometown of Pittsburgh) with allusions to how he felt the day Farrell died:

> At the handing down, the handing down
> Maybe the truth will not be shown
> And the dark will just roll on and on.
> Roll o three rivers where's that star you once
> Held above my faded dreams
> Heart worn more than some I guess
> But I'm still holding at the seams
> Still holding at the seams.
> Scarecrow holds an hourglass
> Above the cross roads for me
> Filled with tears and twilight
> From a friend's dying day
> Here's a turkey feather for his favourite hat
> And a love letter from the ace of spades
> A love letter from the ace of spades
> An anchor and the crown
> Of Queen Anne's lace and chicory
> A charm, a charm to drive away
> All the heartaches I gave
> All the goodbyes and the 'I love you's'
> I said but not in time
> But mine is the heart of the lonesome pine
> And the choices weren't always mine
> The choices weren't always mine

There was an overarching sense of loneliness in the songs, the product of Molina's isolated existence in London. The album's title track is particularly hard for Darcie to listen to today, as it speaks directly to Molina's feelings of guilt and regret about his drinking's ever-increasing toll on their marriage:

> I turned your life so upside down
> I don't know how you stayed or why

Looking always over my shoulder
Exactly what I wanted to find was already mine
Josephine, Josephine

But I saw the horizon
And I had to know where it all ends
I lived so long with the shadows
Lord, I became one of them
Oh, what a fool I've been
Josephine, Josephine

Now I take the hand I took for granted and set it free
Oh, what a fool I've been
Josephine, Josephine

Some folks see the horizon
And never need to know how it all ends
Leave the shadows behind
Don't go chasin' after 'em
You locked the door and put them old records on
I hear you cryin' along
Oh, what a fool I've been
No more will the final words be the tears in your eyes
Oh how I try, oh how I try
Oh Josephine, you are free
Oh Josephine, Josephine

Molina wrote the tune "Song for Willie" after meeting his hero, the country music icon Willie Nelson, outside of a show in Austin, Texas. It houses one of Molina's most poetic observations: "As long as there are sundowns, there will always be the west."

Molina's Gibson SG—marked with his signature Southern Cross in white medical tape—made it to the session, as did his favored Danelectro, which he'd marked with two messages in masking tape: "RIP Studs Terkel" and "Take It Easy . . . But Take It," words made famous by Dust Bowl jongleur Woody Guthrie. Molina also toted a new Fender Jaguar baritone guitar he'd purchased recently in Los Angeles on tour.

The band recorded more than seventy-five minutes of songs, more than what made the final cut of the album. As they huddled together in the control room listening to playback, providing each other notes and suggestions for what they could add or revise, Molina was insistent about producing a double album, thinking of how incensed he was going to be when the label suggested he release half the songs as MP3s. "People don't buy double re-cords and our last record was five records,"[5] Molina said jokingly in the Mr. Squirty voice. "Always fucking self. We're always fucking self," he added with a laugh.[6] Albini chimed in and jokingly suggested they do another five-LP box, but with double-sided LP singles. Once the band and Albini were done taking jabs at themselves and their keen ability to do exactly the opposite of what was trending in the contemporary landscape of indie rock, Molina spoke about his love of Erik Larson's murder-mystery novel *Devil in the White City*, centered on the 1893 Chicago World's Fair, and asked Albini about the best hat stores in Chicago, as he was after a short-brimmed hat like Hank Williams.

Ahead of the session, Jonathan Cargill from Secretly Canadian remem-bered talking to Molina as he was writing some of the songs for *Josephine*, and how excited Molina was about using a baritone guitar again, describing some of the spectral sounds he wanted to glean from its strings and wide body. When Cargill asked what the songs were about, Molina responded, "You know, the usual . . . shadows, ghosts, moons, wolves."[7] After jokingly suggesting that the album be called "Shadows, Ghosts, Moons, Wolves," Cargill added that the artwork could resemble a box of Lucky Charms. "There's no marshmallow equivalent of a shadow," Molina responded so-berly.[8] What did result from the conversation was Magnolia's September 2009 single, "Rider. Shadow. Wolf," captured in the *Josephine* session with Albini, its yellow-and-green sleeve reminiscent of a leprechaun's duds, its Ennio Morricone-esque guitar jangles and trotting drum beats something out of an old spaghetti western.

After he returned to London from the *Josephine* session, he bestowed Darcie with the nickname "Jo" and used it instead of the standard "babe" or other pet names he'd previously employed. Molina never explained it to her, of course, but on the cover of the new album was a fairly clear refer-ence to her: an antique pin featuring an illustrated portrait of a woman with red hair.

⓫

REHAB

Secretly Canadian unanimously agreed that *Josephine* was Molina's crowning achievement with his band Magnolia Electric Co. It was an album that finally captured and synthesized both sides of the songwriter who for nearly twenty years had been penning folk songs, ballads, and rock anthems from a very distinct, midwestern point of view. Released in July 2009, the band's subdued studio tenor paid off in spades, comprising an album that neither veered too far into Neil Young and Crazy Horse, nor stared too far into its own navel. The *AV Club* bestowed an A grade on the album, explaining, "The sympathetic accompaniment of his expansive band—which abandons its onstage Crazy Horse roar to operate in a spare, desolate gray area between funeral-paced country and bloodshot soul on the quietly breathtaking *Josephine*—does nothing to make Molina seem any less alone. On the title track, Molina sings about living so long with shadows that you become one of them, and he really sounds like he's about to be swallowed by the specter of his deepest, blackest memories."[1]

The timing was good for *Josephine* and its throwback country and folk through lines, too. Alt-country and Americana sounds were finding an upswing in popular culture once again via the rise of traditionalist and bluegrass-leaning acts such as the Avett Brothers, Deer Tick, the Punch Brothers, and Trampled by Turtles.

Secretly Canadian had recently added a third label to its label group in Dead Oceans, a folk-leaning imprint that would soon sign such acts as the

Tallest Man on Earth and Phosphorescent, who dabbled in America's musical past. The Avett Brothers, fans of Molina who were on a meteoric rise
and selling out big theaters, invited Magnolia Electric Co. to ready its bolo
ties for the road in May 2009 for a week of shows out west. Jason Groth
counts their first night opening for the North Carolina–based Americana
outfit at the Fillmore in San Francisco as one of the best shows Magnolia ever played, and the second night as one of its worst. When the Avett
Brothers decided to join Molina onstage for "Hammer Down," one of its
favorite MECo songs, Molina couldn't even play his guitar. "It was totally
humiliating," Groth recalled.

By the time Magnolia reached Colorado Springs on May 23 for the city's
annual MeadowGrass Festival, Mark Rice had reached his threshold as
Molina's babysitter. "At a certain point we realized that this whole theory of
being supportive bandmates and living by example wasn't doing anything,"
he explained. Rice had had thoughts of leaving the band as long as one year
prior, but by the time the calendar ticked 2009, there had been so much
touring and so much alcoholic behavior that the bad and good had become
nearly indistinguishable. And Rice was perhaps the most optimistic person
in the group.

**Figure 11.1.   Magnolia Electric Co. at the start of its spring
2009 tour. At this point tensions were mounting due to
Molina's drinking.** *Photo by William Claytor*

The festival in Colorado Springs stood out in particular because it was an unusually pastoral setting for the band, which was used to sleeping in mid-range hotel rooms in more urban locales. The band shared a large cabin, where they each had their own room with a door that locked. The night before they were scheduled to take the stage, Molina stayed awake from sunup to sundown, and drank an entire bottle of Bulleit bourbon in the process. By the time they took the stage, Molina couldn't stand up or hold his guitar. He fired Jason Groth for calling him out on it. The festival had been so generous to the band that they felt obligated to play. "It was epically bad," Rice remembered. A live recording of the set backs up the claim. When the band returned to its home base of Bloomington on May 25, Rice made a decision. He wrote a heartfelt letter to Molina explaining why he had to leave the band and move on with his life. By the time it was delivered to London, Molina had already anticipated its contents. He never opened it.

Rice soon left the band to attend graduate school at the Rhode Island School of Design, where he focused his attention back to his visual artwork. In his stead, Pete Schreiner shifted back to drums, which he'd played in his earliest days with Molina, when they were still called Songs: Ohia. Bloomington-based friend Chris "Sal" Saligoe stood in on bass, getting a swift introduction into Molina's behavior in the process. A month of U.S. tour dates in the summer of 2009 marked the last road trip for the classic Magnolia Electric Co. lineup. It wasn't without its alcohol-related trials.

A photographer from a music magazine had been hired to follow Molina around for the day in Brooklyn, and he and the band were visibly annoyed by it. Molina was also visibly unwell. "He had a bottle of Jameson that he was looking for, but the band had hidden it," Grady explained. Molina told Grady the band had forbidden him from leaving the grounds of the outdoor show, and so the pair of old friends and lovers walked its perimeter, reminiscing about their time in college. "There were so many warning signs that I didn't put together at the time," she said. Molina inquired about her job as a sculpture conservator and expressed how proud he was that she had continued to pursue her passion for art and conservation. "He introduced me as having 'the most awesome job ever,'" she said laughing. "I think the band just collectively rolled its eyes." By the end of their visit, Molina was in tears, mourning the loss of his friend and their intertwined artistic passions. As they said good-bye, he pointed to the stage and explained to Grady that he'd always have her up there, in reference to the number of songs he'd written for and about her over the years.

Figure 11.2. The Magnolia Electric Co. lineup of Jason Groth, Chris "Sal" Saligoe, Mikey Kapinus, Jason Molina, and Pete Schreiner in 2009, after drummer Mark Rice left the band. *Photo courtesy of Ben Schreiner*

Much to the band's surprise, Molina had booked a sleeper coach for the European stint of the summer 2009 tour. They'd always traveled in a van with a hired driver, so the upgrade to a bus seemed lavish and wildly unexpected. Molina's guarantees for the tour were nothing to sneeze at, yet far from justifying the cost of a bus. "He told me not to mention costs or anything to the band as they wouldn't understand," his European booking agent Bas Flesseman explained.

The rental nearly decimated any money the band made on the tour. Some thought Molina wanted a safe place to drink and pass out. Others thought it was an extension of Molina's generosity toward his friends that he wanted everyone to feel comfortable and safe. "I remember at End of the Road Festival he was comparing his bus to Neko Case's bus," Flesseman said. "He wanted to belong to the league of artists that travel in a bus instead of a van." Perhaps more than bus envy was the fact that Molina hated to feel left behind by the artists he once rubbed elbows with on tour and in clubs. Neko Case had once been a country-leaning unknown like himself, hunkering down at beloved Chicago hole-in-the-wall the Hideout, but as he continued the modest club circuit, she was headlining theaters.

Figure 11.3. Molina backstage during Magnolia Electric Co.'s summer 2009 European Tour wearing his Western-inspired suit. *Photo courtesy of Ben Schreiner*

After playing the End of the Road festival in the UK, a young artist from Sweden named Kristian Matsson, who performed under the stage name the Tallest Man on Earth, hitched a ride with Magnolia Electric Co. to Brussels. After chatting with the upstart musician, Molina watched Matsson perform in Brussels ahead of Magnolia Electric Co.'s set at Ancienne Belgique that night. Instead of being energized by the show, Molina seemed defeated and explained to Flesseman that Matsson was better than he could ever be. Regardless, Molina managed to overcome his crushed feeling that night to play one of his best latter-day gigs, though it wasn't without its quirks. During the set in Belgium, Molina wore a Zorro mask, a move that wasn't terribly dissimilar from his self-conscious debut on the Oberlin house show circuit nearly twenty years prior. He held up cardboard signs to the band throughout, with handwritten messages that the audience couldn't see. They said things like "I'm sorry for messing up" and "I love you guys." "The show was so dramatic that it scared me," Flessemen remembered. After the show Molina sat drinking next to a big spinning fan and joked, "That's my biggest fan." Jason Groth remembered that he had never felt sadder than he did during that period, watching Molina drink to his demise.

During MECo's fall 2009 European tour, Groth kept a diary in case it was their last go. Chris Brokaw from Codeine, a band that Jason cited among his favorites, joined them as a solo opener for a week of dates. Over the years, Brokaw's musical vision recast itself from slowcore pioneer to folk-leaning solo singer-songwriter, which perfectly aligned with Magnolia. He met up with the band in Vienna and joined Molina for lunch. The encounter was almost as shocking as when Molina punched him in the heart in Austin, Texas, a couple of year earlier. "I was trying to talk to him, and he sounded genuinely crazy," Brokaw explained. "Having never met him before, I was like, 'Oh my god, Jason Molina is a completely insane person.'" What he later realized was that Molina was really tired and really drunk, rendering his patterns of thinking and speech nearly indecipherable. They reconvened after Molina caught an afternoon snooze, and Brokaw was relieved to discover that Molina was actually sane and a really fun time.

Their September 12 show in Vienna was as good as it could have been, though the band was palpably concerned. "I could tell that I was walking into a situation," Brokaw explained. "Something was going on, but I didn't know what." He recalled that his opening solo sets and Magnolia's sets were generally good and well received by audiences, and he respected that Molina seemed to be constantly creating. In the van, Molina would pull out a notebook, write a couple of lines to a song, and then hand it to Brokaw to review and add upon. They engaged in the back-and-forth all day long as they traveled between cities, something Brokaw had never experienced with anyone before. The pair even discussed Brokaw opening for Molina and Will Johnson during the tour they'd booked for their forthcoming collaborative LP, which they'd tracked during their singer-songwriter Boy Scout retreat in Texas. After a week with Brokaw, Magnolia Electric Co. traveled to Spain to join the Handsome Family—the spectral New Mexico folk duo, perhaps best known for playing the music in the opening credits of season 1 of HBO's *True Detective*—and John Doe & the Sadies, former band for alt-country siren Neko Case. Molina wrote to Darcie from the hotel,

> The Sadies and John Doe and Handsome Family are fucking outstanding. I'm feeling better but only a little. I am just wanting to cry all the time. I know I'm just lonesome and anxious about a lot of things but I think about you all the time and the tiny beast. Then I get sad again because I have no friends and don't know how to find any in England. Then I get sad because I'm surrounded by the guys who I love and all they do is talk about how wonderful things are at home and all of that kind of destroys me.[2]

Despite being surrounded by his friends and bands he respected, Molina felt more lonely than he ever had. In an attempt to dull the pain, he drank. In Seville, Spain, Jason Groth recorded in his tour diary,

> We discovered a square that had a restaurant with cheap tapas and lots of outdoor seating. The octopus and potato salad and the risotto were unbelievably good, but what wasn't good was drunk Molina. He made it through two very tall glasses of red wine on top of whatever else he was drinking during the day, and was talking and talking and interrupting and touching food that he had no intention of eating. He was in full-on drunkarexic mode (i.e., the buzz was obviously pretty good, and food would do nothing but shut it down and put him to sleep). On the way back we stopped at a gelato place and Molina was swerving all over the street. I told him to watch Mikey and concentrate. My biggest concern was him falling into the cobblestone street right in the path of a car or scooter. There were a few close calls. Finally we arrived at the hotel and made sure that our inebriated brother got into his room.

This was Molina's demeanor throughout much of the remainder of the tour, from Spain to Turkey. Molina never expressed his feelings to his band; he only masked them with alcohol and incessant chatter in the van, which at a certain point they worked actively to drown out with iPods and movies. They had no idea how much Molina missed them, assuming that he was only trying to drive them away. It wasn't until they reached Istanbul for their final date on the tour that Jason opened up and admitted to the band that he knew he needed help. They hugged and cried and agreed to support him in any way possible. Molina told them that he wanted to stop drinking and see a doctor. But as the band took a walking tour of Istanbul, Molina sat in his hotel room and drank. He wrote to Darcie,

> I have told the guys that I am taking a long long walk away from MEco and they all seem to be fine with it and there were tears and tears but I have to do this. I still have to make the hard decision to perhaps cancel the Will tour. I don't know if I have all of my flight details yet but tomorrow I will cross my fingers that this computer works since the guys all fly differently. Sorry for the crazy typing. Again I love you and I am not doing very well and am crying a lot. I can't wait to come home and have a smile.[3]

When Molina returned from Europe in November 2009, he became paralyzed by flu-like symptoms. After a hard-worn battle, Darcie convinced him to go to the hospital. It was the first time he'd faced the medical realities of his drinking. He had an inflamed liver, known as hepatitis, and was having severe withdrawal symptoms after an attempt to quit cold turkey. At the hospital the doctor prescribed vitamins, acid reflux pills, and thiamine to help counteract the negative effects the drinking had on his brain function. They referred him to a clinic near his house to help address his issues with depression and self-medicating with alcohol.

After attending one meeting at the clinic, Molina decided it wasn't for him and never went back. A week later he fell in the bathroom, breaking several ribs and sustaining a gash in his forehead that required stitches. Darcie urged him to seek professional help. Professionals urged him to start on a regimen of antidepressant medications, which he refused, taking only the occasional short-run prescription of antianxiety or antipsychotic medications as a band-aid. He believed that the evening effects of antidepressants would kill the creative drive and outlook that came when he was at his lowest lows and his highest highs, which to him seemed more dangerous than his drinking. The biggest problem with that logic was that, because of his constant drinking, Molina hadn't written any new songs in months.

Molina and Will Johnson had worked for months to craft a plan for a European-based backing band and commensurate tour for their joint album, *Molina and Johnson*, which was released November 2. Johnson had planned to meet Molina in Holland to pick up a van and their band after finishing a tour with Monsters of Folk, a sort of "supergroup" collaborative comprised of Johnson, Jim James from My Morning Jacket, Conor Oberst and Mike Mogis from Bright Eyes, and folk rocker M. Ward, who was one half of She & Him with actress Zooey Deschanel. Molina *hated* Monsters of Folk and once remarked, "Will Johnson and I are the REAL monsters of folk!"[4] What he actually hated more than the thought of his friends selling out was the feeling that he was being left behind.

Molina had considered as early as October that he should cancel the tour with Johnson. During the European tour with Magnolia Electric Co., he was desperately sad, lonely, drinking, and missing Darcie and their black-and-white tuxedo cat Bhaji. But the hospital visit acted as the metaphorical nail in the tour's coffin. Shortly after, Johnson received a cryptic message from Secretly Canadian that Molina was sick and couldn't come. "I suspected and respected that what was going on was serious, and so I didn't demand any sort of further explanation from him at the time," Johnson explained. "I was calm about it, but that's not to suggest that I wasn't deeply disappointed. I really liked our record and I was looking forward to going out with Jason and getting to know him better." Soon after canceling the European portion of the Molina and Johnson tour, Molina canceled the winter U.S. dates, too. He also put the brakes on any future tours with

Magnolia Electric Co., leaving very little tour support behind *Josephine*, which had just been released in July.

Jonathan Cargill from Secretly Canadian wrote to Bas Flesseman asking if he thought just the MECo band could play additional European dates without Molina in support of the record, but of course there was no way that was possible. And the band, Will Johnson, and Chris Brokaw were met with radio silence when they attempted to contact Molina. "We all just made other plans," Brokaw explained. "This was a pretty big deal, and the whole thing was just shut down with absolutely no sense of way. It was completely mysterious."

Molina's last solo performance came as a surprise a couple of months after the Molina and Johnson tour cancellations. Chris Brokaw was on tour in the UK with Boston friend Geoff Farina, formerly of the indie-rock act Karate, with whom he'd just released a dual album. After a few dates, Farina had to return suddenly after his dad unexpectedly passed away. With low expectations for a response given the ghosting nature of the previous tour cancellations, Brokaw sent an e-mail to Molina explaining the situation and asked if he'd like to play his show in London at the Luminaire, which happened to be Jason's favorite local venue. "He wrote back two minutes later," Brokaw said.

Darcie accompanied Molina to the show on March 26, 2010. Given Molina's patterns of unpredictable intoxication, she was on high alert. Molina had asked the manager of the club not to announce his presence at the gig ahead of time and spent a long time pacing the sidewalks outside before taking the stage after being spooked by some feedback that plagued the sound check. As was often the case with Molina, he managed to hold himself to a fair degree of sobriety in the company of Brokaw, someone he admired, long enough to belt out a range of solo acoustic tunes, including a cover of Blind Willie McTell's "East St. Louis Blues." Darcie remembered that Molina was doing really well until someone offered him a shot after the set. "My heart just sank," she said. "It was very telling to me how hard it would have been to be someone who has a drinking problem and to be in that profession. That's the first thing people say when you get offstage. Alcohol is always in your face."

She had called Jonathan Cargill at Secretly Canadian in late 2009 with an idea: "Let's Johnny Cash this," Darcie said. "I just wanted someone to take him, to put him in a cabin and dry him out." Darcie, who wasn't someone who found it easy to ask for help, was at her wit's end, trapped in England with a man who would not help himself. She remembered the label being initially reticent about her pleas, even telling her that they had "put it on the back burner" in the midst of dealing with other artists. "I just wanted someone to take him because I didn't know what to do anymore," she added. Knowing that Molina was miserable in London, she had suggested numerous times that they move back to the United States, an idea Molina repeatedly shot down for fear he'd be viewed as a failure.

"For the last year he was in London, all he did was wake up, drink vodka, and pass out," Darcie said. "Maybe smoke a cigarette and scream about something." Soon Jason Groth from Magnolia and Darcie connected over e-mail and began assembling the various puzzle pieces between his home life and his tour life, corroborating stories and symptoms and dispelling myths and lies. What they discovered in the process was that Molina had been actively working to pit his band and his wife against one another. What they concluded was that Molina knew that if the two camps began comparing stories, he'd be in trouble, and his drinking to excess would have been uncovered much sooner.

Darcie also connected with Molina's brother Aaron, who sometimes traveled to Europe for work. He'd battled his own alcohol addiction and eventually quit drinking under the guidance of rehabilitation counseling. "There were times when Darcie couldn't control him, and so she'd have him call me so I could try to calm him down," he explained. He estimated that he was spending about eighty to one hundred dollars a month on phone cards, outside of the inbound calls he received. He and Darcie both became incredibly frustrated by the fact that, legally, there wasn't a lot of recourse for an adult who wanted to harm himself. "Unless someone says, 'I'm going to kill myself,' there's not a lot you can do," Aaron explained. The pair eventually felt so desperate to find help for Molina that they hatched a theoretical plan to get him arrested and then institutionalized due to his mental state, something they never followed through on. They felt utterly powerless to help him, and even more scared for him.

Months after her pleas to dry Molina out, Jonathan Cargill contacted Darcie in March 2010 with concern over a disturbing Facebook message Molina had sent to a mutual friend. It was only then, after a lengthy exchange filled with uncomfortable details, that Molina's fraternal brother at Secretly Canadian finally understood the severity of Molina's condition and resolved to come up with a plan to help him. Though he was in some of his worst states, it would still take Molina a few more years to fully own up to his problem. Instead he often blamed his behavior and physical condition on a host of other ailments ranging from the medically unsound such as "a virus around his heart" or "a fuzzy spot on his brain" to the more straightforward such as AIDS and "the bad kind of hepatitis." As creative as these were, none of them were true.

By the spring of 2011, Molina was up to about 1.5 liters of vodka a day and had tried on his own to get sober no less than fifteen or twenty times. The amount of vodka Darcie had found and poured out could fill a swimming pool. And her efforts were fruitless, as neighborhood corner stores frequently sold Molina liquor on credit. After more than a year off from the band, and at least twice as long dodging Darcie's negotiations and outright pleas for professional help, Molina agreed to attend rehab outside of London in March 2011.

Even after he agreed to go to rehab, getting him there wasn't easy. On the day the couple were supposed to check Molina into the clinic, Molina became so intoxicated prior to their departure that he passed out in the cab on the way to the train station. The angry cab driver threw the couple out in the middle of a busy thoroughfare, leaving Darcie to deal with her husband, who couldn't stand up let alone walk. Eventually an employee of the train station came to assist and explained that Molina would not be allowed on a train in his state. Instead, the couple took an ambulance to the nearest hospital where Molina was detoxed, as they didn't have a car, and no cab, bus, or train would allow them a ride. Darcie still considers it one of the worst days of her life. The next day, a car service from the rehabilitation facility drove to London to pick Molina up for an added cost—money well spent in Darcie's opinion.

Molina lasted six weeks at Providence Projects, about one hundred miles away from London in the coastal town of Bournemouth. After spending time with Molina in one-on-one and group counseling sessions, the doctors and therapists there suggested he stay twice as long. But as the end of the initial run drew near, Molina was all but crawling up the walls. By the time he reached London's Waterloo train station after checking out of the program, he was drunk.

"He called me that day and it was so disappointing," Aaron Molina said. "As an alcoholic, I know that these things have about a 30 percent chance of working, but to not even get off the train before you're drunk was tough." Aaron then came to London to help stage an intervention, during which he chewed out the owners of the local corner market who'd been providing Molina booze on credit. There he discovered that his brother had become known as the neighborhood drunk. It was utterly annihilating to see himself, when he'd been at some of his lowest points with drinking, in his brother, who didn't seem motivated to sober up. "I don't think there was any will," Aaron said. "It seemed like he'd given up." He likened it to that of a slow suicide. And at one point Darcie and Aaron thought they'd lost Molina when they returned home to pools and smears of blood across the couple's cottage and an unresponsive Molina, who was often hard to stir once he'd passed out but this time was remarkably unresponsive. However, his brother finally awoke, and Aaron Molina left London feeling utterly defeated and unsure how much longer his older brother would live.

After years of living with the devastating effects of Molina's drinking, Darcie's fears of her husband ending up a homeless vagrant had been replaced by fears for her own health and safety. After sleeping on the couch for two years, in a tiny mews cottage smeared in the blood, broken glass, and unrelenting screams of a man she no longer knew, whose commitment to destroying his life with alcohol replaced his commitment to his marriage and to his song craft, she made a decision: Molina could no longer live in their Ealing home.

It was April 16, her birthday. She stole Molina's keys and then coaxed him outside for some fresh air. As their home and its white picket fence grew distant in the background, Darcie, racked with guilt, mustered the courage for a very frank conversation. She explained to Molina calmly that he no longer lived in their house and that he'd have to find somewhere else to sleep. After handing over a credit card and explaining its limit and reminding him how much money was left in his checking account, Molina's lioness walked away from her marriage and the man she fell in love with more than a decade ago. "I went home and had a nervous breakdown," she said with tears in her eyes. "I was crying, thinking, that's it . . . we're never going to see him again. He's going to die on the street and we're never going to know."

A few hours later she left the house to meet friends whom she planned to crash with for a few days to stay away from the house. They'd convinced her that seeing a film would help get her mind off the situation. After leaving the house to meet up with her friends, she almost immediately ran into Molina. "Darce, I can't get into the house," he said in the soft, high-pitched voice that had become synonymous with drunken Molina—the drunken soprano, his brother Aaron called it. Darcie reminded him that they no longer lived together. Seemingly unfazed, he replied, "But I have to pee."

He then tailed Darcie down the street screaming until she headed to a nearby police station, at which time he disappeared. Later that night, when she emerged from the movie theater, her cell phone's screen pulsed with alerts. Multitudes of voice mails from neighbors whom she didn't know outside of sidewalk pleasantries explained that her husband had been banging on the door for hours, screaming, and had broken it down. The next evening, having forgotten that he'd made a huge, Jason-sized hole in the front door the night before, he stood at the back door screaming and banging until the landlady, unsure what to do, called the police and had Molina arrested. He spent an evening in lockup and was released with a formal warning the next day.

Over the three years that the couple had lived in the small connected cottage, the neighbors had never phoned the police, even though there had been plenty of noise. It took about a week for someone to come over and repair the door. She'd already shelled out hundreds of British pounds for the innumerable windows Molina had already broken. It was how he got into the house when he forget his keys, crawling through with hands bloodied from the broken glass. "The people from the repair place would actually laugh at me," Darcie remembered.

Calls from hospitals and police officers provided tabs on her estranged husband over the next few days. One night an officer came by with Molina after finding him in a ditch, and the next day Darcie arrived home from work to find him unconscious on the kitchen floor, an unlit cigarette in his mouth as gas from a nearby stove burner saturated the room. At that point there was no clearer—or more dangerous—sign that Molina would never accept their separation, and, thinking on her feet, she coaxed him to nearby Lammas Park to call his friends and to get him out of the house. "He said seemingly everything except the actual problem," Jason Groth remembered.

Darcie then decided to check Molina into a Holiday Inn Express in nearby Hammersmith, where he could stay and safely drink in the bar or in his room. After getting Molina to the hotel, she helped design the first in what would become nearly two years of plans to help unshackle Molina from the devastation of alcoholism, coordinating over e-mail with Molina's friends in Bloomington and Chicago. Though Darcie knew the split from Molina was best for both of them, she never gave up on him and continued to write letters and e-mails and help fund his treatment and cost of living until his last days. She never stopped loving him.

Darcie, Jason's siblings, the members of Magnolia Electric Co., and the former Songs: Ohia players living in Chicago collectively decided to relocate Molina to Chicago where he might benefit from the support of the friends he mourned constantly, who as a group might better succeed in convincing him to dry out. Knowing Molina's colossal pride as a big brother, they knew he would be more likely to face his friends with his problems than his siblings.

Aaron Molina had pleaded with his brother to stay with him, but Molina was too ashamed. "He wouldn't come," Aaron explained. "I was like, come on, I'm the least judgmental person in this situation. I lived in a room with you. I know you." As Molina was too crestfallen to face Aaron, it was especially improbable that he'd face his baby sister Ashley, given his current state. Their dad Bill had suffered a stroke after Jason's mom died and was working through rehabilitation. In general, he could not mentally or emotionally cope with his sons' alcoholism, after living through the effects of it with their mother Karen. Molina's friends valiantly stepped up for what proved to be a long and sullied path to wellness.

"The idea behind it was that Jason didn't have any responsibility or job, so there was nothing for him to stay sober for," Pete Schreiner explained. In Chicago, in the care of his Songs: Ohia comrades, there would be a place for Molina to live and work in an alcohol-free environment, at Dan MacAdam's graphic design and screen-printing studio Crosshair, and in the former Butchershop space on Lake Street, the same loft where the Oberlin friends threw art openings and holiday parties in the late '90s. Schreiner volunteered to be Molina's escort back to the United States and boarded a plane from O'Hare International in Chicago about a week after his initial conversations with Darcie. Molina wasn't filled in on the plan, which to Schreiner felt a bit sneaky. "It was kind of daunting," he said. "On one hand I felt like I was pulling a fast one on my friend. But at the same time, he needed help. If I could convince him of that, well then that's what I was going to do." He arrived the morning of April 24, 2011.

Darcie Molina accompanied Schreiner to the Holiday Day Inn Express where Molina had holed up to explain, in a very calm and collected manner, that Schreiner was there to take him to Chicago. After she left, Schreiner had an endlessly circuitous conversation with Molina, circling round and round the issue no less than fifty times. Molina was physically ragged and palpably embarrassed for Schreiner to see him in such a state. The two had a full day together before it was time to get on the plane to Chicago, with tickets Darcie had purchased just days earlier. "We walked around London the next day, and he was adamant that he wasn't going," Schreiner explained. "He was really frail, physically and mental health–wise. But he'd also been hanging out with some friends of mine that I hadn't seen in awhile. There was some healthy Jason that was clearly still there, and having fun, parallel to this super heavy matter." Their flight left Heathrow at noon the next day, April 25, and when the time came, Schreiner wasn't confident that Molina would be going with him. When it was time to check out, the ever-stubborn Molina never uttered the words "I'm coming" as he followed Schreiner to the Tube station to Heathrow.

After catching the Piccadilly line to Heathrow, Molina found a few pounds on the ground and handed it over to an airport barkeep for a few nips of Jägermeister in an effort to control the shakes during the nearly nine-hour flight from London to Chicago. He had one drink on the plane. When the two friends landed, former Songs: Ohia bass player Dan Mac-Adam was there to greet them. He was shocked by Molina's appearance, how his friend and former bandmate had transformed from a youthful rabble-rouser to a mangled alcoholic, complete with a puffy red nose, blotchy skin, and a paranoid, skittish disposition. After insisting that the airport bar was not a stop they were going to make, MacAdam helped his wobbly friend navigate the halls and congestion of one of the world's busiest airports. Molina was too scared and unbalanced to go up an escalator. "I was, oddly, working at John Mellencamp's house at that time doing some painting work, so I had to get back to that job," Schreiner said. He exchanged pleasantries with MacAdam for a few minutes and felt a great wash of relief after safely getting Molina into the structure that had been put in place in Chicago. "I had this mission to do, and that was it for me," he added. "Then I went back to toiling away at that rich bastard's house."

Once in the car the pair made their way to the Portage Park neighborhood on the city's northwest side so that Molina could grab a quick shower at MacAdam's house. The short-term plan was to put Molina up in a spare room at Crosshair, even though it was technically a working space where overnight guests were not allowed. There, MacAdam would look after Molina during business hours and assign him tasks such as packing boxes, while the rest of the Chicago core of Songs: Ohia—who at that point all had families and full-time jobs—took turns with their longtime friend and creative collaborator in the form of breakfasts, walks, errands, and silly mischief. "We were all trying to engage him with the world so that he wouldn't gaze into his navel and ultimately the bottom of a bottle," MacAdam said.

In the dusty industrial confines of Crosshair, Jeff Panall, Rob Sullivan, and Tom Colley met the pair, and the four friends staged an intervention, explaining that Molina wasn't to leave without telling one of them, that they were tracking his credit and debit card transactions and that Mac-Adam had his checkbook. Darcie had laid out Molina's financial picture to the group prior to his arrival, so they knew what he could afford and what they'd need to come to her for. On his own, Molina had about five hundred dollars in a checking account and about six thousand in royalties on the way from Secretly Canadian, roughly the same amount he received each quarter, though at times it was considerably more. He also had about four thousand dollars in the form of CDs and a small inheritance from his mother. Darcie explained that if he needed money for rehab or living expenses, she'd cover it.

The friends had never spoken so harshly to Jason, MacAdam's protestations about Molina berating a student soundman in St. Louis notwithstanding. Though Molina seemed dumbfounded by the stern quality of the talk, he was surprisingly amenable to the terms of his stay, in what the group would soon realize was a calculated effort to get them off his back. Pretending to agree became his mechanism for getting people to leave him alone so that he could continue drinking in secret, though in the beginning of his stay at the Butchershop he was by all accounts sober. Tom Colley stayed with him the first night, and the friends arranged a regular schedule of lunches and hanging out to distract him from drinking until they found a viable rehabilitation program, as the transfer to Chicago had happened so quickly.

With just a few belongings, an extra pair of pants and shirt at most, they offered to pick up some household items for their friend. Molina insisted on an army-style cot, similar to what he had slept on during his Oberlin days, with a metal base and a thin pad on top. Luckily, Dan Sullivan had just such a thing for camping, which he happily donated, though he admitted he wasn't as involved in the hard work with Molina as his friends were. "At this point those guys all had a longer, college relationship with him," he explained. "I think, too, that there was this undercurrent that my relationship with him didn't end well."

Ever the antiquarian, Molina requested a series of esoteric wares. Fortunately for him the five had gathered enough trinkets, bits, and bobs at junk shops and flea markets over the years to quench their friend's very specific aesthetic. Panall provided an old acoustic guitar, and Molina filled notebooks with lyrics, working out songs which maybe weren't his best but were a better option than filling his body with booze. He frequently consulted a tarot card deck that he insisted had been owned by the magician Harry Houdini. "He was very much playing into this gypsy traveler persona," Panall remembered.

Molina's time at Crosshair wasn't without difficulty, but the group believes he was mostly alcohol free for those days, the occasional beer and a burger aside. There were good times, too, when Molina felt like their friend Sparky, the impish goof they had come to love at Oberlin. Once at the end of a workday, MacAdam invited Molina to an exhibition of Chernobyl photographs, a morbid fascination the pair shared, at the Ukrainian Cultural Institute on Chicago Avenue. The pair eagerly made their way to the city's west side. When they arrived, the exhibit was empty aside from two women who were dressed to the nines and standing near an ornate, traditional Ukrainian cake with just one missing piece. It immediately caught Jason's eye. "You just missed his Excellency," the two Ukrainian women exclaimed, referring to the ambassador who made a requisite five-minute appearance. After the pair perused the harrowing photos, sick but charismatic Molina approached the ambassador's entourage. "He just turned on the charm with these Ukrainian cultural attachés," MacAdam added with a laugh. "And long story short, we downed his Excellency's cake!"

After a couple of weeks at Crosshair, Jeff Panall helped set up Molina on his own in a studio apartment on the far west side, just steps from Panall's home near Oak Park, Illinois. Tom Colley paid Molina's rent, and Darcie reimbursed him. Despite his friends' diligence, care, and daily visits, Molina took a nose dive once he got his own apartment. The minute he was without watch, vodka bottles piled up in his closet, and Molina's wild tales and idiosyncrasies accumulated faster than the dust bunnies under his cot. Molina clung to the idea that Darcie had left him for her lesbian lover, which wasn't true. More important than the truth of the story was that it acted as a distraction from Molina's actual problem of drinking. When friends confronted him about the veracity of the tale, Molina countered that it felt true to him.

Dan Sullivan recalled a trip the pair made to Target to buy necessities. "He was fine one minute and then he was like a child," he said. "He couldn't do anything, not even tie his shoes. He was drunk in this really unrecognizable way." Molina soon made his first trip to West Suburban Medical Center in Oak Park, Illinois, on May 10, where he was subsequently admitted to the J. Madden Mental Health Center in Hines, Illinois, two days later. He spent nine days there in detox and was released, though he'd claim to friends that he escaped.

After being treated at Madden, he met infrequently with a social worker who administered Seroquel, which is most often used in the treatment of bipolar disorder and depression. Though anecdotally many of Molina's friends and family members suspected that he was bipolar, he was never officially diagnosed to anyone's knowledge. And if he was diagnosed at Madden, no one knew, as his records remained private. He spent another tumultuous week in the west side apartment wandering the streets of the Austin neighborhood, a once vibrant enclave of Chicago at the turn of the twentieth century that had succumbed to the trappings of poverty and crime by the turn of the twenty-first. Molina claimed he'd been shot up with heroin and raped, anything to distract from the vodka-drenched elephant in the room. Jeff Panall recalled that one evening he had scheduled time to record music with Molina. But when he showed up to the apartment, Molina was passed out near an empty six-pack and a quarter-empty pint of Jack Daniels.

After tireless conversations and coaxing by Dan MacAdam, Jeff Panall, and Tom Colley, Molina checked into the S.H.A.R.E. rehabilitation program in Hoffman Estates, Illinois. It was an experience Molina likened to prison. There, Molina corresponded with his friends and family via letters. Tom Colley made the forty-five-minute trip to the treatment center weekly to deliver cigarettes and money for laundry, even though he wasn't allowed to see his friend. Dan Sullivan picked up Jason on June 27. The ride home was increasingly harrowing as an incoherent Molina grew ever more mentally distant by the minute. His counselor at the S.H.A.R.E. program had recommended intensive outpatient therapy. "When we got back to his apartment he was dying to get out of the truck," Sullivan said. "He was gracious but definitely didn't want to hang out." That was the last time Sullivan saw his friend Sparky.

Tom Colley's final exchange with Molina occurred back at West Suburban Medical Center. Molina had checked in July 5 after a disastrous encounter with Dan MacAdam, in which Molina was not just drunk but utterly poisoned. MacAdam recalled the gut-wrenching conversation where he insisted that Molina go to another rehab or care facility. "It was the worst three hours of my life," he said.

Gutted by Molina's bottle-shaped tunnel vision, Colley and Panall cleaned out what had become Molina's sad little apartment, smeared with blood and empty booze bottles. They brought Molina's clothes and a list of additional rehab options to the hospital. "He promised me that he would call me once he decided what to do," Colley added. "But he never did. It felt like a bit of a betrayal." Four days later, after a royalty payment from Secretly Canadian posted to his account, Molina checked out of the hospital and into a series of downtown Chicago hotels for the next week, including the Raffaello Hotel, the Holiday Inn Mart Plaza, and the La Quinta. His friends weren't able to reach him on his British iPhone or American burner phone but tracked his movements via his bank account. On July 18, Molina bought an Amtrak ticket after telling his sister Ashley that he was leaving the "bad city."

Molina blacked out in Chicago's Union station before he could board the Amtrak train and was sent to a local hospital. On July 20, Pete Schreiner received a call from Amtrak in New Orleans. The attendant explained that Molina's bag had made it down south to Louisiana without its owner. After being released from the hospital, on July 22 Molina boarded a second train to New Orleans.

By all accounts Molina bought a one-way ticket to New Orleans to die. And on the way he almost did die. In Carbondale, Illinois, Amtrak stopped the train for Molina after he'd begun vomiting blood and turning blue. An ambulance was waiting for him when he got off the train, and he spent two days in the hospital before getting back on the rails to New Orleans. When he arrived in the Big Easy, he became violently ill in the lobby bathroom of his favorite hotel—the luxurious Maison Dupuy hotel in the city's historic Vieux Carré district. He hadn't even checked into his room yet. A panicked employee swiftly dialed 911, and Molina was rushed to the intensive care unit at Tulane Hospital, where he stayed for eight days until he was completely flushed out and pumped full of vitamins and minerals.

Molina spoke with Darcie from the hospital when he was sober and feeling better and explained that he had gone to New Orleans because he wanted to go somewhere where he didn't know anyone. He talked about getting a job and looking for an apartment. He told her he didn't want any calls and wanted to be alone to figure out his next move. After wandering around the French Quarter for a few days, totally ashamed and lonely, Molina decided Bloomington might be the only place that would have him. Jonathan Cargill from Secretly Canadian agreed to allow Molina to stay with him for up to a week while he figured out what he wanted to do. And so Molina returned to the town, the label, and the friends that had launched and nurtured his career.

Jonathan Cargill, who served as the manager and liaison for Jason and Magnolia Electric Co. at Secretly Canadian, remembered talking to Darcie, who relayed that Molina was in New Orleans and planned to head to Bloomington. A few days after that conversation, Molina phoned Cargill, explaining that he'd arrive in Indianapolis the same night.

In the midst of his journey from New Orleans to Indianapolis, Molina was spotted at Union Station in Chicago by Rob Sullivan's friend, who immediately called Sullivan, Molina's former Songs: Ohia bass player and friend from Oberlin. "When I found him he looked kind of terrible but strangely happy," he said. He was wearing a white T-shirt, a vest, and a fedora, an embodiment of the lonesome troubadour image Molina embodied during this time. Sullivan took Molina for a meal at Lou Mitchell's diner in downtown Chicago, where Molina didn't touch his food. He explained to Sullivan that he hadn't been drinking. But when Sullivan pointed out the tall boys of Budweiser in Molina's open backpack, he admitted, "well just enough to manage." After listening to a string of wild stories, Sullivan handed his friend Sparky a twenty dollar bill and never saw him again.

Jonathan Cargill waited in suspense in Indianapolis for two hours as packed buses and trains pulled up, unloaded, and disappeared. Once the final train on the schedule emptied, he circled the periphery several times, searched the restrooms and halls, and had nearly bailed when Molina appeared out of nowhere, a sort of troubadour apparition in a backpack, mustache, vest, and fedora. "My first thought was that he looked like Snoopy's brother, Spike," Cargill remembered.

The palpable nervousness between them was mutual, as neither had seen the other in years, and Cargill was acutely aware of the hardships with Molina thus far. He recalled few niceties during the hour-long ride to Bloomington where Magnolia Electric Co. guitarist Jason Groth and Chris and Ben Swanson from the label joined the pair for brass tacks on Cargill's porch, demanding that Jason admit his problem. The conditions of Molina's stay at Cargill's house were outlined as follows:

1. Molina could stay at Jonathan Cargill's place for one week.
2. In that time he needed to find a job and a place to live.
3. If Molina got drunk at the house he was out.
4. No one would hang out with Molina if he was drunk.

Tough love was doled out in spades over the next nine days, Cargill acting as a father figure to his infantile friend and former bandmate. It's the reason Molina bestowed the nickname "the Defender" on Cargill. He removed all alcohol from his house except for a liter of vodka, which Cargill marked, in order to build an honor system. "I had one rule and that was I would prefer if you didn't drink, but if you need to drink don't hide it from me," he explained.

Molina agreed to the rule and even owned up to drinking too much, even though he blamed a list of fake ailments for his problems in Chicago and New Orleans, such as a new shellfish allergy triggered by lobster risotto. Cargill spent the next week engaging Molina in songwriting and conversation, while Jason Groth and Mikey Kapinus, who both lived in Bloomington, researched detox and rehab programs in the area. Molina even worked a few days in the Secretly Canadian warehouse, processing returns among other tasks, though that didn't last long after he was caught drinking on the job.

Jonathan Cargill and Jason Groth never saw Molina knocking back but were well aware that he was partaking in secret. The tear-inducing scent was unavoidable, and Molina's inebriation continued in its pattern of zero to sixty: one minute he'd be working on a song, and the next he'd be unable to hold a guitar. What astounded Cargill was how early Molina would drink. He recalled an attempt at an early breakfast at Wee Willy's, a favorite greasy spoon diner on Walnut Street. It was around 9 a.m., and Molina

Figure 11.4. Molina in Bloomington, Indiana, during his stay at Jonathan Cargill's house in 2011. *Photo courtesy of Jonathan Cargill*

couldn't sit up in the booth or enunciate well enough to order. Aside from the confrontation on the porch that first day, the Swansons had all but removed themselves from the situation, though they did have a positive lunch encounter with him on August 7. Cargill felt overwhelmed and disappointed, wrangling an incoherent Molina day and night. "This was the guy I admired, who was the cornerstone of Secretly Canadian, and here I am angry at him like a disappointed father because he's crawling around on my floor pissing himself," he explained.

There was a deficit of long-term rehabilitation programs in Bloomington, so Jason Groth, Cargill, and Darcie decided on Fairbanks in Indianapolis, which had a ten-day detox that would buy the three enough time to figure out a more permanent solution. The morning of August 16, Cargill awoke early, around 6 a.m., to discover that Molina wasn't home. He turned up back at the house just before Jason Groth arrived around 7 a.m., drunk and blabbing at the top of his lungs about how he needed to see a doctor.

The timing was perfect as the pair had planned to take Molina to rehab anyway, under the guise of a checkup. Molina handed Jason Groth a prescription from a doctor in New Orleans for something that contained thiamine as well as other supplements related to alcohol withdrawal, claiming it was for a shellfish allergy. When the pair explained that they had already planned to take him to the doctor that morning, Molina almost seemed excited and didn't resist until the trio crossed over State Road 46 while heading north on Walnut Street. "I swore he was going to jump out of the car," Groth explained. "But then he relaxed and said 'Is it inpatient? I don't know if I want to do inpatient.'"

On the hour-long ride to Indianapolis, Molina talked about how much he loved the R&B artist Sade and, upon arriving at his newest rehab center, pointed out the details of the corporate landscape and its "fake lake," an absurd and very Molina thing to do in the heavy situation.

He had a few tricks up his sleeve, too, and attempted to sabotage his intake by telling the nurse that he was bleeding "out both ends and the penis." Thankfully it wasn't her first rodeo, and she called Molina's bluff by sending him to the emergency room where he was deemed fit to be admitted. For Jason Groth, the experience was utterly surreal. "Lying naked in a hospital gown, with [Jonathan Cargill] and I in the room, he talked to us about the most normal stuff. It was as if we were backstage on tour somewhere, just lying down all drunk and sleep deprived and smelly, as if it was no problem at all." By the time Molina was admitted to Fairbanks, it was 4:30 p.m., and he was visibly ill and shaking uncontrollably. He hadn't drunk in at least nine hours but blew a .18 on the breathalyzer (in Indiana, the legal limit for driving is .08). In his room, Molina became terror stricken, and the three friends hugged repeatedly. Groth and Cargill then left to pick up a few things for Molina and used the time as a sort of catharsis and celebration of their friend, choosing items that they felt specifically suited him, including a wolf T-shirt, white tube socks, and a bandana, among other necessities.

As one day turned into ten at Fairbanks, Molina and his family decided it was best for him to be with his beloved grandmother Mary, to whom he was extremely close, and aunt Nancy in West Virginia. "The Indianapolis treatment wasn't working, and Jason wanted to try something completely different," his sister Ashley explained. There in the Mountain State was a Christian-based, thirteen-month inpatient rehabilitation facility that his grandmother, a woman of unwavering faith, had been pushing for. Soon after, Molina's aunt Mary Ellen flew to Indianapolis from her Florida home, and the pair then traveled to Brian's Safehouse in Mount Hope, West Virginia, a facility Molina grew to resent as a "fucking cult." He checked in at 3 p.m. on September 1 without any problems other than that he was running low on funds. The program took away his guitar, and friends and family were not allowed to visit for five weeks. After abruptly canceling his tour with Will Johnson two years prior and vanishing from his prolific writing pace, Molina decided to release his first public statement on Secretly Canadian's website:

> Many of you have inquired as to Jason's whereabouts and well-being since he canceled his tours with Will Johnson in 2009. Over the last two years Jason has been in and out of rehab facilities and hospitals in England, Chicago, Indianapolis, and New Orleans. It has been a very trying time for Jason, his friends, and his family. Although no one can be sure what the future holds, we feel very encouraged by the recent steps Jason has taken on the road towards becoming healthy and productive once again. Unfortunately, because he has no medical insurance, he has accrued substantial medical bills. We are asking all friends of Jason's music to come together with a showing of financial support for him.
>
> Please consider a contribution to his medical fund (via Paypal). Feel free to forward this to any and all appropriate parties. We are hoping to raise whatever funds we possibly can for Jason. He is currently working on a farm in West Virginia raising goats and chickens for the next year or so, and is looking forward to making great music again. Please also show your support and well wishes by sending letters and postcards to:
>
> Jason Molina
> P.O. Box 423
> Beaver, WV 25813
> If you do not wish to use Paypal, please make donations out to Ashley Lawson at the same address.
> With our sincere thanks,
> The Molina Family

Ashley explained that the correspondence Molina initially penned offered fans the chance to donate in exchange for original drawings and handwritten letters, but the label's legal department insisted on redacting that language for fear that Molina would not be able to deliver on such a promise. Nevertheless, fan mail poured into the P.O. box, much of which remains unanswered to this day, a source of anxiety for Ashley, a busy mother of two who also works full-time. One particularly ornate, hand-decorated envelope stood out to Ashley, and she found its contents touching. A woman in Tennessee wrote to Molina explaining that his music served as an indispensable source of comfort and encouragement during an abusive relationship. After listening to the Magnolia Electric Co. on repeat, the woman, who was pregnant, mustered the courage to leave her abuser and check into a women's shelter. A few months later she gave birth and named her daughter Magnolia.

Heaps of other letters arrived, some from friends such as Will Johnson and Mark Kozelek, who wrote to Molina explaining that he would be covering one of his songs. He wished him "love, peace and good thoughts" and included his address and phone number. In turn, Kozelek received from Molina what he described as "one beautiful and thoughtful letter and a painting" and added, "When I was told he was sick and was asked to contribute a song for a compilation to raise money, I said, 'If Jason is sick, I'm sending him a check right now. What's the address? Fuck waiting around for 20 artists to cover songs.'"

Molina wrote volumes of dispatches to family and friends to distract himself from his surroundings, keeping a notebook full of relevant addresses. Darcie in particular received a plethora of letters. "His handwriting was weak and shaky, his jokes weren't funny, his silly drawings were just weird, and his train of thought jumped from track to track and back again," she said. "In contrast to the many many funny, sweet letters he wrote me in the late '90s, these were just painful." A star appeared next to the following entry in his notebook: "Jason Groth/Jonathan Cargill, Best Friends/Owners of my Record Company." Ashley received piles of cartoons for Molina's two nieces and a message via letter including a threat that "Uncle Jason is going to crack skulls if he finds out you bought them Guitar Hero!" Despite making considerable progress, regaining color in his skin, and maintaining a healthy weight, Molina grew increasingly leery of the safe house's religious overtones and controlling staff, who censored his mail and wouldn't let him play music.

They firmly believed that the songs inside Molina drove him to drink. Molina became so desperate to connect with music again that he relented to attending church on Sundays so that he could sing hymns. He was made to read material such as worksheets titled "The Personality of the Holy Spirit in the New Testament," which explained, "Contrary to those who claim the Holy Spirit is only an energy force, the Bible clearly shows that the Holy Spirit has the attributes of a Persin [*sic*]."[5] On notecards Molina scrawled Bible verses such as Matthew 11:28: "Come to me, all you who labor and are heavy laden, and I will give you rest." On September 21, Molina was allowed his first family visitor because someone in the program "graduated." His grandmother, aunt, and uncle snapped a photo of Molina, whose face was full of color and whose head was full of hair again.

Molina received a letter from the artist William Schaff in January. He explained that the Kickstarter campaign for his book was nearing an end and that finally, after five years, their combined project of Molina's mini-album *Autumn Bird Songs* and Schaff's art book *From Black Sheep Boys to Bill Collectors* would be printed and produced that April of 2012 and see its official release in late September that same year. "I am really happy with how much we are going to be able to contribute to your medical fund," Schaff wrote. "I know that 2 grand and a bit ain't much, but still, know it's something." The eight songs Molina contributed for the mini-LP were comprised of just his voice over acoustic guitar, a return to the rough and contemplative posture of *Let Me Go, Let Me Go, Let Me Go*. It sounded more like solo Molina demos than Songs: Ohia and Magnolia Electric Co. songs, but uniquely reflected the fragility of his state when he captured them, as early as five years prior.

That spring of 2012, Molina was diagnosed with MRSA at a neighboring hospital after noticing rather gruesome spots on his skin. Once out of the confines of Brian's Safehouse, the Craftsman-style prison overlooking the Appalachians, Molina refused to return. He proceeded to bounce between his aunt's and grandma's houses until he was kicked out for good for drinking, after which he stowed away in a local bowling alley where he downed shot after shot of whiskey.

Molina wasn't totally broke, but the money that came in did help to pay for his treatment and commensurate living expenses in between royalty checks. It also served as a point of difficulty between Molina and his sister Ashley, when he'd call begging for money and she knew it was for alcohol. Her strategy was to pay his bills directly and divvy out very small amounts of money at a time, or take him shopping herself when he was in West Virginia. She recalled one instance at a local shopping mall where her older brother argued the merits of two-hundred-dollar boots, laughing about how he had a preference for "quality items" until his last days.

After Molina passed away, there was considerable theorizing and stone casting in the press about his lack of medical insurance in the United States and how it ultimately led to his downfall. But Darcie and Molina's friends and family maintain that Molina was his own worst enemy and had ample opportunities to choose to commit to rehabilitation programs in the UK and the United States, which weren't covered completely if at all by insurance. In London, Molina's coverage under the national health-care system didn't extend to his first stint in rehab. Those costs came straight out of his and Darcie's combined incomes, which would have been fine had Molina stuck to it.

A hardship much bigger than his lack of health insurance was that once he'd exhausted his options in London and had failed in his rehabilitation attempts in Chicago, Darcie made the incredibly difficult decision that she and Jason should get divorced so they could both move on with their lives. During a March 17 phone call, she explained to Molina that he couldn't come back to London. The news came as a complete shock to Molina, much to Darcie's surprise, and he didn't take it well. Though they fought on the phone, she explained that she loved him very much, and not wanting to stay married would never change that. Once he relented to the idea that London was no longer an option, the two remained in contact until his last days. Darcie often wrote to Molina to explain that she was thinking of him or proud of him when he was having "good" periods. In her heart she'd always hoped he could pull through. The divorce was never finalized.

After the phone call, Darcie cut Molina off financially. Because he couldn't tour, he wasn't making any money on the road, and he received royalty checks just four times a year from Secretly Canadian. Notoriously bad with money his entire life, at thirty-eight Jason had no savings and no structure or resources to save. In the States he was living hand to mouth, though Darcie did continue to cover his bills during his time in Chicago. In April, from a hotel in West Virginia, Molina wrote to Jason Groth explaining that he was headed back to Fairbanks in Indianapolis under the orchestration of his sister Ashley and bankrolled in part by the donations he had received from friends and fans. After initial talks with his grandmother and aunt about going to Butler Hospital in Providence, Rhode Island, where his brother Aaron now lived, Molina decided that he wanted to try Indianapolis again. What he didn't know was that it would be the last stop on the Molina rehabilitation tour.

⑫

INDIANAPOLIS

After rehab attempts in London, Chicago, Indianapolis, and West Virginia—with a surprise stopover in New Orleans—Jason Molina returned to Indiana's capital, finally willing to do the work. He checked in under the care of Fairbanks in April 2012. He settled into a shared apartment on the northeast side of the city in the Castleton neighborhood, an upper-middle-class enclave dotted with shopping malls and Starbucks. He described the program as "a supportive recovery project that is half hospital nut house and half safe house."[1]

Shortly after arriving he wrote to Jason Groth on April 11, "It is crazy to wake up everyday and be on tour but not on tour. For the first time in my life I am voluntarily leaving behind my guitar, so you know when I get out I'll need an acoustic. Think of me. Not the bad me. Not the sick me, but the simple against all odds me."[2]

After starting the new program at Fairbanks, Molina was stable. He was poor—"butt poor," as Molina would say—but receiving assistance through food stamps and the remaining funds from the donations he'd received. Pete Schreiner visited Molina in Indianapolis shortly after he began rehab. The two friends commiserated over coffee at a Starbucks, and the mood was largely positive. He explained to Schreiner that his group rehab was helping him, though he was frustrated with the shared living situation, which required him to play a mentor role to some of the other guys in the program. The same day, the pair drove south to Bloomington to visit Jason Groth and Mark Rice from Magnolia, and a few other Bloomington friends.

Groth, Rice, Schreiner, and Molina then headed back north to Indianapolis and broke bread at Molina's favorite deli, Shapiro's. Even though it was a happy and heartfelt reunion, Molina turned down the offer to catch the Coke Dares that evening in Indianapolis, for fear he might relapse. He knew his limitations, and being in a room full of people drinking was one them.

Soon after Schreiner's visit, Molina penned his first message to his fans since being confined at Brian's Safehouse in West Virginia. It was posted to Secretly Canadian's website on May 5.

Dear friends and family.

It has been a long hospital year. You all have done so much and given so much to further my cause on this planet that I feel compelled to give you a little note. The response towards my medical fund and other support has been better than I could have ever imagined. I spent my time on the farm which was more like the opposite of a tour of duty, but it was good in its way. I have been moved around quite a bit too, Chicago, England, Indiana, West Virginia and back and forth to each. For the time being I am doing well, still in recovery and still in treatment until probably the summer does its thing. I've been writing a lot of music and eagerly anticipate the new 10" with Will Schaff's book, word is that end of May we might finally get them. It is slow going, but it is going. I did write about 500 letters to many of you who sent me good wishes and more, oddly the facility I was in decided to keep them all instead of sending them. I'll start re-collecting post box information when I am in a place for any length of time. Treatment is good, getting to deal with a lot of things that even the music didn't want to. I have not given up because you, my friends have not given up on me. I do still need your support however that takes shape, good vibes are worth more than you might think. Finally, there are actually some musical projects on the distant radar screen, but for those who understand, I am taking this in much smaller steps than I'm used to. Keep the lamps trimmed and burning!

JM
5 May 2012
Indianapolis

Much like his trajectory in Chicago, where he tended to stay sober under constant watch, Molina's rehab progress pedaled backward when he moved out of the shared living facility associated with the Fairbanks program. Over the summer of 2012, he got his own studio apartment at 7871 Musket Street, a stone's throw from Community Hospital North in Indianapolis. There, he began drinking again and hanging out with people he probably shouldn't have been, guys who were battling their own addictions and weren't a very good influence. Molina sent a few e-mails to Darcie regretfully explaining as much, but reassured her that he was doing his best to write songs. Before Molina was ever sick, he told Darcie on many occasions that if there was ever a time that he couldn't write songs or play music, he would die, and not in a metaphorical sense. He said that writing songs was the only thing that kept him alive. And even in his worst states, his songwriting wheels continuously spun, even if his limited dexterity could not keep up. "It was never a hobby, and it wasn't something he did because he didn't want a real job," Darcie explained. "It was in his DNA."

In e-mails, Molina explained that he'd been watching that summer's Olympic Games, broadcast from London, and had dyed his hair to look like David Bowie. Reading Tina Fey's *Bossypants* reignited his interest in comedy, and he began working on a comedy album while in his rehab program. During his stay, he recorded a few short a capella songs about food. In a Svengoolie-esque voice, he also sang a capella a song he called "Another Crappy Christmas Is Here." In it he replaced the traditional days of Christmas with things like "taking off my pants," "sleeping at the mall," and "PANCAKES!" Chris Swanson from Secretly Canadian thought that at the time of the recording Molina didn't have the dexterity to play guitar. He added that Molina speaking in voices was nothing new, and to his mind it wasn't a by-product of mental illness. "There wasn't a car ride or hang with him where he wouldn't take the Elmo voice to new heights," Swanson said. "The humor was consistent with the Jason I knew."

In late June, Jason wrote again to Jeff Panall, former Songs: Ohia drummer, explaining that now that he had finished treatment, he had plenty of time to reflect. "I am slowly getting enough together to look now at myself and my current life," he said. "It is so hard being alone, I've not really been single in about 15 years, so I get too much time thinking about how fucked up I have been, but that is all over now. I'm playing of all things: a ukulele again. Got a really good one cheap and it just feels right and good."[3]

Chris Swanson visited Molina in July, and they listened to the comedy album he'd recorded. They called it *The Hospital Record*. After playing its eleven minutes, Molina pressed Swanson about what he wanted to do with it, as if it was another album in the can that SC should release. "It was funny and weird and definitely part of the story," Swanson explained. "But it was tough because it was a man who was definitely compromised."

In the conversation, Swanson tried to remain positive and explained to Molina that it was really unique but that it might be heavily scrutinized—

something he might not be ready for in his somewhat fragile state. Swanson was concerned that the press might view it as exploitative, or peg Molina with a Daniel Johnston or Roky Erickson–type mental illness narrative. In an effort to discourage Molina to release *The Hospital Record*, Swanson suggested they release it on cassette, like the old DIY days of the '90s. At first Molina took to the idea and began crafting hundreds of hand-drawn covers, traced from a credit card and adorned with sketchy abstract drawings done in crayon.

During the visit with Swanson, Molina drank a mixture of Gatorade, Coke, and whiskey. Despite the singer's inebriated state, it was the last positive visit Swanson recalled having with his flagship artist. Molina even gave him a copy of Willa Cather's novel *My Antonia*, a generous act that signaled the old Molina still lived inside the frail man before him. When Swanson left, Molina asked when he'd visit again and if he'd send more friends to hang out with. Swanson left promising to return soon with furniture, as Molina's apartment was bare.

A few days later Swanson and Mikey Kapinus from Magnolia Electric Co. reappeared with a mattress, books, comics, CDs, DVDs, and a chair. Molina had just gotten out of the hospital after breaking his foot and was hobbling around his bare-bones apartment. He was disheveled and, in general, seemed in a bad state. The pair took him to Olive Garden for lunch and then to CVS where Molina bought a six-pack of beer. Before they left, Molina attempted to give Kapinus his nicest tape recorder, which he'd been using sporadically to record new songs. At first moved by Molina's unwavering generosity, Kapinus soon thought better of it, knowing Molina could use the distraction from drinking.

About a month later, Molina contacted Swanson and said he didn't want to release *The Hospital Record*. He'd been working on other material with his home recording setup.

Though he was drinking, Molina worked on songs with his ukulele and an acoustic guitar Jeff Panall had mailed to him from Chicago. In notebooks he wrote out the lyrics and chords to "Hickory Wind" by Gram Parsons, "Wild Horses" by Mick Jagger and Keith Richards, and "Stardust" by Hoagy Carmichael, its lyrics a clear testament to his mourning the loss of his marriage.

Molina also wrote out lists of artists and albums. Among them were Randy Newman, Leon Russell, Nick Lowe, Dr. John, Leon Redbone, Harry Nilsson, Gerry Rafferty, Skip Spence's *Oar*, Colin Blunstone, Love's *Forever Changes*, Television, Patti Smith, CAN, Silver Apples, and the Vaselines. In a separate notebook, he mentioned Steve Earle and Tom Waits, two heralded and famously alcoholic songwriters who no longer drink.

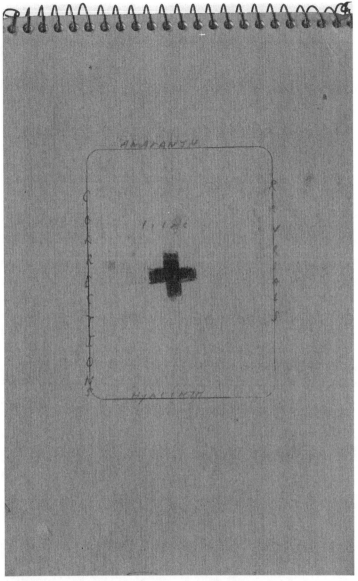

Figure 12.1. One of Molina's last notebooks. *Notebook courtesy of Aaron Molina*

The words of poets, including Robert Lowell, Elizabeth Bishop, Roethke, and John Berryman, appeared handwritten in his notebooks, as did passages of famed occultists, mostly French, including Jules Bois, Jacques Collin de Plancy, and Louis-Claude de Saint Martin. He listed the ingredients of essential oil tinctures and herbal concoctions for spell casting.

Most importantly, he wrote songs again: guitar-and-voice compositions, a return to form for Molina. Two subjects that appeared throughout his last notebooks are something he called the Harper Doe, as well as a woman's name, Mirabel. He also dove back into some of his favorite symbols: the moon, the number 8 train, wolves, ghosts, and owls. He also wrote of someone he called an Anchoress.

In his last notebooks live pages of short songs traversing these themes, a couple with the word *Master* written above them, meaning he'd recorded them to tape and sent them to Secretly Canadian. "Mirabel" acts as a sort of lament of his mistakes and the loss of his marriage. In the song he addresses Darcie directly by using the name Josephine and worries that she now hates him. "The Harper Doe" is similarly shorter in length and sorrowful in tone. In it he explains that no one can keep his heart, in between recounting experiences with wolves, anchors, and the conductor of the number 8 train. "Hawk and Buckle" and "Anne Biahayha" again reference his sorrow, the moon, and a woman named Anne. Whether the reference is to Anne Grady remains unknown.

Molina provided a series of tapes to Secretly Canadian with intent to release them as two sides of a 7" single under a new name, Magnolia Engine Works. This proposal was particularly touching to the band Magnolia, since it indicated that "Magnolia" had special significance to Molina, that their bond really meant something, enough for Molina to carry it through to new works.

Though he was convening with his notepads and guitar again and creating work in line with his past successes, Molina continued to drink, and in excess. What he didn't realize was that the drinking would very soon catch up to him. His body couldn't take much more.

On March 16, 2013, at 7:12 p.m., a fifty-five-year-old man named Michael Pettijohn called the Indianapolis Metropolitan Police Department to report finding Jason Molina dead. Pettijohn, who as of March 2016 lived at the Street Reach homeless shelter in Myrtle Beach, South Carolina, told the police he was a friend of Molina's and had spoken to him the day before. None of Molina's friends or family members know Pettijohn, who told the police that he occasionally stayed with Molina when he was in Indianapolis. When Pettijohn showed up to Molina's place that evening, the door was unlocked but latched from the inside. Upon arrival the coroner declared Molina's death due to natural causes.

Mikey Kapinus recalled that Molina was out of communication with his friends for the last months of his life, oscillating between turned off cell service and turned off Internet service. Molina's brother Aaron had spoken to him two days prior to his death after conducting a wellness check with the police. In the last weeks of Molina's life, Aaron often called the Indianapolis police when Molina wouldn't answer the phone. He described the two-hour waiting period, from the time he called the police to the time he was asked to call back after they'd checked on Molina, as thoroughly harrowing. He added that he knew Molina was in a bad place, as was his tendency when he'd become noncommunicative, but he never expected that his body was ready to give out. That spring, knowing of Molina's declined state and sporadic communication, Chris Swanson had been putting a plan in place to move him back to Bloomington, as life alone in his apartment in Indianapolis clearly wasn't working. Molina had been bucking between it and the emergency room at nearby Community Hospital North all winter.

The coroner in Indianapolis contacted Molina's grandmother in West Virginia after finding her phone number in Molina's cell phone. This of course doesn't account for the lists of friend and family phone numbers Molina had written in notebooks, as his Luddite tendencies often prevented him from learning or wanting to learn new technology, such as entering phone numbers into cell phones. The frequency with which he lost and misplaced cell phones often prevented him from spending too much time on their setup as well.

After the police reached Molina's grandmother Mary, word spread to Molina's aunt and sister Ashley, then to Darcie, his father Bill, Jason Groth, Jonathan Cargill, Chris Swanson, and the rest of the members of the Magnolia Electric Co. The plan for publicly releasing the information was to have Secretly Canadian issue an official statement so that details of Molina's death would not be misreported or misconstrued. But first, Jason Groth and Darcie worked together to compile a list of names of friends and family members they wanted to contact in person to make sure they heard the news from them directly, before it reached the Internet. During each call they explained the situation and asked each person not to share the information until they were sure all of Molina's family and close friends had been made aware. They explained that they had been working with the label to draft an official statement to the public, and to not write anything or post anything on the Internet until the statement came out.

The last person to make Darcie and Jason Groth's list was Henry Owings, the friend of Molina's who had designed the cover of the Magnolia Electric Co. compilation album *Fading Trails* and who sang onstage with Magnolia Electric Co. during his wedding celebration in 2004. Darcie remembered that Owings and Molina were friends and asked Jason Groth to call him with the information they had been passing on. Jason Groth remembered that when he relayed the news, he and Owings both broke down in tears. Owings asked why the authorities called Molina's grandmother. "I said I think that was the only number he had in his cell phone," Groth explained.

"To me that wasn't a surprise because Jason lost so many cell phones, and Henry knew that." He remembered asking Owings not to do anything with the information and not to write anything about it. He offered to text him as soon as Secretly Canadian made the announcement.

Owings remembered having a quick exchange with Jason Groth on the phone. "He just said, 'Jason's dead,'" Owings recalled. "I can't remember the exact words, but it was something like 'he did it' or 'it happened.' You just dread those calls." He then remembered hanging up, saying good-bye to his wife and young daughter as they headed out the door, and then sitting down and crying. He explained that he felt like he didn't do enough. "In light of that, emotionally, I was really hot under the collar," he said. "I can't remember exactly what I wrote, but I remember just being really fucking angry. I remember thinking, 'god damnit Jason,' and I typed that into Twitter." He then called a few local friends who knew Molina, like the owner of the 40 Watt Club in Athens, where Molina had played more shows than could be counted on two hands.

He then posted a eulogy to Molina on his website, chunklet.com. He explained that it was an avenue to allow everything that was in his head to flow out and added that he wanted the message to come from the heart and not a press release. On March 18 Owings wrote a blog post that included the following passage:

> Even with all of his friends never leaving his side, he cashed out on Saturday night in Indianapolis with nothing but a cell phone in his pocket with only his grandmother's number on it. Of course, she was the first to be dealt the tragic news.

> Jason leaves behind him an enviable body of work that will be continually rediscovered because what Jason wrote wasn't fashion. It was his heart. It was his love. It was his demons. And ultimately, it brought his life to an end.

Music news outlets stretching from the United States to the UK almost immediately picked up on the post. Websites such as *Pitchfork*, *NME*, *Paste Magazine*, and the *AV Club* all recycled the line about the cell phone, and today the line, and Owings name, continue to live online in tandem with Molina's death. "Was I thinking in terms of anything other than my emotions and the loss of a friend? No," Owings explained. "In retrospect could I have done things differently? Sure."

Jason Groth still lives with the guilt of having provided the misrepresented intel for the infamous line. "Sometimes when I'm showering in the morning and I'm thinking about this, because that happens, I feel so bad," he lamented. "Because had I not called that dude, it would not have turned out that way . . . it would not have been the first thing that informed all of those other things." Owings added that if he had in any way hurt Darcie or Molina's family, he would apologize until his "heart bled."

In response to the rapidly firing news of Molina's death, Secretly Canadian hustled to post the following statement:

We are deeply saddened to announce that Jason Andrew Molina passed away in his home in Indianapolis this past Saturday, March 16th of natural causes at age 39. Jason was a world class musician, songwriter & recording artist. He was also a beloved friend. He first caught international attention in 1996 when he began releasing albums under the name Songs: Ohia. In 2003 he started the band Magnolia Electric Co. Between those two bands he released over a dozen critically-acclaimed albums and—starting in 1997—he toured the world every year until he had to stop in 2009 to deal with severe alcoholism. Jason was incredibly humbled by his fans' support through the years and said that the two most important words he could ever say are "Thank you."

This is especially hard for us to share. Jason is the cornerstone of Secretly Canadian. Without him there would be no us—plain and simple. His singular, stirring body of work is the foundation upon which all else has been constructed. After hearing and falling in love with the mysterious voice on his debut single "Soul" in early 1996, we approached him about releasing a single on our newly formed label. For some reason he said yes. We drove from Indiana to New York to meet him in person, and he handed us what would become the first of many JMo master tapes. And with the Songs: Ohia *One Pronunciation of Glory* 7" we were given a voice as a label. The subsequent self-titled debut was often referred to by fans as the *Black Album*. Each Songs: Ohia album to follow proved a new, haunting thesis statement from a prodigal songwriter whose voice and soul burned far beyond that of the average twenty-something. There was organ-laced, sepia-toned economica (1998's *Impala*) and charred-hearted, free-form balladry (1999's *Axxess and Ace*). There were the dark glacial make-out epics of 2000's *The Lioness* and the jungle incantations of 2000's *Ghost Tropic*. There was the career-defining agnostic's gospel of 2002's *Didn't It Rain*, an album about setting roots that also seemed to offer solace to a world that had recently seen its bar on terror raised. It was followed in 2003 by a thrilling about-face, the instant classic Magnolia Electric Co., which took Jason's songwriting to '70s classic rock heights. The move was such a powerful moment for Molina that Magnolia Electric Co. became the new moniker under which he would perform until 2009. With Magnolia Electric Co., Jason found a brotherhood in his bandmates, with whom he built an incredible live experience and made a truly classic album in *Josephine* (2009).

We're going to miss Jason. He was generous. He was a one of a kind. And he had a voice unlike any other.

A few days after Molina died, Jason Groth and Jonathan Cargill from Secretly Canadian traveled north to Indianapolis from Bloomington to clean out Molina's apartment, where they found a sad room covered in blood, cigarette butts, and music magazine cuttings, but also a corner recording setup and a few new tapes. A pot of old spinach and chickpeas sat on the stove, a sign of one of Molina's many attempts to improve his health through avenues other than quitting drinking.

Today, Molina's complete works, including live shows, master tapes, and unreleased material, lives in a massive collection at Secretly Canadian's headquarters. It spans Molina's earliest recordings with his high school bands the Spineriders, Green, and Bleem, very early Songs: Ohia demos, songs written for solo projects and Magnolia Electric Co., and material that runs all the way to his last days in Indianapolis. That Molina was famously prolific is no simple anecdote; it is estimated that the label has about one hundred tapes, containing masters for many unreleased demos, as well as studio material that was never released. One such demo project was something Molina called Lamb and Flag, which were songs he had written and intended to perform with Duluth, Minnesota–based indie-rock act Low. The unreleased Magnolia Engine Works project remains in the collection as well.

The hand-drawn and assembled paper materials that composed the covers of many of Jason's albums are also at SC headquarters, including the drawings provided by Molina's friend William Schaff for the front and back covers of *The Magnolia Electric Co.*, which were scaled for CD and LP. There's the postcard of palm trees that graces the cover of *The Lioness*, as well as handwritten instructions from Molina for how he wanted the disc to appear. "S:O pretty large + my name rather large as well (for ego reasons)," he wrote in a sketch of the *Lioness* CD. The doily and the pin from the *Josephine* cover rests with its respective archive, as does the inspiration for the *Sojourner* box.

Molina's body was cremated, and vessels for his remains were designed and produced by William Schaff at the request of Molina's family. He crafted one wooden box for each of Jason's siblings and one for Darcie. Each family member chose symbols for Schaff to draw, which illustrated their personal relationship with Molina—owls, moons, and the number 8 train, among them. On Darcie's box is a drawing of the couple's black-and-white tuxedo cat Bhaji, who died in April 2014, one year after Molina. She's convinced that their cat child was therapeutic to Molina in his darkest hours, and she admits she wouldn't have made it through all the tumult without him.

A memorial service for friends and family was held May 11, 2013, in Bloomington at the Buskirk Chumley Theater. Brothers Chris and Ben Swanson from Secretly Canadian spoke, as did Molina's brother Aaron; Tom Colley from the Chicago-based, Oberlin-originated friend crew; and Darcie. At the service, members of Magnolia Electric Co. and Songs: Ohia performed covers of their favorite songs from Molina's oeuvre, like "Blue Factory Flame," "Dogwood Gap," Tenskwatawa," "The Big Game Is Every Night," "Bowery," "Just Be Simple," "The Pyre," "Whip-Poor-Will," "Shenandoah," and "Northstar Blues." Versions of "Hold on Magnolia" bookended the service. Jonathan Cargill's cover of "Soul" sent shockwaves through the room. Not many had heard Cargill sing before, and his vocal resemblance to Molina was uncanny. It was as if Jason was singing through his "Defender." Max Winter from the Oberlin College friend group penned a tribute to his friend Sparky and posted it online. It stands out among friends and family as an astute characterization of Molina:

> I think it's fair to say that we all saw different sides of him. And, in turn, Jason, who was uncommonly perceptive, sensed this and showed each of us the side that we were already predisposed to see most clearly and respond to most honestly. He was as complex a man as I have ever known. "Just Be Simple"? Sure, it's a great song, but, yeah, right. Sparky was about as far from simple as they come. He was large and multitudinous: commensurately inspiring and frustrating, goofy and gloomy, spontaneous and studied, generous and self-absorbed, loyal and flaky, wise and naive, trusting and paranoid, outgoing and reserved, honest and totally full of shit, and every blessed and profane thing in between. And it's all there in his music.

The same night the group from the private memorial convened with extended friends and fans at the Bluebird nightclub in Bloomington for a wider celebration of Jason's life. Dave Doughman of Swearing at Motorists, Edith Frost, and members of Molina's high school band the Spineriders, among others, took to the stage to perform their favorite Molina songs. The evening culminated in a four-song sweep from *The Magnolia Electric Co.*, with members of Songs: Ohia who recorded the album at Electrical Audio, along with Jason Groth, Mark Rice, and Pete Schreiner from Magnolia, taking the stage. For the song "Farewell Transmission," "Old Black Hen" singer Lawrence Peters stepped in for Molina behind the microphone, with backing assistance from Jennie Benford. "I don't want it to end," Benford said as the song concluded. Traditional funeral services for family members were held at Boyer & Cool Home for Funerals in Lorain, Ohio, on March 23.

Figure 12.2. Jennie Benford and Lawrence Peters from the Magnolia Electric Co. session sing "Farewell Transmission" with backing by Dan MacAdam, Rob Sullivan, Pete Schreiner, and Jason Groth. *Photo by Robert Loerzel*

In the wake of Molina's death, innumerable online tributes spread in waves throughout the Internet, forming a sort of collective memorial tide pool, its many artists and writers and fans comprising a unique coterie of residents united under a love of Molina. Memorial albums sprang up, too, with friends and fans covering songs from Molina's catalog. William Schaff worked with Graveface Records, the label that issued Jason's *Autumn Bird Songs* with William's art book, to produce *Weary Engine Blues*, a thirty-six-track album that includes covers by Alasdair Roberts, Scout Niblett, Damien Jurado, Will Johnson, and Mark Kozelek, who chose to cover Jason's song "It's Easier Now." "My guess is that Jason was suffering badly," Kozelek explained. "'It's Easier Now' is probably how it is, when you're suffering badly, and you finally go." Will Oldham contributed "The Gypsy He-Witch," a song he recorded during the Amalgamated Sons of Rest session in 2001, with Molina and Alasdair Roberts. With the release, William Schaff included an intricate hand-drawn map he'd made for Molina when he was alive and struggling, which never made it to Molina amid his rehabilitation journey. In a press release for the album, Schaff explained,

Back in January of this year [2013], I received a message from a friend of Jason's, Tara Samaha. Like so many of us were, she was concerned. She was concerned for his safety, mental and physical health after receiving an alarming email. She felt he needed a map to help him through these troubled times and then asked that I make him one. I did. Sadly we were never able to land a concrete address for Jason, where we knew he would get the map. I know that he had lost things important to him over the past few years, for various reasons, so I wanted to be sure this got into his hands, and no one else. That said—sadly—the map was never delivered to him.

Upon learning of his death, the map sat in my studio; it felt cold, and now useless. A guide made for a friend who can no longer see it. Ryan Graveface and I thought of how, thanks to folks like you, we were able to raise a considerable amount of money for Jason's medical bills through sales of the book, *From Black Sheep Boys to Bill Collectors*. We thought maybe there is still a way for this map to be useful. Not as it was originally intended, a map for one man, but as a tool to commemorate this man, and continue to help his family, especially in such dark times as these. 100% of the profits from this print will be going to Jason Molina's family. We now have a chance to give back to the family that gave us Jason, who in turn gave us all so much.

Another tribute album, *Farewell Transmission*, features an electronic rendering of the album's namesake by Louisville indie-rock band My Morning Jacket, who recorded a split EP with Molina, before they were selling out massive theaters and headlining Lollapalooza. "*The Magnolia Electric Co.* album is one of the greatest albums of all time, start to finish," My Morning Jacket frontman Jim James said. "He has songs that I cherish and love from other works, but this album I hope becomes known in a broader way as time goes on." James added that he often thinks of Jason being "reborn," maybe with the same problems, but that in his next life, "the world may have evolved enough that he can get the help he needs, deal with and conquer his demons and live a long and happy life."

The tribute album *Through the Static and the Distance: The Songs of Jason Molina* featured Molina's friends Dan Sullivan, performing under his solo moniker Nad Navillus; Peter Hess; and Eoin Russell from the *Black Album*. Other tribute albums poured in from musicians stretching from Texas to the UK. Live tributes were played at clubs all over North America, from Charlotte, North Carolina, to Maine and all the way to Seattle. So much money was raised through commemorative efforts that Molina's family was able to pay off all of Molina's medical bills, legal fees related to his estate, and even the travel costs for his family members traveling to and from his funeral services. The Molina family received enough queries

Figure 12.3.   The map drawn by William Schaff for Molina. *Drawing courtesy of William Schaff*

that Darcie began referring interested donors to charities like MusiCares, which provides financial assistance to musicians for medical bills and drug rehabilitation programs.

Surprise televised tributes were aired as well. Band of Horses played "I've Been Riding with the Ghost" from *Magnolia Electric Co.* on the Jimmy Kimmel late-night show on April 20, 2013, proudly wearing black-and-white Magnolia Electric Co. T-shirts. Later, Glen Hansard rounded up the cast from his first-ever session at Electrical Audio for one of The Late Show icon David Letterman's last broadcasts. On Tuesday March 17, 2015, Hansard, vocalist Jennie Benford, Dan Sullivan, his brother Rob Sullivan, drummer Jeff Panall, and Rob Bochnik from the Frames, who engineered

Hansard's first Electrical session, played "Being in Love" from *The Lioness*. It was to mark the release of Hansard's Molina tribute album, *It Was Triumph We Once Proposed . . . Songs of Jason Molina*.

For the album, the same group convened at the Wilco recording loft in Chicago, where Jeff Tweedy volunteered engineering time to record its five tracks as a tribute to Molina. By the time the album was released, Molina's medical bills were squared away. As such, Hansard plans to donate the proceeds to build a Jason Molina memorial rehearsal space at Oberlin College, Molina's alma mater.

In its tribute to Molina, the *New York Times* deemed Jason a "Balladeer of Heartbreak" and a trailblazer for acts such as Mumford & Sons, which he would have hated. Those who knew Molina, and those who knew him through his music, remember his song craft and its intrinsic work ethic as unique, undying, and inspiring as his spirit, which lives on among his friends and admirers who continue to speak his name and sing his songs. A seemingly endless trail of live recordings, handmade protection spells, drawings, and historical trinkets and ephemera that Molina left behind provide a constant source of sleuthing and story swapping for fans and family members alike, a sort of curated legacy meant to be continuously unlocked.

"I was just very caught off guard," Mark Kozelek explained. "My memories of him are positive and uplifting. He was just so young, and such a nice person." In response to the news, Kozelek wrote a song he titled "Sometimes I Can't Stop." It appeared on his collaborative album with indie-rock band Dessertshore, which was released August 20, 2013. In its lyrics Kozelek explained that he couldn't understand why the world takes away the good ones and repeated his observation that Molina's life was like the line from *To Kill a Mockingbird*, that Molina was innocent and only wanted to sing his heart.

Despite the downtrodden tag that was so often affixed to Molina, the real tragedy of Jason Molina lives not in his songs but in his short life, and the many songs he would never get the chance to write. His only personal measure for success was in his continued ability to create, and only in the loss of that ability did he lose hope. Only then did he become "paralyzed by the emptiness," as he sang in "Blue Factory Flame," a song in which he also clearly laid out his last wishes:

> When I die
> Put my bones in an empty street
> To remind me of how it used to be
> Don't write my name on a stone

Bring a Coleman lantern and a radio
Cleveland game and two fishing poles
And watch with me from the shore
Ghostly steel and iron ore ships coming home

No matter how far he'd come, or the extent to which he struggled, Jason Molina from Ohio remained proudly rooted in the trailer park shores of his childhood. Today, his spirit stands tall in its breezes. Near the facility where his mother Karen passed away, and a stone's throw from where the fabled old man Mean Joe lived, the branches of a towering silver maple tree skitter in Lake Erie's winds. It grew from a sapling the Molinas planted more than forty years ago, when young Jason scoured the shoreline for treasure and performed songs for anyone who'd listen. With his kid-sized shovel, Molina dug the hole that incubated the tree sapling, which germinated from a fallen helicopter seed near the Molina trailer.

Like the tree's roots that burrow through the landscape of his youth, Molina's body of work continues to take root in the collective consciousness of independent music fans and makers across the globe, its poetic themes of simplicity, love, loss, and hard work as relatable as they are mysterious, as forlorn as they are hopeful. "I built my life out of what was left of me / And a map of the old horizon," Molina once sang. Though he's gone, his catalog lives to be rediscovered, the songs animating his character—Molina via moons, stars, wolves, trains, and hard work—steered by plaintive tenor guitar and electrified country. What's left of Molina is an alluring and tragic sonic map, filled with twists and turns, with triumphs and tribulations and every uplifting and sorrowful thing between them, from the heavy metal bass player to the many-sided man with the big voice.

NOTES

This book is based largely on original interviews conducted with numerous family members, friends, bandmates, and colleagues of Jason Molina between 2013 and 2016. All quotations not otherwise cited throughout this book come directly from these original interviews. I was also provided access to the Molina archive at Secretly Canadian. Direct quotes from Molina were sourced from previously published material, as well as e-mails, letters, and video footage provided by sources.

CHAPTER I

1. From original interview with Ashley Lawson.
2. Jason Molina, as quoted in "Deepening the Mysteries of Ohia," *Wingnut* fanzine, vol. 3, 1996.
3. Ibid.
4. Ibid.
5. Ibid.
6. Jason Molina, as quoted in Dylan Metrano, "Meet Me Where We Survive, Jason Molina Interviews," chapbook printed in 2015.
7. Jason Molina, as quoted in "Deepening the Mysteries of Ohia," *Wingnut* fanzine, vol. 3, 1996.

CHAPTER 2

1. Jason Molina, as quoted in "Deepening the Mysteries of Ohia," *Wingnut* fanzine, vol. 3, 1996.

2. Reilly Lambert, as quoted in the Spineriders bio for Misra Records, July 24, 2014, http://oldsite.misrarecords.com/tag/lorain-ohio.

3. Jason Molina, as quoted in an interview for a student video project by RAW, 1997, https://www.youtube.com/watch?v=GpG8Te3WxJc.

CHAPTER 3

1. Jason Molina, in a recording of the WOBC broadcast by Tom Colley, October 18, 1994.

2. Ibid.

3. Ibid.

4. Jason Molina, as quoted in "Schubas Backstage Interview with Jason Molina Part 1 of 2," https://www.youtube.com/watch?v=HIEcLcES3lU.

5. Jason Molina, as quoted in "Deepening the Mysteries of Ohia," *Wingnut* fanzine, vol. 3, 1996.

6. Will Oldham, postcard to Jason Molina, August 30, 1995.

7. Jason Molina, as quoted in an interview for a student project by RAW, 1997, https://www.youtube.com/watch?v=GpG8Te3WxJc.

8. Jason Molina, e-mail to Edith Frost, October 7, 1996.

9. Jason Molina, postcard to Anne Grady, July 1996.

CHAPTER 4

1. "The Midwest Has a New Music Haven: Indiana," *Billboard*, May 4, 1996.

2. Ibid.

3. Jason Molina, letter to Anne Grady, July 31, 1996.

4. Jason Molina, letter to Anne Grady, July 1996.

5. Jackie Linge, as quoted in "College Students to Appear on National Talk Show," *Oberlin Review*, February 14, 1997.

CHAPTER 5

1. Jason Molina, letter to Anne Grady, July 1997.

2. Jason Molina, letter to Anne Grady, September 1997.

3. Ibid.

4. Ibid.

5. "Songs: Ohia Impala," *CMJ New Music Monthly*, July 1998.

6. Jason Molina, letter to Anne Grady, TK date.

7. Jason Molina, handwritten note given to Anne Grady.

8. Jason Molina, as quoted in "Q&A with Jason Molina Summer 2004," jasonmolina.com, July 14, 2004, http://content.jasonmolina.com/post/22207847804/press-molina-qanda2004.

9. Jason Molina, as quoted in Dylan Metrano, "Meet Me Where We Survive, Jason Molina Interviews," chapbook printed in 2015.

10. Ibid.

11. Ibid.

12. Jason Molina, as quoted in the one sheet for the Songs: Ohia album *Axxess & Ace*, March 15, 1999, http://www.secretlycanadian.com/onesheet.php?cat=SC024.

13. *Pitchfork* review of *Axxess & Ace*, https://web.archive.org/web/20000816190733, http://www.pitchforkmedia.com/record-reviews/s/songs-ohia/axxess-and-ace.shtml.

14. Jason Molina, as heard on the "Duyster" radio show, Studio Brussel 94.5 FM Belgium, April 20, 2003.

15. Jason Molina, postcard to Anne Grady, October 1998.

16. Jonathan Cargill, as quoted in Dylan Metrano, "Meet Me Where We Survive, Jason Molina Interviews," chapbook printed in 2015.

CHAPTER 6

1. Jason Molina, in "Songs: Ohia January 30, 1999 CD Exchange Bloomington, Indiana," video, https://www.youtube.com/watch?v=uJoY1w98XSM.

2. Jason Molina, in video recording of Glen Hansard session with Songs: Ohia. Recorded by Zoran Orlic, May 23, 2000.

3. Ibid.

CHAPTER 7

1. Jason Molina, quote as remembered by Darcie Molina.

2. Jason Molina, as quoted in Dylan Metrano, "Meet Me Where We Survive, Jason Molina Interviews," chapbook printed in 2015.

3. Jason Molina, as quoted in "In My Room: Jason Molina of Songs: Ohia," *CMJ New Music Monthly*, January 2001.

CHAPTER 8

1. Jason Molina, quote as remembered by Alasdair Roberts, October 18, 2014.
2. Alasdair Roberts, as quoted on pitchfork.com, http://pitchfork.com/news/58066-jason-molina-song-september-11-recorded-on-911-with-will-oldham-and-alasdair-roberts-unearthed.
3. June Panic, as quoted on exclaim.com, http://exclaim.ca/music/article/june_panic.
4. Damien Jurado, as quoted on spin.com, http://www.spin.com/2016/03/damien-jurado-visions-of-us-on-the-land-interview-seven-favorite-albums-kraftwerk.
5. Ibid.
6. Ibid.
7. Ibid.

CHAPTER 9

1. Jason Molina, as quoted in press archive on jasonmolina.com, http://content.jasonmolina.com/post/22207847804/press-molina-qanda2004.
2. Pete Schreiner, as quoted on commfolkmusic.com, https://commonfolkmusic.wordpress.com/2014/05/03/remembering-jason-molina-peter-schreiners-tribute.

CHAPTER 10

1. Jason Molina, as quoted in Schubas Backstage Interview with Jason Molina Part 1 of 2, https://www.youtube.com/watch?v=HIEcLcES3lU.
2. Ibid.
3. Jason Molina, as quoted in unreleased footage from "Recording Josephine," shot by Ben Schreiner, November 4–8, 2008, in Chicago.
4. Mark Rice, as quoted in unreleased footage from "Recording Josephine," shot by Ben Schreiner, November 4–8, 2008, in Chicago.
5. Ibid.
6. Ibid.
7. Jason Molina, quote as remembered by Jonathan Cargill.
8. Ibid.

CHAPTER 11

1. AV Club review of Josephine, July 21, 2009, http://www.avclub.com/review/magnolia-electric-co-emjosephineem-30595.

2. Jason Molina, e-mail to Darcie Molina, October 2009.
3. Jason Molina, e-mail to Darcie Molina, October 2009.
4. Jason Molina, quote as remembered by Bas Flesseman.
5. From a worksheet given to Molina while at Brian's Safehouse, provided by Aaron Molina.

CHAPTER 12

1. Jason Molina, e-mail to Jeff Panall, April 22, 2012.
2. Jason Molina, quote as remembered by Jason Groth.
3. Jason Molina, e-mail to Jeff Panall, June 24, 2012.

INDEX

ABOUT THE AUTHOR

Author Erin Osmon. *Photo by Aiyana Taylor*

Erin Osmon is a writer based in Chicago. Her work has appeared in dozens of newspapers, magazines, websites, and journals dealing with music and culture. She also writes long-form liner notes for reissues of historic albums. A native of Evansville, Indiana, Ms. Osmon grew up in the Midwest underground music scene. She discovered Jason Molina's music in 1998 after the song "Vanquisher" from the first Songs: Ohia LP made rounds on a mixtape among her high school friends. This is her first book.